ABNER DOUBLEDAY:
His Life and Times

"Abner Doubleday: His Life and Times Looking Beyond the Myth is a well-researched and skillfully-written book on an often overlooked 19th century officer and gentleman. Doubleday, a graduate of the U. S. Military Academy, served the Union from the firing on Fort Sumter through to the bloody fields of Gettysburg. Gone are the baseball myths and other oft told tales of the man. Here rather, author JoAnn Bartlett shows the reader the real Abner Doubleday."

Blake A. Magner
Independent Historian

"It isn't often that you find someone outside of the family doing great family history work. In this case JoAnn has persevered and from what I've observed has thoroughly researched and produced a work of great national as well as family history."

Larry Doubleday
Second cousin, three times removed from Abner Doubleday

ABNER DOUBLEDAY:
His Life and Times

Looking Beyond the Myth

JoAnn Smith Bartlett

To order additional copies of this book, contact:
Xlibris Corporation
1-888-795-4274
www.Xlibris.com
Orders@Xlibris.com
45829

Contents

To:

With apologies to Abraham Lincoln, twenty years and four computers ago, I began this book. Along the way four very special people encouraged me, supported me and kept me going on a journey I never expected to travel. All of them have passed on and will never see the final result of what they so carefully nurtured. As a writer, words should come easily. However, I can't find the right words to express what they meant to me, individually and as a group. They will be forever in my debt. This book is dedicated to:

Lenora Senedeker: You suggested Abner; I said, "Why not?" You paved the way to meet Brian.

Brian Pohanka: A guiding hand, a cheering voice, a faithful heart within a gentle spirit.

Glenn Armitage: You never gave up the dream.

Daniel Bartlett: You were the center of my universe; a research partner, photographer, best friend and my husband. As my sounding board, my driver and my biggest fan, you gave me more than you could have ever imagined.

INTRODUCTION

The creation of this book has been fascinating and enjoyable, but a very long journey. It began with a simple telephone conversation with a very dear friend and mentor, Lenora Snedeker. The book exists because I was too naïve to understand the scope of my undertaking. My journey took me to places I had only heard about: the National Archives, the Library of Congress, West Point and many colleges and universities. Along the way, I met some very remarkable people that would have never crossed my path had I not been working on this particular book.

When I began this work I, like millions of other people, thoroughly believed that Abner Doubleday invented baseball. And, that was all I knew. As time passed, and my research became more intense, I began to understand the man, the world he lived in and the creation of a myth that will live for many more years. Although we will never hold the entire picture in our hands, my understanding of the man changed my outlook considerably.

His brothers, Thomas and Ulysses, and other family members served in the Civil War too. I also found no less than four Abner Doubledays in the course of my research. I also found at least three Ulysses Doubledays! Therefore, the father of this book's subject is always written using his middle name, Ulysses Freeman. Not only did I need to untangle the names, but also their deeds and signatures made all the more complicated by one man who signed his name, A. Doubleday (a distant cousin, Dr. Ammi Doubleday of Binghamton, New York). The Doubleday family loved to use the same name several times. At one time, it was customary to honor another relative by naming a new baby after that beloved relative. While, this is a wonderful family tradition, it becomes a huge challenge for a researcher.

As this work progressed, Abner was no longer seen as a sports legend, but as a real flesh and blood man, who held to his standards, was misunderstood by many of his contemporaries, and perhaps worst of all, did not receive recognition for his contribution to the Union cause in the Civil War. He was a rare general—an abolitionist. The writing of this book, which began so innocently, became an effort to tell his story—all of it that could be documented. I hope my readers will see the man I discovered.

Abner was ahead of his time. In an era when military officers didn't exhibit compassion for the troops they led, Abner tried to be sure the men were comfortable when possible. He commanded African American troops during a time it was extremely unpopular and showed concern for their welfare. He embraced new technology.

He endured the contempt of fellow officers and Southerners; the loss of his field command after the Battle of Gettysburg; and the politics of those who were in command above him and he never changed his views to be "popular" with his peers and fellow officers. Many of the men who served with him spoke kind words about him. Abner had access to President Lincoln in ways that have not been explored until now.

In writing this book, I also developed a theory about Abner. I believe that he has not received credit for certain photographs taken during the Mexican War. Knowing where he traveled and being intimately familiar with his handwriting, I am relatively certain he took some of the very early photographs that have been designated as "unknown photographer." Ultimately, the theory will be left to another author who I dearly hope will pursue that line of research.

I also have a better understanding of how Abner became the man who invented baseball. His grandparents and uncles lived in and around Cooperstown, New York. While I can't prove Abner ever walked the shores of Otsego Lake, I also cannot prove he didn't. And, who better to credit with creating the national pastime than a hero of the Civil War with ties to the area. After all, another Abner Doubleday rests in Lakeview Cemetery, but a short drive from the National Baseball Hall of Fame.

As with any study of the past, it becomes the author's task to sift through the research to find the truth. And, there is always more than one truth, depending on who is making the comment and why. I have attempted to examine Abner's era without modern-day prejudices. We do a great disservice to our collective ancestors by using modern day eyes to draw conclusions about the past. I have made every effort to tell Doubleday's story through his own words, documents, letters and military records. I hope this will be the beginning of a new effort to understand a man who was as complex as any modern person. It is entirely possible other gems of information remain hidden in someone's attic.

Early in my research, I contacted several Doubleday family members. They have shared information with me and I cherish their support and friendship. At the end of the book you will find one relative's version of Abner Doubleday's story. Sadly, Abner and his wife did not have children who might have had family stories and documents to share.

This work is entirely my own and so are any errors that may exist. I have used Abner's own words when it seems appropriate. In other quotes, I have left the original spelling of the writer. In a few cases I have included words we would not use today in an effort to illustrate life through the eyes of a nineteenth century person, not as an affront to any person, gender, race or other cultures.

So let's return to a time when entertainment was singing by the piano, when railroads were young and Indians were roaming the Texas plains; a time when the horse provided transportation and the telegraph was the quickest way to communicate over long distances, a time when America was growing and nearly everyone experienced anxiety and pain in the process.

ACKNOWLEDGEMENTS

Any writer's listing of those who assisted in the writing of a book is fraught with the possibility that someone will be left out. So let me say right here, I have not left anyone out deliberately. I can only blame a faulty memory and not a lack of appreciation for the assistance so freely given. These are only a few of the many people who assisted me along the way and are in no particular order.

Dr. Richard J. Sommers of the United States Army Military History Institute in Carlisle, Pennsylvania: You provided suggestions and support for a very green researcher. Our first meeting was less than auspicious; our last meeting kept me floating on clouds for several days when you liked certain passages of this book. You are a legend, a fountain of information and I am thankful for your assistance. Not to be forgotten are your colleagues, Richard Keough and Pam Cheney. Michael Winey and his staff were very helpful in locating photos. Thank you all.

Next are two Gettysburg Licensed Battlefield Guides, Tim Smith and Wayne Motts. Words are not enough to state how much you both gave me. You were sounding boards and teachers; friends and mentors. I cherish having you both in my life during my magical years in our beloved Gettysburg. I miss both of you more than you know.

Archivist Mike Musick was at the National Archives for many years and gave me numerous tips as I learned how to accomplish Civil War research. You gently "pushed" me in the proper direction. Your colleagues were equally knowledgeable and helpful. Since your retirement and change of staffing, I miss all of you when I visit the Archives.

Donald Pfanz, of the Fredericksburg National Military Park provided insight to that famous battle. You pointed out information about the battle, the citizens and the participants. I greatly enjoyed our conversation about the National Park Service in general and discovering little gems of information in the library.

I am red-faced as I write my appreciation for the help given by John Hennessy. You loaned me your personal copy of Abner's diary from Harpers Ferry. Although, I did make a couple of attempts to return it, it is still in my possession. I hope you can forgive this oversight. I profoundly apologize and remember the great conversation we had about Abner Doubleday.

Next is Scott Hartwig, of Gettysburg National Military Park. You were gracious even when I called at the last minute with a burning question. You gave of your time and expertise. You clarified terms that were foreign to me. I deeply appreciate your assistance.

I spent a few precious minutes with Carol Reardon and your few words of encouragement will never be forgotten. You encouraged me to use my full name as an author to demonstrate that men are not the only people who can write about the Civil War.

To Louise Arnold-Friend, I give a huge thank you. As librarian at United States Army Military History Institute, as a battlefield guide, as a fellow human being, you assisted and encouraged. I will always remember our trip to Ford's Theater. Not to be forgotten too, is Gettysburg National Military Park Ranger Becky Lyons. Your death has left a huge hole in the lives of many including my own. You mentored me; you sat with my terminally ill husband so I could run errands and not leave him alone. You were a dear friend. I hope your people will continue to call my people.

To Marion Brophy I owe a huge thank you. You found a deed to Doubleday property in the charming Village of Cooperstown. You helped sort out the many Doubledays I discovered. Your assistance was most valuable and welcomed.

I must not forget members of the Abner Doubleday Society: Glenn Armitage, John Cromie and Bill Short. Each sent me material about Abner Doubleday and invited me for an unforgettable weekend in Abner Doubleday's home town of Ballston Spa, New York. I am forever grateful.

To Bill Schwartz, of Gettysburg, Pennsylvania and Rod Sutton, of Sidney, New York, fellow photographers, thank you for assisting with the images in this book.

To Tom Ryan of the Gettysburg Discussion Group I am also grateful. You took the time to read a portion of this work and offer suggestions. Anytime someone offers his/her time to help, is an honor for the author.

To my friend, Lewis Warner, I owe a great deal. You helped with finding obscure documents, provided a treasured photograph, called me often in a show of support, befriended my late husband and I and you have so much enthusiasm I wish it could be bottled and given to every school child that is struggling to understand why history is important. I treasure your friendship.

To Al Gambone, a fellow author, I owe a great deal. You provided information and encouraged me to go forward. You were a true gentleman. You had planned to write your own Doubleday biography, but backed out so I could go ahead. Thank you so much and your death leaves a large hole in the world of Civil War authors.

To Sue Greenhagen a huge thank you. You took time to read my manuscript and offered suggestions and corrections. You gave me tidbits of information. You kept me on track and gave me so much more. We giggled, sweated the small stuff and shared our love of the Civil War. Hats off to you.

To my fellow reenactors I wish to express my gratitude. To be surrounded with artifacts of the past, to provide an interpretation of people's lives and continuing to share knowledge with the general public is a very special activity.

Families and friends are to be cherished, especially when they provide assistance (knowingly and unknowingly) along the path traveled by any writer. They comprise a truly large group of people whose names would fill an entire page. Please know that you are appreciated, loved and not forgotten. A special thank you to Richard Finneman for your generous assistance.

Along the way there have been countless, and sometimes faceless, librarians. I asked unusual questions and you never batted an eye—well, maybe once or twice. I have benefited from your patience and knowledge. The world is a better place because of your chosen career. From small public libraries to colleges and universities, and West Point, librarians hold a special place in my heart. The most recent of this very large group include Lori Chien, Lisa Matte, and Lisa Kinna of Jervis Public Library. Saying thank you isn't enough.

"Our generation has been stirred up from the lowest layers and there is that in its history which will stamp every member of it until we are all in our graves."
Henry Brooks Adams to Charles Francis Adams
July 17, 1863

CHAPTER 1

"To the Happiness of the Men"

The Twenty-fourth United States Infantry's Colonel Abner Doubleday prepared to send a letter to the army's Office of the Adjutant General in the nation's capital. Doubleday was in command of Fort McKavett, Texas in 1871 and after nearly thirty years in the army, he knew a contented soldier was less likely to desert his post. This unit of infantry was one of the country's regular (non-volunteer) army regiments. It was also a regiment of African Americans, known at that time as "Colored," or as "Buffalo Soldiers."

> [I] request permission to purchase a few portraits of distinguished generals, battle pictures and some of [John] Rogers groups of Statuary particularly those relative to the action of the colored population . . . . This being a colored regiment, ornaments of this kind seem very appropriate. I would also like to purchase baseball implements for the amusement of the men and a Magic Lantern for the same purpose. The fund is ample and I think these expenditures would add to the happiness of the men.[1]

It appears that permission for the purchases was withheld and it wasn't because of money for as Doubleday stated in his request that the post had enough funds to cover the costs. At that time, the Buffalo Soldiers were seen only as "Colored" and therefore inferior. While this is outrageous to us now, nineteenth century eyes were blind to the humanity of African Americans as well as the Indians. These letters tell us the kind of man Doubleday was and how his Negro troops were treated. By showing concern for his troops, he demonstrated that he was a man truly ahead of his time.

The wording of his request is striking: Baseball implements. The man who supposedly invented the sport dubbed "America's Pastime," did not say he wanted baseball equipment, he did not say he wanted bats and balls. No, he wanted to buy **baseball implements** for his Buffalo Soldiers. The nickname Buffalo Soldiers allegedly came from Native Americans who saw the tightly curled hair of African American soldiers to be similar to the hair of a buffalo. These men might have to fight the Comanches or the Apaches, but when they returned to the fort they could have played, if the request of their commander had been granted.

A few months later, Doubleday wrote another letter:

> There is a universal complaint by officers of companies. There is a general ignorance of Colored troops and a lack of grammar to do all writing. There is no present method to instruct the men and the Chaplain is of little use. The enlisted men of this regiment are most anxious to be taught. I recommend a competent man—white or black—with the rank of sergeant be assigned to instruct the men.[2]

Negroes from the Southern states had usually been forbidden to learn reading and writing. Once again, we get a glimpse at Doubleday's treatment of his Buffalo Soldiers.

In nineteenth century Texas the only air conditioning was a stiff breeze that pushed dust over the land and into buildings as it encircled animals and people. There were no tall buildings gleaming in the broiling sun of summer. The Spaniards were long gone, but the Native Americans, at that time always called Indians, were tenaciously hanging onto their land and their heritage. Following the Civil War, many men headed west. Not all of them were upright citizens. There were also bands of cattle drovers, thieves, gamblers and rogues as well as the good people of the East seeking a better life in a new land.

There were many Indian raids along the Rio Grande between this new sprawling land and old Mexico. United States Army regiments were sent to protect its citizens and the growing number of railroads; not an easy assignment with too few soldiers and too many robbers. The mail was one important delivery; there were others. The troops would accompany freight trains, stagecoaches and cattle drives that made the dangerous trek through the countryside. If the robbers didn't attack, Indians might. The army itself was experiencing its own problems involving a lack of clearly defined authority over commands in far away garrisons and no standard policy dealing with what was seen as the "Indian problem." The land itself could be either friendly or the enemy. There were no shopping malls or supermarkets for supplies. Military men and civilians alike depended on waterways, good grazing land, shady trees and strong horses, mules or oxen to pull wagons heavily loaded with supplies.

Fort McKavett was built about 1852 in west Menard County about 160-odd miles northwest of San Antonio. It was not only home to the infantry, but occasionally served as home to companies from the Ninth and Tenth United States Cavalry regiments.

Duty called, and civilians-turned-soldiers answered. Frequently they were not only soldiers expected to keep order, but they were also the men who had to build or rebuild the very forts they lived in. McKavett had been abandoned for nearly ten years before the Buffalo Soldiers reported to the post. In addition to their regular duties, they now assumed the roles of carpenters and stone masons. While they were in essence building a "new" fort, they lived in tents. Luckily water wasn't a problem; the fort sat close to the San Saba River and there was a refreshing spring nearby.[3]

There are certain types of employment that almost guarantee a life of boredom punctuated by moments of sheer terror with an adrenaline rush followed by exhaustion: law enforcement officers, firefighters, emergency personnel and members of the military for example. The soldiers serving in Texas and other Western regions were very experienced with the many conditions they faced daily: the Indians could attack at any moment; there could be grass fires or any number of things that could happen. In between, they sought ways to relieve the boredom and their commander tried to help improve the general morale among his men. The number of available soldiers changed frequently as illness and desertions caused their numbers to dwindle.

An eight-page letter by Doubleday to the army's Department of Texas at San Antonio offers a look at Fort Brown, one of several forts he visited while making the rounds of army posts in his area. In 1872, a group of local citizens, near Fort Brown, called on him to express their concern over the actions of a man known only as Cortina. Cortina wasted no love on Americans. He and his followers threatened death and carried out this threat many times.

Those living in the region were justified in their fear. Doubleday wrote that Brownsville was American, but was populated with American-hating Mexicans. Doubleday provided an assessment of the situation and resources should there be trouble. He requested more men be assigned to his command.[4]

The retention of soldiers was nearly as difficult as keeping some form of peace on the frontier. Only the year before a captain from the Twenty-fourth United States Infantry wrote home: "I have got tired of hunting the noble 'Red Man' on foot. I want to leave the infantry and am an applicant for an appointment to the Pay Department of the Army. I have in five years marched over 5,000 miles and want a change."[5] The dust, the Indians, marauding Mexicans, poor housing and boredom caused many men to leave—either by transfer or by simply walking away.

In another two years, Doubleday would retire. He had given his country thirty years of his life. Mary had been the dutiful wife, going with him from post to post whenever possible. The years were taking a toll on him and he was trying to keep up with his work. Occasionally, his failing health required him to take medical leave.

Doubleday applied for retirement in late 1872, but it took several months and appeals to have his request granted. One of the many appeals was written by Mary and addressed to Julia Grant, the wife of President Ulysses S. Grant. Mary was not well either, and told Mrs. Grant that medical treatment she needed for her illness was unavailable on the frontier. Doubleday was losing sleep and using the "Necessary" (bathroom) frequently. He had an enlarged prostate and a bladder problem. Mary's neuralgia was so bad she couldn't walk across the room, he wrote. It was time to go home, wherever that might be back East.[6]

Retirement eventually took the couple to Mendham, New Jersey located about forty miles south of New York City. There they built a new home on Hilltop Road. His Mendham neighbors described Doubleday as a, "very religious man who never drank or used profane language." The retired general was "dignified and courteous in manner, with a cough that was shattering, booming." One citizen described Doubleday as never walking. "'He always marched, hands behind him, slowly and in perfect form, back and forth on the brick-paved veranda. His little wife, dressed in black, was always a pace or two behind him.'"[7]

Another description of Doubleday made its way into print: "The general was tall, and had become somewhat portly . . . . I always found him to be a stately, old-school gentleman, whose fine military bearing combined with a naturally open and genial countenance and disposition to make an attractive personality. A sanguine temperament, inclined to aggressiveness, suggested reserve power, self-reliance and initiative in emergencies or when otherwise fully aroused." He was described as having "strong perceptive faculties, [and] was a keen observer." This writer states Doubleday demonstrated how he fired the first cannon at Fort Sumter.[8]

Doubleday's retirement years gave him time to become involved in Theosophy, to dabble in Sanskrit, and to work on his memoirs; there were so many stories to record.

Endnotes

1   Colonel Abner Doubleday to E. D. Townsend, Adjutant General United States Army, Washington, D.C., June 17, 1871, pg. 132, Letters Sent, RG 393, Records of the US Regular Army, Mobile Units, Twenty-fourth United States Infantry, National Archives and Records Administration (hereafter NARA), Washington, D.C.

2   Ibid, Nov. 21, 1871, 148

3   Col. M. L. Crimmins, "Fort McKavett, Texas," *Southwestern Quarterly*, July 1934, 28-39

4   Abner Doubleday to United States Army Department of Texas, San Antonio, October 6, 1872, 111-115, Letters Sent, RG 393, Records of the US Regular Army Mobile Units, Twenty-fourth United States Infantry, NARA, Washington, D.C.

5   Captain Corbin, letter, Halstead-Maus Family Collection, December 12, 1891, archives branch, United States Army Military History Institute (hereafter USAMHI)

6   Mary Doubleday to Mrs. Ulysses Grant, March 2, 1873; Abner Doubleday to Lt. Gen. Phillip H. Sheridan, April 25, 1873, RG 94, Letters Received by the Appointment, Commission and Personal Branch, Adjutant General's Office 1871-1894, NARA

7   Joan Barbaro, *Daily Record*, Mendham, N.J., Oct. 23, 1963; the Doubleday house no longer exists

8   "Reminiscences and Portrait of General Abner Doubleday," *Freeman's Journal*, Cooperstown, N.Y. Oct. 1939

CHAPTER 2

"Keep him moving"

The old general leaned forward in his chair. His ink-stained fingers guided the pen across the pages of his journal. He was gathering up his memories and setting them down for posterity.

The memories were called forward, sometimes they came easily; sometimes he had to rely on brief notes he had made during those years. Names, images, moments suspended in time like photographic snapshots in an album found life as Doubleday's pen scratched its way across the paper.

Doubleday's contemporaries included South Carolina born James Longstreet, Virginian Thomas Jonathan "Stonewall" Jackson, the fiery-tempered Pennsylvanian George Gordon Meade, the excellent horseman, Grant of Ohio, and the Illinois lawyer, old Abe himself, President Lincoln.

Doubleday's life was filled with special moments—on and off the battlefield. Should he tell the story of a prank he and his fellow officers pulled at a ceremonial parade in New York City? What about the laughable moments with Jackson; or the not-so-great moments of battles during war? In the kaleidoscope of memory, a horse leaped forward to take center stage.

It was 1851 at Fort Hamilton, New York, near Brooklyn's Verrazano Narrows Bridge. Doubleday had orders to relieve the man later known as "Stonewall," Thomas Jonathan Jackson. Jackson was a "staid, quiet" man who moved awkwardly. He was not known to have a funny-bone, either. Jackson's uniform never quite seemed to fit his lean frame as it should, and he rarely wore civilian clothing even when he visited the city, said Doubleday. A pious man, Jackson had a long sharp nose and piercing eyes.

Jackson had many health concerns that he attempted to solve in unusual ways. He believed one arm was longer than the other, and would hold the "longer" one in the air to "balance" his circulation. Jackson's quirky ideas regarding his health became legendary throughout the military and remain so even now. Pepper was to be avoided at all costs. Jackson, with Doubleday and Doubleday's friend and fellow soldier, Otis Tillinghast, and other officers were seated for dinner. Tillinghast was seated next to Jackson. Tillinghast buttered his bread and added a dash of pepper to his food.

Jackson's eyes flashed as he spoke to Tillinghast, "You have put your knife covered with pepper next to my plate!"

"No, it didn't touch your plate," Tillinghast replied. "It may have touched your bread, but not your plate, and I don't think it has any pepper on it."

Jackson grabbed his bread, ripped it into shreds, and threw it in the fire. "Never mind. It's not important," Jackson said as his actions revealed his anger.[9]

Jackson was a trusting man—he found it impossible to believe that anyone could harm an animal. Jackson's fine horse caught the eye of a jockey. The unidentified jockey talked Jackson into a horse trade. Poor Jackson didn't know his new horse was known as a balky mount. Shortly after his arrival at Fort Hamilton, Doubleday indicated he was interested in buying Jackson's animal. Asking if he could ride the horse, Doubleday went to the stable and was surprised to see a small crowd of onlookers. He mounted the animal and an easy half mile later, Doubleday headed back to the stable where he returned Jackson's horse. The crowd had vanished and Doubleday looked for Jackson to have a talk. Doubleday asked if the horse had any problems or "faults." It took Jackson a few seconds before he answered, perhaps a little sheepishly. "Well, when I got him, he would stop and throw out his front legs," Jackson admitted. "I haven't tried to keep him from doing it though." Saying the horse no longer stopped unexpectedly, Jackson and Doubleday agreed on a sale.

Not long after buying the horse, Doubleday was out riding his new mount when he became aware that they were too far forward of his artillery section. Doubleday halted the horse. The horse stopped, and threw its legs out; refusing to move. Doubleday got the animal moving again, but when he stopped a second time, the horse refused to move.

Doubleday spurred the horse and they took off down a ravine and through some brambles. Upon returning to the stable, Doubleday looked for Jackson. Jackson told Doubleday, "You shouldn't have stopped. Keep him moving and you're alright."

Doubleday stopped writing and likely smiled at the memory. Poor Jackson. He died eight days after being wounded on May 2, 1863, by his own men at the Battle of Chancellorsville. Jackson was only thirty-nine years old.

Doubleday's pen paused. A carriage in a parade rolled out from his memory.

Around 1851, there was a very important parade in New York City. Members of the army and navy had been invited to participate. General Winfield Scott, nicknamed "Old Fuss and Feathers," who had commanded the American troops in the Mexican War, and New York's Whig Governor Hamilton Fish, named in honor of Alexander Hamilton, were expected take part in the event. However, many officers did not place ceremonial duties high on the list of enjoyable activities. Previous experiences had not been pleasant affairs, Doubleday said. It was hard to compete with the splendid uniforms of militia members who rode good looking horses. The army regulars wearing their plain-looking uniforms were expected to march on foot in muddy streets. The ladies viewing the parade would find little to catch their eyes among the army contingent, in Doubleday's opinion.

The men decided not to attend the parade, but their colonel convinced them to change their minds. The army would be represented by three officers: Doubleday, his close friend James Ricketts, and William French, all reported to city hall where they waited to take position in line. The navy men waited too—until they were called to take their place in comfortable carriages.

The three army officers could not help but notice there was an empty carriage designated for navy officers. Wouldn't it be a waste if the carriage didn't get used?

The three men decided to become temporary "naval" officers. When they opened the carriage door, there was a surprise inside. A man was sitting in one corner. The man said he was a tailor in the Bowery, near the livery stable where the carriage had been parked. Since the tailor had never been in a carriage, he decided it wouldn't do any harm to experience a carriage ride as far as city hall before returning home.

It didn't take long for Doubleday, Ricketts and French to figure out that the tailor was not a well-educated man. French questioned tailor about politics and other topics of general interest. The man did his best to appear knowledgeable although it was clear he was not. This went on for more than an hour as the procession traveled through the streets of the city. Doubleday, Ricketts and French were amusing themselves during what would have otherwise been a very boring ride.

Once the parade stopped to honor the attending dignitaries, many of the officers became very annoyed with the delay. The speeches were so lengthy, at least one officer ahead of them hopped out of the carriage he was in and walked to his nearby home. This left his carriage companion (a general) alone and consequently, very unhappy. The general instructed an aide to find a new carriage companion. The aide asked Doubleday, Ricketts and French if one of them would join the general, but the wording of the invitation was not received well by the officers. They respectfully declined. The aide returned saying the general was being very insistent.

The tailor from the Bowery was about to get the carriage ride of a lifetime. It didn't take much convincing by the three army officers to talk the tailor into joining the general. The tailor wasn't sure it was appropriate, but soon gave in. In his excitement, the tailor missed the step on his way out and landed in the muddy street. Picking himself up again, he headed to do his duty and opened the door to the general's carriage.

A few questions by the general were soon replaced by the storming of one very angry general. The general exited the carriage calling for his cavalry to open the lines, allowing the general to travel down Bleeker Street.

The tailor was now all alone in the carriage, surrounded by cavalry, and the parade began to resume its march. There was no way out for the tailor and he became the center of attention as the carriage moved forward.

Looking for all the world like an important person, the tailor was mistaken by the watching crowd as Governor Fish! Hats were tossed in the air. Hip-Hip-Huzzah was heard three times as the "Governor" was cheered. By now Doubleday, Ricketts and French had to be laughing so hard their sides hurt. The troops were called to attention—after all the "Governor" was passing! Present arms! Blow the trumpets, dip the flags, and bang the drums!

The very anxious tailor was trying to spot a way out of his dilemma. The parade had worked its way back to City Hall where a group of distinguished men were ready to greet the "Governor." The carriage drew to a halt, the door opened and the tailor ("Governor") fell out once more. Instead of standing upright, the tailor crawled into the crowd, stood up and took off running

Doubleday, Ricketts and French returned to the fort where they told their fellow soldiers, the parade wasn't so bad after all. You can only imagine the three of them trying to keep straight faces while they answered questions about the parade as they reported for duty.[10]

So many memories, so many years gone by, Doubleday must have mused. There were so many memorable moments in Doubleday's thirty-years in the army. But not all the memories were of amusing incidents. He had seen too much blood, too much war and too much trouble to hold only happy memories.

Endnotes

9   Abner Doubleday diary, 1846-1858, (hereafter A.D.), Abner Doubleday papers, New York City: New York Historical Society, n.p.

10   Some have suggested this was a funeral procession in November 1849 for military personnel James Duncan and William J. Worth. Although that is possible, it is hardly likely that Abner and his companions would dishonor the memory of their comrades by pulling a practical joke. Another possibility might have been the parade to honor the birthday of George Washington in 1851. Abner used his notes when he wrote his diaries and the dates are rarely inaccurate.

CHAPTER 3

"I was brought up in a bookstore"

"I was brought up in a book store and early imbibed a taste for reading. I was fond of poetry and art and much interested in mathematical studies. In my outdoor sports I was addicted to topographical work and even as a boy amused myself by making maps of the county around my father's residence which was in Auburn, Cayuga County, New York. He was a bookseller and editor there," said Doubleday of his early years.[11]

He was born in Ballston Spa, New York. When he was only five months old his mother, Hester Donnelly Doubleday was busy getting her three children ready for church where they were to be christened. Thomas was three years old, Ruth Maria was two and the infant, Abner. The two older children probably toddled about, tugging at their clothing as Hester checked Abner's diaper one last time before leaving. The family was in their small, but adequate home preparing for the ceremony that would take place at the First Presbyterian Church. Since it was early November in that northern village, Hester made sure each child was dressed warmly for the short trip by carriage to the service that Tuesday evening. Once there, in the soft glow of candles and oil lamps, Hester and her husband, Ulysses Freeman Doubleday, placed their three children in God's care. The family had lived in Ballston Spa since 1816, the year without a summer, and the very same year Ulysses Freeman bought a newspaper, *The Saratoga Courier*, and established himself as a full-fledged printer. By 1819, the family had grown for a third time. This second son would make his mark in the military, surpassing both his father and grandfather before him. Doubleday first saw the light of day on June 26, 1819. His parents had met and married in Albany, the state's capital, five years before. Doubleday has long lingered on the fringes of history, a shadowy figure that appears on center stage often enough to arouse curiosity. On a hot day in July 1863, he made an everlasting contribution to his country in a small Pennsylvania town called Gettysburg. In order to better understand the man and his life, we must first understand his early years and the influences during that formative period.[12]

The year Doubleday was born, King Louis XVIII sat on the throne in France and the United States purchased Florida from Spain. This action was the result of Andrew Jackson's invasion of Florida, a place Doubleday would become all too familiar with later as the Seminole Indians tried to retain their land. Jackson would be a future occupant of the White House as America's seventh president and his election would represent the common man rather than the gentrified, aristocratic men of influence and substantial means. Doubleday was not the only baby born in 1819 who would reach prominence. Americans Julia Ward (In 1843 she married Samuel Gridley Howe who was a backer of John Brown's 1859 raid on Harpers Ferry. In November 1861, she wrote "Battle Hymn of the Republic."), and Walt Whitman (who became a well known poet) were born that same year as well as a baby girl, Victoria, who became the Queen of England, and another baby boy, Albert, who would be Victoria's prince; as adults, all would greatly influence that period of time and make their marks on history. It was the time when steamboats were not only traveling on the Mississippi River, but making maiden voyages on the Missouri River. Just days before Doubleday's first birthday, Alabama became a state putting a twenty-second star on the nation's flag.

This third child of the family would not be the first Doubleday to serve his country. Doubleday's father, who was born in New Lebanon, Connecticut, December 15, 1792, joined the army seven years before this second son arrived. For the sake of clarity, the father will be referred to as Ulysses Freeman, thus separating him from his son Ulysses, who would be born in 1824, when Abner was five. Ulysses Freeman was a soldier in the War of 1812 and saw action at Sackets Harbor, New York. Doubleday's grandfather was Captain Abner Doubleday who served in the American Revolution. The earliest record of Ulysses Freeman indicates he was christened October 3, 1802, at the Presbyterian Church in Cooperstown, New York. It was this background that would place the future general, erroneously, on a baseball field in Cooperstown.

The Village of Cooperstown was named in honor of Judge William Cooper whose son, James Fenimore Cooper, gave it a permanent identity when he wrote of "Glimmerglass" lake and Natty Bumpo's adventures in the first great American novels. "Glimmerglass," was really Otsego Lake, the headwaters of the Susquehanna River which flows a leisurely 444 miles to the Chesapeake Bay. There were many Doubledays who lived in the Cooperstown area of Otsego County. By the peaceful waters of the lake, Ulysses Freeman grew to manhood. In future years, another relative would become a prominent Cooperstown citizen. Doubleday's Uncle Seth

Doubleday served as a justice of the peace and postmaster; Seth also was a founder of the Cooperstown Universalist Church there much later; the building still stands on Pioneer Street. Inside, the architectural features of an old church are clearly visible. Other Doubledays would also settle throughout Central New York, in Cortland and Broome counties. Five of Abner's great uncles and his great-grandfather had served in the American Revolution

When he was old enough, Ulysses Freeman entered the printing trade while still in Cooperstown where he learned his trade as an apprentice under H.H. Phinney.[13] It was hard work for a young man. The firewood needed to be placed in the stove to keep warm in winter, sheepskin had to be made soft enough to wrap around the ink balls used to hold the press' ink; it was a distasteful job. The sheepskin had to soak in urine and needed daily tending, by wringing out and then being placed for more soaking to achieve the proper softness.[14] Ulysses Freeman next achieved journeyman status with Seward and Williams in Utica, New York, a community northwest of Cooperstown. In 1814, he went to Albany, where he worked for Webster and Skinner. That same year he won the hand of Hester Donnelly, a daughter of Captain Thomas Donnelly, who had been a sergeant-at-arms for the state House of Assembly.[15] They were married October 10, 1814.[16] Two years later Ulysses Freeman decided to strike out on his own and in 1816 bought *The Saratoga Courier* in Ballston Spa.[17]

Ballston Spa, in Saratoga County, is in the northeastern portion of the Empire State. The community is on the edge of the famous "Forever Wild" Adirondack Mountains and a few miles from the Vermont border. Slightly further north of Ballston Spa is the more famous Saratoga Springs, where a Revolutionary War battle took place and many would someday go to enjoy the "healing powers" of the waters there. The Hudson River begins at Lake Tear of the Clouds in the Adirondack Mountains and flows 315 miles south through Albany and past the United States Military Academy at West Point before its water reaches New York City and the Atlantic Ocean. As Abner grew to manhood, the Hudson River would be connected by way of canals and other waterways to open up the western part of the state and continue on to the Great Lakes.

The fledgling businessman and his wife settled down and started a family in their Ballston Spa home. Their first child, born February 18, 1816, was a boy, named Thomas Donnelly Doubleday, in honor of Hester's father. The next child was a girl, Ruth Maria, who arrived the following year. Then Ulysses Freeman and Hester had their second son, Abner, named for his grandfather, the Revolutionary soldier on his father's side of the family.

This Doubleday, too, would win fame many years later on other battlefields. He was only a few months old when his father decided to buy *The Cayuga Patriot* in Auburn, Cayuga County, New York, where the Finger Lakes ran through the center of the state. [18] Auburn sits at the north end of eleven-mile long Owasco Lake, one of the Finger Lakes.

The newspaper had its beginnings in 1814 from, the Wagon Shop on Lumber Lane (now Osborne Street) and had a reputation as being "'anti-federalist, and Democratic-Republican'" in its politics. Its motto was "*Pro-Patria.*"[19] Ulysses Freeman "was distinguished for the strength, originality and accuracy of his mind; for purity of purpose and integrity of character. He was one of the most prominent journalists of the [Cayuga] county."[20]

Considering the harsh winters in New York State, it's possible Hester and the children did not move west until the spring following the purchase of the Auburn newspaper. Ulysses Freeman most likely elected to stay in Auburn and publish his newspaper until the family could be reunited. Auburn was on the edge of the New York western frontier. The Doubledays were not the only family on the move. It was a time when many left home and hearth for what was then considered the West. Auburn was growing and fast becoming an important community. The Auburn Academy was established and constructed seven years before Doubleday was born. [21] Auburn had been incorporated only four years earlier under the leadership of future governor, Enos T. Throop. Auburn would also have another notable person in the nineteenth century, William Henry Seward, who not only sat in the governor's mansion, but who became a United States senator, and the secretary of state for Lincoln as well as a friend to the man who became a general during the Civil War. [22] When Auburn was chosen for the construction of a state prison, it was well on its way to becoming an important place on the map. The cornerstone for the new prison was set on June 28, 1816, three years before the Doubleday family arrived. [23] The prison was plainly visible when the family arrived at their new home. The community was expanding rapidly and included a state bank and a Theological Seminary. By the following year, Auburn had what was known as the Colombian Garden "with an amphitheater for circus performances, a ten-pin alley, a stage and galleries for the drama, and arrangements for fireworks and music."[24]

When Ulysses Freeman took over *The Cayuga Patriot*, it was the second newspaper in Auburn. The *Western Federalist* had been the first to be established. According to one source, none other than Thurlow Weed[25] had set type at the *Patriot* before Ulysses Freeman purchased the paper. [26] The same year Ulysses Freeman bought the *Patriot,* the *Western Federalist* was also purchased and its name changed to *The Republican.*[27]

Ulysses Freeman didn't limit himself to printing the news; he offered "demi and foolscap and blank books" at his book store nearby.[28] Items such as "Dr. Jebbs Celebrated Linament" and "toothache pills" could be purchased too. He offered the popular "Dr. Reeler's Aromatic Female Pills" for the ladies of Auburn. One could also find *Ballou's Sermons, Rob Roy* and *Children of the Abbey,* pocket bibles, school books, stamps, inkstands, slate pencils and drawing paper in the shop. Quarto Bibles were three cents, as were some toys. Ulysses Freeman printed almanacs, too. You can almost see Doubleday as a child at his father's print shop carefully watching the printing press churn out a steady supply of broadsides and other reading materials. Doubleday, who would usually have a book nearby even when at war, gained an appreciation of books at a tender age.

By the time he was three in 1821, Missouri had received statehood as a slave state, while Maine became a state free of slavery, through the Missouri Compromise. It was also a year when Ulysses Freeman began to make his mark in other ways as an Auburn citizen. Even though Ulysses Freeman was operating his two shops and seeing to his family's needs, he and twenty-eight other men formed the First Universalist Society in Auburn on April 21, 1821. While it probably had little immediate effect on his three-year old son, the activities must certainly have been discussed at the dinner table.[29]

The Auburn church found itself blessed with notable speakers and preachers such as Pennsylvanian Quaker Lucreatia Mott who brought her anti-slavery message to Auburn. Mott's sister, Martha Wright, lived in Auburn, so it was a convenient lecture site.[30] Mott not only spoke out against slavery, but also in favor of extending the vote to women. At this time, women weren't allowed to speak publicly or to even have custody of their own children. It was a man's world and any attempt to change it would be considered nothing short of scandalous.

With these types of influences swirling about the heads of the Doubleday children, it may be assumed some part of these teachings became a part of them as they grew and matured. It could even be argued that young Doubleday absorbed much that would later label him as an unusual man, a Radical Republican (one who favored ending slavery).

Little is known about his early education. By the time he was five in 1824, the Auburn Academy, which had been affiliated with the Theological Seminary there, reopened as a separate school under the guidance of "Mr. John A. Savage, late principal of the Academy at Delhi, [New York] in the county of Delaware." A student in English was charged three dollars tuition; students of the classics paid a dollar more.[31] Since both of Doubleday's brothers were recorded as receiving their schooling in Auburn, it would seem logical to believe he did also, but according to a Doubleday descendant, he may have attended school in Binghamton, New York, possibly living with a relative, Dr. Ammi Doubleday. Among Doubleday's admission papers to West Point is a letter by his father who states he taught his son.[32] Through the years, it has been said that Doubleday went to a school run by Mr. Duff in Cooperstown. One source says, "In December 1838, Mr. William H. Duff, a graduate of Trinity College, Dublin, opened a classical and military academy for boys." Duff's school closed three years later. At this time, Doubleday was already a cadet at West Point.[33] Could historians have gotten the wrong Doubleday? Abner D. Doubleday was born about 1829 in the Richfield Springs/Pierstown area of Otsego County, New York, not far from Cooperstown. What if this Abner attended Duff's school? Not much is known about this Abner, except when he was thirty-four years old in December 1863, he enlisted to serve with the Second New York Heavy Artillery during the Civil War. His health caused him to have a short military career and he was discharged for disability in January 1865[34] and later moved to Michigan.

Educational books in those days did not feature cute, colorful pages. Classes began with a prayer and a "Salutatory Oration in Latin." That was followed by discussion and more oral recitation work.[35] Teachers were strict and the ruler not only measured length, but was liberally used by instructors to strike a student's knuckles or palm to measure the student's ability to apply himself to his studies.

In 1824, the same year the first sections of the Erie Canal were completed, a new newspaper, the *Free Press* opened shop in Auburn and took journalistic pot shots on the *Cayuga Patriot*.[36] It was also the year Doubleday got a new baby brother, Ulysses, who became his right-hand man during the Civil War years. As Doubleday was growing toward adulthood, his father was becoming more and more vocal in politics through his weekly editorial column in the *Cayuga Patriot*. Since the *Cayuga Patriot* now had more competition, it was time to make some improvements. Ulysses Freeman notified his readers in 1825 he would take a trip to New York City for the purpose of buying a new press and equipment. It was a time of advancement, and most likely this new printing press was steam-powered. He asked his customers to pay their subscriptions as a means to finance the venture. In October of the same year, Ulysses Freeman addressed the political scene. His editorial column made this observation: "Truth is ever simple and consistent; honesty always holds one language, does not tell one story today and another story tomorrow."[37] It was a lesson not only for his fellow Auburn citizens, but for his children too.

We also get another look at the father through Ulysses Freeman's writing concerning the worthiness of apprentices. In the May 24, 1826, edition of the *Cayuga Patriot*, sounding like the adults of every generation, Ulysses Freeman said apprentices "rambled about at will late at night and Sundays. The heart sickens to see a generation of young men raising up, many of them in a fair way to become vagabonds and pests to society." A few days later on June 7, 1826, Ulysses Freeman gave notice in his paper that his own apprentice, Jehiel Hart, had run away. "All persons are forbid harbouring, trusting or employing him under penalty of the law. If said boy returns, he must overcome his disorderly habits or he will be severely dealt with." Clearly, he was not a man to be trifled with. After all, it was a time when young men were sent to tradesmen to learn a marketable skill, and since the youths were under a contract, they were legally obligated to fulfill the requirements.

The years sped by, and the Doubleday family of Auburn was growing, but not without sadness. William James was born in 1822 and died as an infant; two years later, a girl was born, Hester Elizabeth, who would die at the age of three.[38] She was not the last little sister Doubleday and his family would mourn. Thirteen year old Jane Ann died June 12, 1843.[39] Diseases spread rapidly and antibiotics had not yet been discovered. Another sister, Amanda, arrived about 1826. She later married a Baptist preacher, the Reverend Herman James Eddy, on August 14, 1842 at Scipio, New York. Her husband, sons, nephews and brothers would all take part in the Civil War.[40] Ruth Maria married Dudley P. G. Everts on January 21, 1835 in Auburn. Of course, all this wasn't known in 1827, when Ulysses Freeman took on his partner, Isaac S. Allen. Together, they published the newspaper until Ulysses Freeman was elected to Congress and headed for the nation's capital and a seat in the House of Representatives. Allen bought the paper, and operated it by himself for the next two years.

The 1830s were a time of change. The Industrial Revolution had begun and with it a public awareness of sweat shops, children laboring for little compensation, temperance, education, religion and slavery. Auburn was in the middle of what became known as the "Burned Over District." This region, although not designated geographically, stretched through Central New York from Utica to Rochester, and was a region where traveling evangelists held revival meetings frequently and often called for an end to the drinking of alcohol, and an end to slavery as well as addressing other issues of the day.[41] There were a great many issues for Doubleday and his family to sort out. Less than 100 miles from Auburn, in Utica, a United States congressman, Samuel Beardsley, led a mob to break up an anti-slavery gathering in that city. Young Doubleday, called by his friends "Old Two-Days," must have learned a great deal outside the classroom too.[42]

In some ways the seeds of the late 1820s and 1830s planted changes that grew to a fateful harvest thirty years later. In a broader sense, it could even be compared to the civil rights issues 100-plus years in the future. Nearly every facet of life was undergoing changes: education, religion, farms, science, politics, manners and morals. New discoveries would have profound effects in the future. In 1831, a baby girl was born and named Helena Petrovna (Blavatsky). She would eventually found the Theosophical Society, a group that Doubleday would be associated with. By 1829, Louis Jacques M. Daguerre was working on the development of photography. As this new discovery matured, it would capture the serious faces of young men going off to a future war that pitted neighbors and families against each other. Hydropathy, the treatment of disease by water, began the same year, and won many followers including a young man destined to bear the nickname, "Stonewall" whom Doubleday would meet years later in the army.[43] Phrenology, the study of a person's character by reading bumps on their head, was considered high science. Explorations into the spirit world were taken very seriously by a small segment of citizens.

When Ulysses Freeman headed for Washington, District of Columbia, as a new congressman to take his seat in the Twenty-Second Congress, Doubleday was twelve years old. It was an exciting time for him to grow up, although he and his family probably would not have seen it that way. History doesn't seem like history when you're alive as it is made. When he was only fourteen, Doubleday began a school of sorts himself: he organized his father's apprentices into an evening class where he instructed them in the subject he excelled in—mathematics. As a mathematical scholar, he was thinking about entering the field of civil engineering. Many youths went into the ministry. The second greatest field was that of studying law. There were medical schools, but the field had not yet taken on the aura of a profession and for a few fortunate youths, an appointment to the United States Military Academy provided a formal education and even a future career.

While his application to West Point was being considered, young Doubleday was off to the wilderness surrounding Lake Simcoe in the Canadian province of Ontario. There he worked at surveying for the proposed Toronto & Lake Huron Railroad that would open a new path for business and citizens. However, an insurrection between reformers and the government broke out and Doubleday returned home to find his letter of acceptance to West Point.[44]

As Doubleday was considering his future, his father wrestled with Washington politics, national issues and the growing pains of a young nation. At the opening session on March 4, 1831, Ulysses Freeman officially began his freshman term in the House of Representatives representing the citizens of the Twenty-fourth District. The district was a long, narrow band of communities, including Auburn, running north to Lake Ontario.[45]

During his two separate terms, Jacksonian Democrat Ulysses Freeman found himself in company with Senators Henry Clay, from Kentucky, Daniel Webster, of Massachusetts, Thomas Hart Benton from Missouri and future president James Buchanan of Pennsylvania. In the House of Representatives his colleagues were Edward Everett who would more than thirty years later speak at the dedication of a national cemetery in Pennsylvania, and the grand old man from Massachusetts and former resident of the White House, John Quincy Adams, along with future president Franklin Pierce, of New Hampshire, future mob leader Beardsley of Utica; Francis W. Pickens and Waddy Thompson Jr., both firebrands advocating slavery from South Carolina and another firebrand and future Virginia governor, Henry A. Wise. Jackson's vice president was the Red Fox of Kinderhook, another future president, Martin Van Buren, the man who led the Albany Regency, the group taken to task by Ulysses Freeman in his paper six years earlier.[46] Many of these politicians were on the road to national prominence. It was the golden age for newspapers. The *Albany Argus* was known as the Regency's mouthpiece. William Lloyd Garrison began printing *The Liberator,* an anti-slavery publication in Boston. In addition, a trickle of petitions opposing slavery were making their way into Congress.

In the nation's capital, Ulysses Freeman found a temporary home at the boardinghouse of Mrs. Kennedy on Third Street. His tablemates included his fellow representative Joseph M. Harper of New Hampshire and two senators, Isaac Hill, also of New Hampshire and one from his own state, William L. Marcy. This was the same Marcy of the Albany Regency whom Ulysses Freeman had taken to task in his paper and would later contact when his second son was in serious trouble.

The Auburn congressman had only been in office a few months when an event in the South took place that had long-term effects. In August 1831, a slave named Nat Turner and his followers began a killing spree of white slave owners and their families in Southampton County, Virginia. When the butchering had ended, sixty people were dead and in pieces from being hacked with axes and hatchets. Almost immediately, the whites retaliated and it didn't matter if the unlucky black person in front of them was guilty or not. Death became a heavy summer harvest that year. [47]

In May 1834, Ulysses Freeman signed his name as "corporator" and stockholder with a group of businessmen. They were going into the business of railroading. By then Doubleday was fifteen, and having his father involved in railroading must have been exciting. The Auburn and Syracuse Railroad charter called for the first payment due contractors in 1836. The rails would connect with the Erie Canal and enable the movement of cargo to the interior of the state more easily.[48]

Then on March 27, 1835, barely into the first session of the Twenty-fourth Congress the hotheaded Virginian, Henry A. Wise, drew a pistol on Congressman Jesse A. Bynum of North Carolina over the bank question. On the issue of slavery, Wise told his fellow representatives that Congress did not have the power to end slavery within the District of Columbia. Wise even asked the Northerners to join Southerners in rejecting petitions such as the one presented by Fairfield.[49] Wise would continue to be a thorn in the side of those from the North, including Doubleday, for years to come. And in one those crazy quirks of history, Wise's second wife would be none other than Sarah Sergeant, of Philadelphia. Sarah's sister, Margaretta Sergeant married a man who would also be a thorn to Doubleday, future Union General George Gordon Meade. Yes, one of Meade's brothers-in-law was Henry A. Wise, who would govern Virginia from 1856 to 1859, the eve of the Civil War.[50]

Although history does not record a statement by Doubleday's father in the debate regarding slavery in the nation's capital, Ulysses Freeman did vote in favor of the Gag Rule, thus postponing the very issue his sons would be intimately involved with during the Civil War. The slavery issue would take up the time of legislators for years to come. In 1836 South Carolina's legislator in the House of Representatives, James Henry Hammond, gave a sizzling speech told his fellow legislators that abolitionists should "expect a felon's death" if that person was caught spreading the anti-slavery message in the South.[51] Why the congressman from Auburn voted as he did is uncertain, but by joining the majority he cast his stone into troubled waters and his sons would experience the floods to come. The young general-to-be was surrounded with many influences that would affect the Doubleday family in ways no one could have predicted.

Endnotes

11 Abner Doubleday, letter, Nov. 20, 1887, Abner Doubleday papers, The National Baseball Hall of Fame, Cooperstown, New York

12 Ulysses Freeman Doubleday, obituary, *New York Times*, March 24, 1866. The house, owned by a local attorney, still stands in Ballston Spa. A fading historical marker is next to the street.

13 Ibid

14 Henry Mayer, *All on Fire, William Lloyd Garrison and the Abolition of Slavery*, (New York: St. Martin's Press, 1998), 23

15 Ulysses Freeman Doubleday obituary, *New York Times*, March 24, 1866

16 Abner Doubleday papers, National Baseball Hall of Fame, Cooperstown, New York.

17 Nathaniel Bartlett Sylvester, *History of Saratoga County, New York*, (Interlaken, New York, Heart of the Lakes, reprint, 1979) 102

18 A. Sylvia G. Faibisoff, ed., *"Biography of Newspapers in Fourteen New York Counties* (Cooperstown, New York: New York Historical Association, 1978), 52-53

19 Ibid

20 Elliot G. Storke, *"History of Cayuga County, 1879,"* (Syracuse, New York), 55

21 D. Morris Kurtz, *Auburn, NY: It's Facilities and Resources*, (Auburn, New York: The Kurtz Publishing Co. 1884), 21

22 Kurtz, 23; Lenora Snedeker, *Memories at Willowbrook*, (Oxford, New York, 1995), 24

23 Kurtz, 23

24 Kurtz, 25

25 Thurlow Weed was a prominent nineteenth century journalist who eventually became a powerful man on the political scene and helped Abraham Lincoln become president.

26 Kurtz, 21

27 Kurtz, 26

28 *Cayuga Patriot*, Aug. 2, 1820

29 Storke, 206-207

30 Joel H. Monroe, *Historical Records of 120 Years at Auburn*, (New York: Auburn, 1913), 102; "Mott and her sister," *Pennsylvania History*, April 1965"; Ira V. Brown, *The Woman's Rights Movement In Pennsylvania, 1848-1873*, 153

31 *Cayuga Patriot*, Nov. 16, 1824

32 Hyland Kirk, *Heavy Guns and Light, The History of the 4th New York Heavy Artillery*, (New York: C.T. Dillingham, 1890), 435-436 states Thomas was

"educated in Auburn." It also gave the same information for Abner's younger brother, Ulysses.

33   S. M. Shaw, ed., *A Centennial Offering Being a Brief History of Cooperstown,* (Cooperstown, New York, 1886), 148

34   Abner D. Doubleday, pension records, NARA, Washington, D.C.

35   Carl Russell Fish, *The Rise of the Common Man 1830-1850,* (New York: The Macmillan Co., 1950), 204

36   Kurtz, 26

37   *Cayuga Patriot,* Oct. 5, 1825

38   William James Doubleday, *Cayuga Republican,* died about Oct. 16, 1822, age 13 months, Hester Elizabeth Doubleday died Dec. 10, 1830

39   Jane Ann Doubleday, daughter of Ulysses F. and Hester died June 12, 1843, aged 13 years, 3 mo. and 7 days. North Street Cemetery, Auburn, NY; Abner Doubleday papers, National Baseball Hall of Fame.

40   Gertrude Baker, *Marriages Taken from the Otsego Herald, Western Advertiser and Freeman's Journal, Otsego County, NY,* (New York: Unknown, 1932), Vol. 1; Ruth Eddy, *The Eddy Family in America,* (Boston: Unknown, 1930) 417

41   Filler, 33. This district was an area from Utica to Rochester "which was peculiarly sensitive and responsible to revivalism and religious experimentation."

42   *Auburn Weekly News and Democrat,* Dec. 25, 1873

43   James I. Robertson Jr., *Stonewall Jackson,* (New York: Macmillan Publishing, 1997), 178-179. Jackson and his second wife enjoyed the waters at Rockbridge Alum Springs upon returning from their honeymoon, they stopped at Saratoga Springs, New York (known for its healing water), but only went for a boat ride on Lake George.

44   "Search of the Life of a Fort Sumter Hero," *Weekly Patriot and Union,* Harrisburg, PA, October 10, 1861

45   Kenneth C. Martis, *The Historical Atlas of United States Congressional Districts 1789-1983,* (New York: The Free Press, 1982)

46   Schlesinger, *The Age of Jackson,* 177-178

47   Stephen B. Oates, *The Fires of Jubilee Nat Turner's Fierce Rebellion,* (New York: Harper & Row Publishers, 1975), 69-100

48   *History of Cayuga County, New York 1789-1879,* 46

49   United States, *Register of debates in Congress,: comprising the leading debates and incidents of the second session of the Twentieth Congress: : together with an appendix, containing important state papers and public documents, and the laws enacted during the session: with a copious index to the whole.,1833,* 2027 Washington [D.C.]: Printed and published by Gales and Seaton.

[50] George Gordon Meade, and George Gordon Meade. 1913. *The life and letters of George Gordon Meade, major- general United States Army.* (New York: Charles Scribner's Sons, 1913) 17

[51] United States, Francis Preston Blair, John C. Rives, Franklin Rives, and George A. Bailey. 1837. *The Congressional globe . . . [23d Congress to the 42d Congress, Dec. 2, 1833, to March 3, 1873]*, Washington: Printed at the Globe Office for the editors [etc.].February 1, 1836

CHAPTER 4

"His character and habits are decidedly good"

By his late teens, Doubleday was taller than most men, standing about six-feet tall. He was slender, had dark wavy hair and a booming voice. It was June 11, 1838 and he was seated at a table. He dipped his pen into the ink bottle, wiped off the excess dark liquid and began writing:

> Sir, I offer myself for the appointment of Cadet in the Military Academy at West Point, and request that my application be considered when the next selections shall be made to fill Cadet vacancies in that Institution. I was born in the State of New York; and now reside in the village of Auburn, County of Cayuga and State of New York. I was eighteen years of age the Twenty-Sixth day of June last; and my character and qualifications will appear from the following recommendations.
>
> Yours respectfully, Abner Doubleday

Doubleday carefully dried the ink, folded the supporting documents and letter before placing them all in the envelope addressed to Secretary of War Joel P. Poinsett. [52] In May 1838, with those few simple words to Poinsett (who had also been a minister to Mexico and discovered a plant with red leaves that was named for him: "Poinsettas"), Doubleday put the wheels in motion that would evolve into a long career. The young man's letter also referred to a statement by his father. Ulysses Freeman said his son had spent summers employed in the Corps of Engineers on three railroads, the Utica-Schenectady, Toronto-Lake Huron and Auburn and Rochester. Ulysses Freeman wrote that he had been teaching his son for the last six months: "[He] is instructed in mathematics, algebra, geometry, trigonometry and measureation for drawing." As might be expected from a father, Ulysses Freeman said that his son's character and habits were "decidedly good." The two letters were accompanied by a third, and although the signature is illegible, the writer states he too, has known Doubleday for several years and agrees with the assessments of the father. On the surface there appears to be an agreement between Doubleday and Ulysses Freeman about the son's future. The experiences Doubleday had while surveying for the building of railroads had him thinking about becoming a civil engineer. He may have also been influenced by having a father who fought at Sackets Harbor and a grandfather and six great-uncles that fought in the American Revolution, giving the military an appeal for a young man.

West Point is located on the west side of the Hudson River, about fifty-five miles north of New York City. Many of the stone buildings there look as if their very architecture defines military fortification. They are built on the side of Storm King Mountain, less than twenty miles from Newburgh, New York, birthplace of Doubleday's mother. As the famous educational home to the officer corps of the United States Army, it offers spectacular views of the river and its valley. When one visits, it is easy to see why the spot was chosen during the Revolutionary War to defend the river and Upstate New York from invading British. Seeing the immaculate grounds of today, it is difficult to visualize cows grazing across on the fields, but an order was issued the summer of 1839, Doubleday's first summer at the military academy, banning cattle from running loose within the walls of the school.[53]

About the same time this order was given, slaves on board the *Amistad* revolted and took over the ship and thus began another chapter in the fight for freedom by enslaved Africans. In the White House, President Van Buren was dealing with the Mormon War in Missouri and approved measures that would lead to the "Trail of Tears," forcing Cherokees and other bands of Indians on what would be, for many, a death march from their land in Georgia that took place over several years, ending about the time Doubleday began his West Point years.

As Doubleday began wearing the uniform of a West Point cadet, the public was beginning to hear about slavery from two sisters who had seen slavery as part of their everyday lives. Angelina and Sarah Grimke were touring Northern cities spreading the message of slavery's evils and gave the Anti-Slavery Movement momentum. Doubleday soon found himself immersed in his studies and learning the Army way of life. As he learned his lessons, West Point itself was the center of a political battle. In the early 1830s none other than the three-term buckskin-wearing Congressman David Crockett, of frontier fame, in his typical disdain for those he perceived as wealthy, raised the question of the government educating the "sons of the rich and influential . . . while the sons of the poor . . . are often neglected."

Crockett, who would later die at the Alamo in far-off Texas, had called for West Point to be abolished.[54] As the son of a former congressman and publisher, Doubleday certainly benefited from his background. However, these sons of the affluent slept on the floor in their barracks.[55] Among the eighty-five plebes in Doubleday's first year at the Point were: William S. Rosecrans, John Newton, John Pope, Isaac Bowen, Lafayette McLaws, Seth Williams, Napoleon J. T. Dana, John McCalmont (who would become a lifelong friend of Doubleday) and James Longstreet, McCalmont's roommate.[56] Sixteen-year old Newton soon discovered how serious the military was about following orders. He was court-martialed for being off the post without permission during his first summer encampment; before his formal studies even began.[57]

. Upperclassmen in the fall of 1838 included: Henry W. Halleck, James B. Ricketts, George H. Thomas, John F. Reynolds, Richard B. Garnet, Richard S. Ewell, William T. Sherman, and Don Carlos Buell.[58] As Doubleday became an upperclassman himself, he would find Ulysses S. Grant, Christopher C. Augur, Nelson W. Green, Alfred Pleasonton, John P. Hatch, and Winfield S. Hancock close on his heels. Many would win future fame, and Green would later cross Doubleday's path again in a most unexpected way.

Doubleday's grades at West Point show him as an average student. His academic record places him after his first year as thirtieth in his class of eighty-five members.[59] By June 1842 and at the completion of his West Point years, he is listed as twenty-fourth in a class of fifty-six graduating cadets.

It is his record of demerits and financial accounts that shatter the legend that he invented baseball the summer of 1839. In fact, Doubleday does not mention baseball until 1871 in his request for several items including "baseball implements" for his Buffalo Soldier troops.[60]

It is claimed he laid out the bases in a Cooperstown field with Abner Graves the summer of 1839. A closer look at the facts shows that claim to be the type of story that legends are made of; small truths or cases of misinformation that have been greatly expanded.[61] A look at the demerits Doubleday received reveals he was not in Cooperstown, but participating in the required summer encampment. For example, a partial listing shows him as receiving the following demerits:

July 2:   One demerit for having rust in the barrel of his musket at inspection;

July 9:   Eight demerits because while on sentinel duty, Doubleday allowed someone to pass his post without stopping him;

August 8:   One demerit for a messy tent;

August 24:   Two demerits for having his shoes and pants were out of order.

The records also show he paid for dancing lessons to the tune of $3.70 and then he attended the end-of-summer ball.

In the summer of 1839, Abner Graves, who made the claim that Abner laid out the bases in Cooperstown for the game that became the national pastime, was only five years old. In considering the claim, you have to ask why an eighteen-year-old boy would be playing with a five-year old. What if Abner Graves had the wrong summer? What if he was off by a year and it was 1840? And in the most interesting "what if" of all, what if it was it was Doubleday's cousin, ten-year old Abner D. Doubleday who lived in Richfield Springs, New York, a short distance from Cooperstown? Still, he is not listed as having any demerits for the summer of 1840. However, a look at his financial accounts for July and August shows he spent $8 to the storekeeper, $9.13 to the tailor, $2.50 to the shoemaker and $.74 cents to the barber. He also paid $.13 to have his quarters cleaned. If he was in Cooperstown inventing baseball, why would his room need cleaning and why would he pay the barber? He also paid nearly $5 dollars to attend the annual end of summer ball. The facts are similar for the summer of 1841, the only exception being that he also paid a small sum for his attendance at cotillion parties as well as the ball. If this is not convincing enough, perhaps the words of his life-long friend, John S. McCalmont who offered a tribute to him less than six months after Doubleday's death, say it best: "He was rather averse to out-of-door sports and retiring in his manner."[62]

It was while he was at West Point we first glimpse Doubleday's sense of humor. Being careful not to identify the erring cadet, he recalled an incident in French class. A hapless cadet was attempting to translate the French phrase *Le somimuel du merchant* (the sleep of the wicked) and after several moments decided Samuel the Merchant was correct. As Doubleday put it, "The French professor [Hyacinth R. Angel] fairly jumped out of his chair in amazement."[63] A look at Doubleday's finishing grade in French, placed him forty-sixth overall of the seventy-six classmates in their second year at the academy. During this academic year, he ranked third in the drawing class of Robert W. Weir. Weir was part of the Hudson River School and one of his paintings is in the Capitol rotunda in Washington, D.C.

A portrait of a young woman, titled "Virginia," hangs today in an office at the United States Army Military History Institute in Carlisle, Pennsylvania.

The painting is said to be the work of Doubleday. Although some may doubt the artist, the fondness of drawing maps even as a child and the many hand-drawn maps in his papers at the National Baseball Hall of Fame and at the National Archives indicate his fine ability with pen and paper.

The military academy had previously experienced a series of events that lead to clashes between the cadets and those in authority, and as Doubleday took his place, changes were happening at the top command along the Hudson River. A new superintendent, Major Richard Delafield, was chosen to oversee both men and academics. The cadets, who had been in the habit of frequenting Benny Havens' tavern two miles from the school, would now find their quest for alcoholic beverages made more difficult as a stricter hand increased the infractions for such behavior. The ruling didn't affect Doubleday for those who knew him said he never indulged in alcoholic beverages either as a cadet or officer, proving indeed, "his habits are decidedly good." Despite the changes made by Delafield, not all added to the discomfort of the cadets. He introduced iron bedsteads and made it possible for the cadets to pay $.40 each month for a more comfortable night's rest.[64]

Little is found in West Point records about Doubleday. Other than a small notation about his missing gloves, and the fact the son of a bookseller/printer borrowed only three books from the West Point library in four years, there is little to learn of his days there. His medical records reveal that he was treated for pain in his side four times, a sprain, an ulcer and toothache.[65]

He and his fellow classmates, graduated from West Point on June 30, 1842. Doubleday received his first assignment with the regular army's Third United States Artillery. Before going to his first post, he had three months leave. His military career would take him to many posts and he would participate in two major wars that would change America and cause many of these new army officers to march into their nation's history books.[66]

Endnotes

[52] Abner Doubleday, Cadet Application Papers, West Point

[53] Post Orders, Vol. 1, Feb. 19, 1838 to June 3, 1842, Order 48, 138, West Point

[54] Thomas J. Fleming, *West Point, The Men and Times of the United States Military Academy*, (New York: William Morrow & Co., 1969), 98-99

[55] Ibid, 6

[56] John S. McCalmont papers, *Cullum's Register of Officers and Cadets of the U.S.*, Special Collections, West Point, Box CV1141-1165, #1142

[57] John Newton papers, United States Military Academy, archives

[58] McCalmont papers, West Point

[59] Cullum's Register of the Officers and Cadets of the U.S. Military Academy, June 1939, 14-18

[60] Abner Doubleday to Adjutant General of the United States Army, Washington, DC, June 1871, 132, letters 70, 17, letters sent Vol. 1, RG 393, Record of the US Regular Army Mobile Units, twenty-fourth Infantry.

[61] Abner Doubleday papers, Statement of Cadets Accounts, January 1, 1838 to June 30, 1841 and July 1, 1841 to August 31, 1844, two volumes, also listing of demerits, U.S. Military Academy.

[62] John S. McCalmont, Twenty-Fourth Annual Reunion of the Association of Graduates of the U. S. Military Academy, June 9, 1893, (Saginaw, Michigan: Seeman & Peters, 1893, 89

[63] A.D., n.p.

[64] Fleming, 96-97

[65] Jack D. Welsh MD, *Medical Histories of Union Generals*, (Kent, Ohio: Kent State University Press, 1996), 101

[66] Abner Doubleday, library records show Abner borrowed *Science of War*, by Plates, Vol. 1 & 2 in 1840; *Sacroix Calcul Differential*, in 1840, and *Gwilt's Equilibrium Arches* in 1841; U.S. Military Academy. Also, 40 cents in 2002 dollars equals $6.49, Inflation Calculator, (WWW.Westegg.com)

CHAPTER 5

"A higher toned organization"

Doubleday's family was delighted to see him. After four long years, this second son was home, even though it was for only a short time. Now, he was Second Lieutenant Doubleday, and home was where he didn't have to salute anyone or worry about demerits. "Life at West Point was very secluded," he told them. This home was not the one Doubleday knew so well. Ulysses Freeman had bought a farm in Scipio, New York, about eleven miles south of Auburn just before he left for West Point.[67]

There had been a financial panic in 1837 and we can only speculate as to why Ulysses Freeman traded his printing press for a plow. He was probably struggling from the recession that hung over the nation. That summer Doubleday's father was tapped to be judge of bee hives and the best honey at the Cayuga County Agricultural Society's yearly fair.[68] While area newspapers didn't take notice of the new officer, they did record the marriage of his sister, Amanda, who walked down the aisle and married Reverend Herman James Eddy, a Baptist preacher, on August 14, 1842 in Scipio.

At the end of his furlough, Doubleday headed south to report to Captain and Brevet Lieutenant Colonel Thomas Childs commanding Fort Johnston, Smithville, North Carolina. The fort, no longer standing, was sited along Cape Fear River, a short distance from the Atlantic Ocean. Doubleday said the trip was long and tiring.

He was greeted by Childs and fellow West Pointers who were already at the post. Doubleday described Childs, "[He] is [a] handsome man, of steady presence and pleasing manners. He had gained laurels as a mere boy in the War of 1812 with Great Britain and in the War of 1836, which lasted several years against the Seminole Indians in Florida. He was a strict disciplinarian, but his severity was a matter of duty and always tempered with kindly impulses." Childs was well liked and his home was a meeting place for many including, "some of the most influential families in the state," Doubleday said. Soldiers and citizens would gather together for parties, picnics and fun in the nearby water. Evening parades attracted many, as the band was comprised of "Germans who had studied music and who had been selected from the recruits," Doubleday continued in his diary.[69]

It is at this first assignment that we glimpse what may have been the influence of the Temperance Movement on Doubleday. He noted, "Our men as a general thing behaved well but on pay day, which came every two months, they gave us a great deal of trouble, for they were sure to be drunk and disorderly. These payments at long intervals are, in my opinion, very demoralizing and destructive of discipline. It is much better to pay small sums weekly than large sums every two, four or six months. The latter inevitably leads to gambling, drunkenness and other excesses"[70]

As Officer of the Day and responsible for good order on the first payday after arriving at the fort, Doubleday found himself filling a guardhouse with drunken men, with some even being tied up and gagged. There had been a drunken spree of men at a small post with little else to do. In addition, he was assigned to be a member of a garrison court martial panel. It would be the first of many courts martial boards where Doubleday would have to render an opinion concerning the behavior of his fellow soldiers. Doubleday was selected again for court martial duty the following summer and left by a steamship for Fort Moultrie at Charlestown, South Carolina, the town supported by rice and tobacco. In 1861, Doubleday would find himself again in Charleston where he would first taste fame. The responsibility associated with participating in courts martial was a heady matter for a man in his mid-twenties and untested on a field of battle.

As the ship approached Charleston Harbor, Doubleday was surprised to see soldiers drilling on the beach at sunrise. He learned that the oppressive heat later in the day was cause for early drill at Moultrie. While there, Doubleday soon found himself in the company of more West Pointers: Second Lieutenants Daniel H. Hill, William T. Sherman, George H. Thomas, John F. Reynolds, and First Lieutenant Braxton Bragg. These men under the department command of General Walker K. Armistead, the father of the future Confederate General Lewis Armistead, caused Doubleday to remark, "I do not believe there ever was a higher toned organization in service than the Third U.S. Artillery at that time, made so by the example of Sherman, Thomas, Bragg and others. Each officer looked upon any stain upon the regiment as vital to himself. The command had just returned from Florida where it had spent several years campaigning in the swamps and [by-ways] against the most wily, treacherous and cruel of all the Indian tribes. The contrast of their late hardships and wild life, with the elegant hospitality of Charleston was very gratifying and acceptable." With the court martial proceedings completed and several parties later, Doubleday returned to Fort Johnston after only a few days.

Officers were expected to fill many roles in their careers, especially when in isolated areas. At the fort, Doubleday applied his drawing skills as he assumed the duties of an architect. He designed a new hospital for the garrison. It must have been a good design, for Doubleday said the post doctor was satisfied.[71]

While he was at Smithville, Doubleday was also focusing on a new technology, photography. He made a camera obscura. "Some of the servants saw it and reported that I had made a machine that turned every body upside down."[72] Such an event caused no little excitement among those who saw the inverted images. It would not be the last time Doubleday became involved with photography.

The year 1843 saw the development of a new invention: Samuel F.B. Morse built the first telegraph line from Baltimore, Maryland to Washington, D.C. It was also the year a group of young college students known as the Lane [Seminary] Rebels lead by Theodore Weld, held a sit-in at the Seminary run by Lyman Beecher in protest of the Seminary's stance against addressing the slavery issue. The students transferred to Oberlin College where their views were tolerated. For Doubleday, the year brought personal sadness. His thirteen-year old sister, Jane Ann died. Being so far from home, the news hit twenty-four year old Doubleday hard. True to nineteenth century style, he wrote a poem about his little sister's death and poured out his grief to newly-wed Amanda:

> Yes, where is she whose present could awake
> The hearts deep chords to notes of joy and grief,
> Whose love, nor time, nor absence e'er could break.
> Whose voice was sweet as melody of Eve.
> Ah me! When the memory recalls the past,
> Those twilight hours when shone the harvest moon,
> And hand in hand a spell around us cast
> Beneath the old home porch till midnight's moon
> In conversation long and sweet, we parted too soon. [73]

Duty kept Doubleday traveling between Fort Johnston, Fort Moultrie and other nearby posts. In 1844, he even did a tour of duty at Fort McHenry in Baltimore. It is there that he probably met First Lieutenant William

Shover, also a member of the Third United States Artillery. Indicating the two men became friends, Doubleday corresponded with Shover's widow, Felicia about 1852 and again during the Civil War. By 1845, Doubleday was sent north to Portland, Maine under the command of Colonel Ichabod Crane. He would only be there for a few months before he received orders to head south, then west.

Endnotes

[67] A.D., n.p.

[68] *Auburn Journal and Advertiser*, July 20, 1842

[69] A.D., n.p.

[70] Ibid

[71] Ibid

[72] Ibid

[73] This poem is in the possession of the Doubleday family.

CHAPTER 6

"A note of arrogance and menace"

Doubleday walked up the plank of the *Lexington*. The ship softly rose and fell with the waves in New York harbor. The ship would be his home for the next month as it sailed toward south Texas. "I was headed for a situation that was filled with a note of arrogance and menace," he said. He had orders to go to Mexico and war.[74]

As the politicians decided the country should look westward, its army prepared to head for Texas and the Mexican border. In spring 1845 Doubleday, who had been at Fort Preble, Maine, near Portland, soon received orders and headed to New York harbor and eventually St. Joseph's Island off the coast of Texas. His new assignment would be a big change from the fog and cold rocks by the Atlantic to the sun and warm waters of the Gulf of Mexico.

The war with Mexico was brought on by many things including the desire to add more land to the United States and a perceived threat that Mexico would solve part of its debt problem by selling the California Territory to Great Britain. There were people who thought annexing Texas would extend slavery. The Massachusetts transcendentalists spoke out against making Texas a state because of the slavery issue, and Henry David Thoreau refused to pay taxes to the government that was taking action he didn't agree with, making him an early non-violent activist.[75]

Doubleday traveled to New York City readying for the trip southward. He had been assigned to Company A of the First United States Artillery commanded by Captain Giles Porter. Companies B, C, D, E, I, and K were also onboard.[76] These seven companies left September 2, 1845 on the ship under the command of naval Lieutenant Frank Elison. During the month they were at sea, the soldiers played cards or chess and even participated in a glee club.[77] Although Doubleday did not identify the man who organized the singers, it was probably none other than First Lieutenant John Bankhead Magruder (West Point Class of 1830), who later became a Confederate general.[78] Magruder was known for his geniality and the telling of jokes after the tables had been cleared and "the wine and cigars" appeared.[79]

Three hundred and seventy-two enlisted men plus officers sailed out of New York Harbor. By early October, they arrived on St. Joseph's Island located off the southernmost point of Texas near where the Rio Grande empties into the Gulf of Mexico. Among the officers were 1842 West Point classmate and Maine native, Second Lieutenant Seth Williams, and Ohioan First Lieutenant Irvin McDowell of the First United States Artillery. In fact, the Mexican War would be the bloody training ground for the Civil War.[80] Williams had graduated from West Point with Doubleday; McDowell had graduated the spring Doubleday wrote his letters of application to the military academy. McDowell had been a tactics instructor at West Point when war with Mexico broke out, but was now serving on the staff of Brigadier General John Ellis Wool. Wool had a reputation as a very capable officer and the Newburgh, New York native had been wounded in the War of 1812. As the men took up their new duties, the commander of the First United States Artillery Colonel Ichabod Crane, and his adjutant and future Civil War general, Joseph Hooker (West Point Class of 1837), were in Florida temporarily before heading to Mexico.[81]

Once the vessel set anchor in the harbor and the troops headed for land, some of the soldiers barely got their land-legs back before they were on the move again, this time to Corpus Christi to join the main body of the army. In this group was Second Lieutenant George Gordon Meade, who although born in Spain, was from an influential Philadelphia family. Meade was in the Corps of Engineers and on the staff of General Zachary Taylor, who became president five years later in 1849. Meade became a general in the Civil War and expressed an intense dislike of Doubleday that will be seen in a later chapter.[82] However, Doubleday and Porter returned to the island where they had orders to guard the multitude of temporarily stored army goods. In December 1845, Texas was granted statehood by Congress. The Mexicans, quite naturally, opposed the move. Back on St. Joseph's Island, by the end of the year three men had died and seven had deserted from Corpus Christi. Up to that point, life for the men had been pretty boring with little to do. Then in early January 1846, the army was divided into two brigades under fifty-one year old New Yorker General William J. Worth, and Georgian Colonel David E. Twiggs, who was four years younger than Worth. Twiggs would later serve during the Civil War as the oldest Confederate commander. Doubleday noted the two commanders, Worth and Twiggs, "were not very friendly to each other."[83] Twiggs was viewed by some as "one of the worst kind of men, though possibly a good fighter."[84]Worth was known as an excellent horseman and was honored several times for his bravery.

For the men, there were drills and parades and battles with the weather. In early December, Meade wrote his wife, "It has been storming and raining incessantly for the last three weeks."[85] Doubleday said the wind from the north blasted across their camp and the men had to continually "fortify" their tents against the "blasts."[86] He wrote:

> No person who has never been in that region can appreciate the force and severity of a Texas norther. The change of temperature which sometimes occurs in the course of twenty minutes is incredible. Often while taking a siesta in consequence of the tropical heat which prevailed, I have heard the roar of the approaching tempest. I would hardly have time to call to the men to come with axes to drive down my tent poles before the very blast would be upon us. In fifteen minutes perhaps the rain would be hanging in icicles from all the brushes in the vicinity. Stoves and camp fires would be an immediate necessity. The storm would rage for three days and then all would be serene again.[87]

There was no water fit to drink and in the words of one soldier, it was hot enough to "roast a haunch of venison in about five minutes time."[88] The men were not without entertainment however. Magruder "sent for a theatrical company." [89] Meade wrote home that New Year's Day of 1846 was spent in enjoying eggnog, racing and the theater. His opinion of the entertainers was expressed this way: "They are a company of strolling actors, who murder tragedy, burlesque comedy and render farce into buffoonery, in the most approved style."[90]

Adding to the colorful landscape of people, local hunters were present riding their wild horses. Several of these men would bring in mustangs to sell to officers at $2.50 each[91]. The mustangs ran in herds and were very small when compared with American horses, Doubleday noted. The Texans would lasso the horses but the animals weren't really broken to ride. Then in an attempt to regain control over the mustangs, the horses would be "creased," shot with a gun across the neck near the spinal column. The horse would then become easy to overtake, if not killed outright. (Thankfully this practice died out eventually.) The army quartermaster saw the horses as an inexpensive alternative to American horses. When First Lieutenant Braxton

Bragg requested horses for the artillery, he was given these weakened animals. Bragg commented this exercise was a "beautiful example of the goodness of coincidence" in allowing these undernourished animals grass to live on "since they had not strength to draw their own forage."[92]

The island was abundant with deer and quail and the men often went hunting. Doubleday even thought there was "a species of tiger roaming about." Doubleday described the animal as striped, but smaller than the "Asiatic animal." Just what animal he saw remains a mystery, but that meant hunting was not without its own dangers. During one of his hunting excursions, he found a cave that was apparently the home of one such animal. Bones were lying about, so Doubleday wisely decided to leave quietly. However, during the three-mile walk back to camp, he was followed by a pack of coyotes.[93]

At the end of winter the men were sure they would begin their advance into Mexico. Taylor and the main body of his troops headed for Matamoras in early March.[94] With the army preparing to meet the enemy, Doubleday and his fellow soldiers were sent to Point Isabel to guard the relocated supply base.[95] The company remained at Point Isabel as the "bombardment of Fort Brown and the battles of Palo Alto and Resaca" occurred.[96] To twenty-seven year old Doubleday left behind guarding the supplies, it likely seemed as though he was never going to see action.

Once Matamoras, located a few miles up from the mouth of the Rio Grande, had been captured, Doubleday decided to be a curious tourist and visit the city to learn something of the manners and customs of the Mexicans in their own country. A few years later, this knowledge would be invaluable to him in a way he could not have imagined.[97] The sightseeing trip was not without incident. Doubleday, who was briefly detained from leaving at the same time as a few members of Texas cavalry, told them to go ahead, he would catch up. However, Doubleday found to his surprise, he was on a separate trail:

> I was not aware that there were two roads a mile apart separated by large ponds. The Texans went one way and I gallopped on the other expecting every minute to overtake them and wondering that I saw nothing of them. When I reached the battlefield of Resaca at the bend of the road where the batteries had been posted, I suddenly found myself in the presence of a party of Mexicans who were evidently there to despoil the corpses of the slain. In the best Spanish I could muster, I simply told them to get out of the way, that troops were close behind who wanted to kill them.[98]

Doubleday credits the fact he was in uniform to the quick departure of the plundering Mexicans. He was certainly glad to reach his Matamoras and Bragg's camp, where he received a warm welcome from Bragg, and the men of Randolph Ridgley's battery.[99]

Eventually, the soldiers would occupy the town for a time before advancing further toward Mexico City. Matamoras wasn't much better than a camp. Fellow artillerist and West Point classmate Isaac Bowen called it "filthy, beggerly and uninteresting."[100] That may have been true for Bowen, but Doubleday was determined to get the most out of the experience. While in Matamoras and still a bachelor, Doubleday decided to attend one of the nightly dances, a fandango. It proved to be more of an adventure than he had anticipated. The American officers removed their swords and laid them aside "to dance with more freedom."[101] As the American soldiers kicked up their heels with the Mexican maidens, the Mexican men began looking over the weapons and passed them to the rear. Then someone in the crowd who spoke both languages called to the soldiers that the Mexicans were planning to take the swords planned to use them to kill the American soldiers. The officers quickly drew their pistols, scrambled to retrieve their swords and called it a night.

Describing the Mexican women, Doubleday said, they were not the "better class of females." Many of the American soldiers were not prepared for a culture that allowed women to have bare bosoms.[102] Several of the married American officers wrote home and tried to reassure their wives that the Mexican women held no appeal.[103]

Doubleday had yet one more misadventure before seeing military action. He tried to swim across the Rio Grande and soon found himself caught in a swift current that swept him far below the entry point. He became quickly exhausted and thought his military career could be ending there in the river. Some friendly Mexicans pulled Doubleday to safety.[104]

Doubleday had been guarding supplies for about seven months. He watched other soldiers leave for intended combat. Bored and frustrated with the possibility of missing action, he requested and received a transfer.[105] As a second lieutenant, Doubleday joined Company E under the command of First Lieutenant James B. Ricketts (West Point Class of 1839). Ricketts was a native of New York City and two years older then Doubleday. They soon formed a friendship that would last for years. Serving with them was Brevet Second Lieutenant Thomas B. J. Weld (West Point Class of 1845). Together, the formed part of the artillery battalion under Doubleday's very first commander, Captain and Brevet Colonel Thomas Childs, of the Third United States Artillery.[106]

Endnotes

[74] William L. Haskin, *The History of the First Regiment of Artillery Fort Preble, Portland, Maine*, (B. Thurston and Co., 1879), 304 ; A. D., n. p.; Post Returns and Regiment Returns, and M617, Roll 675, and M727, Roll 3, National Archives, Washington, DC

[75] Henry David Thoreau, *On the Duty of Civil Disobedience*, (Chicago: Ill.: Charles H. Kerr 1989; reprint of 1849)

[76] Haskin, 304-5

[77] A. D., n. p.

[78] A. D., n. p., Abner writes in his diary about a man as "M". See also Haskin, 305. This portion of the regimental history was contributed by Abner.

[79] Ibid

[80] Ibid

[81] Returns from Regular Army Artillery Regiments, June 1821-January 1901, M 727, Roll 3, NARA, Washington, DC

[82] George Gordon Meade, and George Gordon Meade. *The Life and Letters of George Gordon Meade, Major-General United States Army,* (New York: C. Scribner's Sons, 1913), Vol. 1, 25

[83] A. D., n. p.

[84] Caleb Coker, ed., "The News From Brownsville", *Texas State Historical Assoc.,* 1992, 40. May 7, 1848 letter by Helen Chapman

[85] Meade, Vol. 1, 37

[86] A. D., n. p.

[87] Ibid

[88] Isaac Bowen papers, letter to his wife, May 20, 1846, United States Army Military History Institute (hereafter USAMHI), Carlisle, PA

[89] A. D., n. p.

[90] Meade, Vol. I, 43

[91] A. D., n. p.

[92] Ibid

[93] Ibid

[94] Haskin, 305

[95] AD, n. p.

[96] Haskin, 305

[97] AD, n. p.

[98] Ibid

[99] Ibid

[100] Bowen, letter to his wife, June 8, 1846, USAMHI

[101] AD, n. p.

[102] Ibid

[103] Napoleon Jackson Tecumseh Dana, and Robert H. Ferrell, *Monterrey is ours!: the Mexican war letters of Lieutenant Dana, 1845-1847*, (Lexington, KY: University Press of Kentucky, 1990), 142

[104] A. D., n. p.

[105] Haskin, 305

[106] A. D., n. p.

CHAPTER 7

"Bullets whizzed arond us"

Doubleday described the early morning scenes of army life:

> There is something exceedingly romantic in these early marches.
> The sudden burst of martial music as the different bands strike
> up the reveille, in the deep darkness of the forest, ending with the
> bugle calls of the light artillery and cavalry, the loud shout, the
> merry laugh, the hundred fires which spring up suddenly lighting
> up the green woods and glinting back from bayonet and sword,
> the bustle of preparation, the striking of tents, present a scene in
> the highest degree picturesque.[107]

Shortly after the mid-July transfer, Doubleday made his way to
Matamoras to re-join his company.[108] In September, Doubleday and his
comrades began the approximately 150-mile march toward Monterrey
and the interior of Mexico. Doubleday, Ricketts, and the other men in the
company were assigned as rear guard. Several hours before daylight, camp
was broken. Doubleday and his company got up early even though they
were to be last in the line. Who could sleep through the din surrounding
them anyway? Fried pork, hard crackers and coffee under their belts, the
men soon assembled to move forward. Doubleday's comrades watched as
the rest of the men formed lines. The men moved out as if presenting a
parade; they were all in an eager mood and high spirits; laughing and joking
as they began their march.

The Matamoras to Camargo march was one of determination. "The
heat was intense," Doubleday said. As the army advanced and several of
men suffered sunstroke in the unrelenting heat, the beauty of the land was
temporarily forgotten.[109] John R. Kenly of the Maryland Volunteers wrote,
"I saw men toward night (of the third day's march) frantically digging with
their bayonets in the dry bed of a water-course in the vain hope of finding
water beneath the surface. I saw men fall down in convulsions on this march,
frothing at their mouths, clutching the sand with their hands, and left to

lie until nature and the shadows of night restored them to consciousness and strength."[110] It wasn't just the heat they had to endure. The pack mules caused much frustration said Lieutenant Ulysses S. Grant of the Fourth United States Infantry. Because the army had a great many items to prepare for the march, "It took several hours to get ready," said Grant, "by the time we were ready some of the mules first loaded would be tired of standing so long with their loads on their backs. Sometimes one would start to run, bowing his back and kicking up until he scattered his load; others would lie down and try to disarrange their loads"[111].

On the way, the Americans passed the barely cold fires of the Mexicans who were ahead of them. In the distance, they could see the Mexican lancers. The Americans arrived at Walnut Grove on September 19.[112] As the American soldiers advanced toward Monterrey, General Taylor split his forces. Considering the Mexicans outnumbered the Americans, it was a calculated gamble on Taylor's part. At Monterrey, the prominent landmarks included the Bishop's Palace on the side of Independence Hill and to its left the Citadel Fort, and to the right was Federation Hill. The Saltillo Road wound its way between the two hills parallel to the Santa Catarina River. Taylor sent General Worth's division and the Texas Rangers, under Colonel John Coffee Hays, to circle to the north and west around Monterrey so that Worth's men would approach the city from the Saltillo Road. Butler and Twiggs would provide a diversion on the east side of the city. At 2 p.m., September 20, the Sabbath, Hays' and Worth's men began their advance on Monterrey. The route was flanked by enemy forts and batteries placed on the high ground surrounding the city.[113] Dividing their troops was, "a most hazardous enterprise, as we would be entirely isolated and the enemy would be posted between us and the remainder of the army." said Doubleday in his later years.[114] Advance troops had reported the streets of Monterrey were barricaded. Walls of the buildings were thick with holes cut for the mouths of cannon and the roofs were flat with parapet-like fortifications.

As they forged ahead expecting to be shot at any minute, Doubleday got his first look at the Citadel, an enormous building built on a site once intended for a cathedral. All was quiet as they tramped forward. The American skirmishers moved toward the road leading to the rear of the enemy fortifications. The suspense soon ended. The heights above them were "swarming with armed men and it had to be stormed," Doubleday said.[115] Doubleday stared at the Bishop's Palace through a borrowed spyglass. "The last rays of the sun were reflected from a forest of bayonets."[116] Looking at the structure, Doubleday thought taking the building was a "hopeless task."

He was about to participate in his first large-scale battle. Monterrey would not be easy to take. Surrounded by high ridges on three sides, the American troops would be forced to cross open land from the north. Supplies had to be brought across the Santa Catarina River to the rear of Monterrey. The Bishop's Castle dating back to 1786, was an imposing building and a reminder of the Mexican war with Spain. There was another ridge, Federation Hill, and two Mexican forts in the eastern portion of town. When the Mexicans planned their attack, they didn't consider the rear of the ridges as points for possible attack. Mexican commanders were sure the slopes were too high, nearly perpendicular; it would prove to be a miscalculation they would regret. [117]

After four hours and seven miles later, General Worth called a halt a short distance from the Saltillo Road before continuing forward attempting to learn more of the situation ahead. As he and a few members of his staff had ridden a short distance, they realized a group of Mexican horsemen had gotten behind them and the rest of the army. The horsemen stopped just long enough for the Americans to race to safety. Had the enemy continued its charge, the Mexicans may have captured Worth.

The sun went down, but the men remained in place. The Americans settled down for the night with their right flank resting on the slope of a mountain, and the left flank ending in the protection of thick undergrowth. Just before midnight, the Mexicans inside Citadel Fort sent up "sky-rockets and fired twenty-one guns in rapid succession. Then we saw a fire ball sail high in the air," Doubleday said. Thinking an attack was beginning, the men became alert. Satisfied with their show, the Mexicans then settled down. [118]

Duncan's Battery acted as advance troops and guarded the main road. Doubleday wouldn't get much sleep. He and Ricketts tried to find a decent place to sleep. "The ground was covered thick with thorny bushes and broken pieces of limestone from a quarry in our rear," said Doubleday. Since the men did not realize they would be separated from their supplies, "We were utterly destitute of blankets and suffered severely from the cold," he continued. For Doubleday, the night was much too long. He suffered from "neuralgia (severe pain along a nerve) in the face" and could not sleep except for "short intervals." Regardless, he and Ricketts had their evening assignments. A staff officer assigned Ricketts as brigade officer of the day and Doubleday as officer of the brigade guard. Informed that the guards had been posted several hours, Doubleday got up, put on his sash and sword and went out to inspect the sentinels. It was pitch black and he spent considerable time stumbling around in the darkness, often tripping over a sleeping soldier. With his clothes torn, and after nearly falling over the edge of a cliff, Doubleday gave up all hope of finding the guards and lurched his way around in the darkness until he found his way back to where Ricketts was lying. Doubleday told Ricketts about stumbling around in the dark, and Ricketts decided not to attempt an inspection either. Doubleday was sure he could be arrested for breach of an order, but nothing came of it the next morning.[119] Not able to sleep, Doubleday wandered from his makeshift bed on the ground to the warmth of the campfire. There he would talk with other men around the fire as they discussed what they thought would happen in the morning.[120] The night was not a quiet one. The Americans could hear the Mexican guards calling out every half hour. Some of the Mexicans troops sent up rockets, causing the Americans to think a night attack might begin.

The Morning of September 22, 1846

As soon as it became daylight, the advance resumed: Colonel Hays' Texas horsemen and Captain Charles F. Smith's troops of the Second Artillery led the way. Behind them were Captain James Duncan's flying battery in the center, Childs' artillery battalion on Duncan's right, and the Eighth Infantry on Duncan's left; in the second row were Lieutenant William Mackall's battery and the Seventh Infantry. Doubleday, who had never been in mountainous country, said the countryside was beautiful. Private Carr White, from Ohio, wrote to his sister, "Oh! it is the prettiest sight you ever saw to see about two thousand soldiers all dressed alike with Bright and shining guns, swords, & belts white as snow, if you could see them marching and hear their music."[121] However, gazing at the landscape was put aside for more pressing business.

The Americans drew closer to the city where they could see fluttering Mexican flags. It wasn't long before the Americans were spotted by the Mexican troops under Commander-in-Chief Pedro de Ampudia. These were Mexican lancers, 1,500 of them commanded by Lieutenant Colonel Juan Najera. Worth ordered the advance troops to dismount and take cover, but before the men could get out of their saddles, the enemy charged. The lancers ran into a group of Texas troops led by Ben McCulloch. Quickly, Duncan and his flying artillery came to the aid of the Texans and began shooting grape canister at the lancers. The Mexican cavalry slowly moved to their rear giving the appearance of retreating, as the Americans advanced.

The Mexicans were soon out of sight, but not for long. As the Americans moved steadily forward, the Mexican Lancers soon thundered into action in an all out charge. Duncan's battery went into action and turned the lancers back to the loud cheers of the American soldiers. Worth's men had one man killed and two wounded. A number of Mexicans lay dead, the number of wounded was unknown.[122]

While this was taking place, Worth was attempting to learn more about the enemy's positions. He ordered Childs to send a company up the mountainside to get a good look. The duty fell to Ricketts, Doubleday and Weld to climb up several hundred feet above where they had just faced the Mexican lancers; they could see that the roads leading to the city were heavily guarded. From their vantage point, the trio could see both Independence Hill and Federation Hill. Halfway down the Independence Hill stood the Bishop's Palace. It had been prepared for an attack. Federation Hill boasted a fort and a battery. They could see Worth's men pushing the retreating Mexicans even further. The battery on Federation Hill fired on the Americans. Several Americans were wounded and the Eighth United States Infantry's Captain Henry McKavett was killed. The Mexican battery soon discovered Doubleday, Ricketts and Weld's presence and opened fire on them. Their aim was good and the three men were soon covered with dirt and gravel.[123] "The sound of these projectiles was anything but pleasant," said Doubleday.[124] In the distance, he saw a line of cavalry along the Saltillo Road; they were headed to reinforce the Mexican soldiers in Monterrey.

Weld scrambled down the mountain to tell Worth of the approaching enemy reinforcements. After delivering the information, Weld was nearly hit by a Mexican shell as he was climbing back up the mountain. Another shell hit the ground where Doubleday and Ricketts were standing. Many more shells followed them, but no one was injured.[125] The sounds of shelling got even louder; Mexican soldiers had gotten to the foot of the mountain where Doubleday and the others were located. The Americans soon returned fire. With their position becoming dangerous, Childs ordered them to descend from the heights. Worth then ordered them to form as an advance picket for half an hour before returning to the artillery brigade then in the cornfield.

Once back in the cornfield, Doubleday soon saw a "hasty funeral" for McKavett. Doubleday was a friend of the captain and noted McKavett had predicted his own death. Doubleday could not face the terrible reality of McKavett's fate. "I turned away when the body was brought up for I had no desire to see what lay beneath that bloody blanket," said Doubleday. McKavett, an orphan, was buried in the cornfield. Years later, Doubleday would command Fort McKavett, named in honor of his fallen friend. As the burial of McKavett was taking place, Captain Charles F. Smith and four of his companies moved forward to silence the enemy's guns. [126]

While Doubleday, Ricketts and Weld were watching from the mountainside, Federation Hill was stormed successfully. The Americans held their prized real estate, and plans were made to take Independence Hill in the morning. The soldiers knew that even with the hills in American possession, the city would not be easy to capture.

The fighting subsided and Ricketts, Weld and Doubleday found an enlisted man to cook a meal for them; they had not eaten in two days. That taken care of, sleep was the next concern. It was raining hard, soaking all the soldiers, and Doubleday, who had not slept much, looked for a place, but found other soldiers and officers had already filled up one area. "Col. Childs however kindly loaned me his overcoat and displacing some saddles near him, made room for me by his side," Doubleday said.[127] Around midnight, Doubleday received word the heights above the Bishop's Palace would be stormed. There would be no sleep for Childs that night. At 3 a.m. the colonel would lead a charge up the heights, but since Doubleday's battery was not involved he got some much-needed rest.

The Morning of September 23, 1846

At daylight, Ricketts, Doubleday and Weld received a special assignment. Placed under the command of Captain and Brevet Major Harvey Brown of the Fourth United States Artillery, they were headed to Los Molinos, seven miles from Monterrey. Reports had been received that a large body of enemy cavalry was heading toward Monterrey from Los Molinos (meaning "the flour mills"). Thinking it could be Mexican politician and soldier, Antonio Lopez de Santa Anna (who had a colorful, checkered career in both arenas); the Americans were to stop the enemy's reinforcements from reaching their goal.

Accompanying Doubleday's battery was a section of light artillery under Lieutenant Irons and a company of dragoons under Captain Mahon. Los Molinos sat at the foot of a mountain that rose behind them nearly "perpendicular for several thousand feet." A torrent of water fed the mills and the white limestone buildings where the water works ran were covered with highly polished cement. The beauty and serenity of the countryside made Doubleday almost forget why he was there; the fighting seemed far away. Doubleday and the men rested as Captain Graham wrote his report about the enemy in front of them. The presence of the Americans scared the Mexican reinforcements off and the Americans later discovered it prevented a pack train of 180 mules loaded with flour from joining the Mexican troops in the city.[128]

Doubleday and the other men who had gone to the mills had completed a successful mission and returned for new orders. Evening was approaching as the Americans reached the city. When they arrived some of the Texans told them the Castle had been taken and in the distance, they could see the Stars and Stripes flying above its walls. Childs had captured one of the Mexican batteries positioned there. The men who had fought so hard were now laughing and singing; others were drinking coffee and relaxing, something not done for the last two days. Nearby, their guns were stacked and ready to be grabbed if needed. The Saltillo Road into leading into Monterrey was in the hands of the Americans.

New orders sent Doubleday's company to the "highest point of [Independence] hill where they joined Lieutenant James G. Martin with his two guns of Taylor's Light Battery."[129] Worth's men were behind the castle; the Seventh United States Infantry was holding Federation Hill.

High on Independence Hill, Doubleday, Ricketts, Weld, Martin and the enlisted men prepared for a possible night attack. Hungry, Doubleday and Martin made their way down the mountain to the castle in search of food. Their meal would be a cup of coffee. They made their way back to the mountaintop where they endured another cold night. The fire died out. Since they didn't want the Mexicans to see where their camp was located, the fire was not restarted. No blankets, nothing for warmth, "Martin then proposed to pitch a captured Mexican tent." The unfamiliar shelter took some time to erect and soon Doubleday and Weld decided to test it for sleeping. Sandbags were used as a floor to lessen the effect of the rocky ground beneath them. The sand was wet and anything but a warm, soft mattress. It would be another miserable night, but the lack of sleep during the two previous nights took hold and they slept soundly for a short time. The timbers of the tent gave way and Doubleday narrowly missed injury. "Weld never stirred," and the men thought he was badly hurt. The men dragged him from the tent none the worse for wear, but very angry at being disturbed much to the laughter of the troops. Doubleday went back to sleep and was "dreaming of home" when Ricketts shook Doubleday to waken him for guard duty. Doubleday checked the sentinels and the main guard. Thoroughly chilled he went back to the camp and "sat by the embers of the fire." There lost the in the timeless thoughts of soldiers, Doubleday likely remembered family and friends.[130]

The quietness of the night didn't last; a sentinel sounded the alarm about 1 a.m. The Mexicans were approaching in an attempt to reclaim the hill. The men were up at once and the noise of their preparations scared off the enemy.

Later during the night as Doubleday went among the men waking them up for duty, he approached one group that appeared to be sleeping men. He discovered it was a group of dead Mexicans. The remainder of the night passed without incident. In the morning Doubleday went for a closer look at the corpses he had found in the night. "They were dressed simply in uniform coat and pantaloons without underclothes of any description." Doubleday gazed upon the faces of death, in all its ugliness. "One had a laugh still upon his face, the muscles seeming to become rigid before the expression could change." [131]

At daylight Childs was already leading the American troops toward the Monterrey. The Mexicans were not about to give anything away for free. Ricketts' company remained at their position for a short time, in case the Mexicans attacked from the rear. Orders to move forward arrived and Doubleday's company joined with Lieutenant Edmond Bradford's company of the Fourth United States Artillery to act as skirmishers at the bottom of the hill. From there they pressed forward in support of Childs' men in the city. Reaching Monterrey, the Americans would learn about the dangers of street fighting. They pushed forward and made their way through the city streets. Childs was so far in advance, he couldn't be found. As they searched for Childs, they advanced to the public square where they found a chapel with an adjoining cemetery. The walls of the cemetery had been opened to hold barrels of the cannon hiding there. Held in reserve, Doubleday and the others were soon moving forward again, "platoons filling up the entire width of the street." Eighty yards in front of them the Mexicans had thrown up a protective barricade; others were in many of the buildings and on rooftops. Soon the Americans were shooting and looking for cover.

As they approached the barricade, the shooting became more intense. The battle forced the men to change formation and they ran along the sidewalk to escape flying balls, grape shot and bullets. As the American soldiers ran into a store, several men fell from the enemy's fire. "Before I went in, two balls struck the wall near my head," Doubleday said. It was time to storm the barricade.[132]

The men rushed forward taking shelter "under the wall of a bakery," said Doubleday. They stayed there several hours while the Texans cleared the rooftops and pushed the Mexicans back. Opposite the bakery was a house with an inner court planted with orange trees. As Doubleday and the men moved inside the courtyard, grapeshot filled the air. Deciding to get a closer look at the action ahead, Doubleday borrowed a spyglass. As he was peering through it, one of the men shouted a warning. Just in time, Doubleday stepped back from the open doorway where he had been standing. Grape shot hit the very spot where his feet had been planted. Another day came to end and they were ordered to occupy a building across from the courtyard. This new location had passage that lead to open fields and would provide the Mexicans access back into the city and the rear of the main body of the American army. To Doubleday, the situation looked anything but promising for the next morning. "The enemy greatly superior to us in numbers were now cooped up in a small part of the city," said Doubleday. Orders for the night were, "To hold it to the last." As Doubleday moved into position, a shell fired by Americans in the rear lines, exploded in the kitchen area across from him covering him with pieces of adobe. He and the others had not eaten for two days. Their search for a meal produced coffee and a few grapes.[133]

As night fell, both sides settled down to rest. Doubleday who had barely five hours sleep in the last two days, tried to lie down in the narrow archway, along with all the other men. The best he could do with his six-foot-plus frame was to avoid the sharp stones and sleep sitting up. All night more American soldiers passed through, making sleep nearly impossible and the night seemingly endless.

In the morning, he learned the heights had been taken and the Mexicans had gone inside the palace for safety. Using the enemy's sandbags for leverage, they positioned a twelve pound howitzer into place and fired into the palace. With the shelling, the Mexicans left rapidly. A small party of troops took the castle and they were soon joined by other American troops. As the Americans chased the Mexicans from their hiding spots in the buildings, it was a very brave Lieutenant Ayres that jumped through the window of one such building before he could confirm a lack of danger.

The Americans began pounding the Mexican troops. The early shells missed the enemy, but hit American troops. The next American shell landed in the cathedral where General Ampudia was hiding along with a large quantity of ammunition. Pandemonium followed as the Mexican leader mistakenly thought the Americans were attacking in force and ordered return fire. It was several hours before the firing came to a halt.

The next morning, September 24, the Americans advanced even further through the city. The firing slowly gave way to silence. By noon, they learned the fighting had officially ended. The Americans were told to reassure the few remaining Monterrey citizens they had nothing to fear. After several days of fighting, Doubleday and his comrades didn't resemble anything like officers and gentlemen. "Our faces were scratched from forcing our way through thorny bushes and our clothes from the same cause presented a very dilapidated appearance," he said. Their clothing was "stained with specimens of every kind of mud from sleeping in roadways and on the wet ground. Add to this, beards of several weeks growth and we could not have been very prepossessing." [134]

The Battle of Monterrey was over. Private Carr White wrote home, summing up the battle, "It was a terrible time the Bullets whizzed arond us like so many Humin Birds. But I guess we whiped them at last."[135]

Endnotes

[107]   A. D., n. p.

[108]   Haskin, 305

[109]   A. D., n. p.

[110]   George Winston Smith and Charles Judah, eds., *Chronicles of the Gringos,* (Albuquerque: The University of New Mexico Press, 1968), 75

[111]   Ibid, 77

[112]   Haskin, 306

[113]   Ibid

[114]   Ibid

[115]   A. D., n. p.

[116]   Ibid

[117]   David Lavender, *Climax at Buena Vista,* (Philadelphia: J.B. Lippincott Co., 1966), 102-103

[118]   Haskin, 307

[119]   A. D., n. p.

[120]   Ibid

[121]   Jon E. Lewis ed., *Mammoth Book of War Diaries & Letters,* (New York: Carroll & Graf Publishers, Inc., 1999), 82-83

[122]   Lavender, 109

[123]   Haskin, 309

[124]   A. D., n. p.

[125]   Ibid

[126]   Ibid

[127]   Ibid

[128]   Ibid

[129]   Ibid

[130]   Ibid

[131]   Ibid

[132]   Ibid

[133]   Haskin, 313; and A. D., n. p.

[134]   A. D., n. p.

[135]   Lewis, ed., 82-83

CHAPTER 8

"Superhuman exertions"

After being warned of the enemy's presence, Doubleday left Saltillo to join his company. Along the dusty road, he was struck by the silence, not even a dog barked an announcement of the moving figures. "It's so quiet it's like the people and animals have turned to stone." He later said of the experience "It was more impressive to me than the solitude of the desert or the ocean had ever been" [136]

The army of occupation was comprised of the Louisville Legion, the Ohio Regiment, General Tom Marshall, his staff and thirty of his Kentucky cavalry, and Doubleday's Company E under the command of Captain James H. Prentiss. There was a daily uneasiness that they would be attacked, and that concern was fueled by many alarms including one from a drunken soldier that turned out to be yet another false alarm. Although the American officers and troops didn't know it, Mexican General Antonio Lopez de Santa Anna was about to pay a visit with his ever-increasing army, as many as 15,000 men. General Zachary Taylor's army numbered about 5,000 available soldiers. Once Monterrey had been taken, the Americans occupied the city. They began to settle in for an unknown duration and several soldiers took over some of the city's homes as temporary residences. Doubleday and many of the American troops stayed at the Citadel Fort.

Doubleday rode to Saltillo to see a few acquaintances. It was during this visit to Saltillo that he saw a Mexican family he had become friendly with. Fearing for their safety, he urged them to leave the city.

The family left the very next day, the same day that his company received orders to outfit as a heavy artillery unit with four cannon: two eighteen-pounders and two twelve-pounders. Getting ready for their duty took a full day and it was almost dark when they were ready. "By eight P.M. of the same day, by almost superhuman exertions, we had obtained horses, adjusted the harness, equipped the guns, and packed the ammunition in the wagons," said Doubleday.[137] They gathered up every available man; those who were well enough to leave the hospital and even the drunks in the guardhouse, and set off for Los Molinos. It was dark as they began their march.

About three miles out, one of the eighteen-pounders overturned in a gully. After struggling with the huge cannon and finally getting it upright again, the march resumed. When they reached the mill, Doubleday banged on the door until the miller let the sleepy men inside and showed them a store counter that became a bed shared by Doubleday and Ricketts. After his recent experiences, Doubleday was determined not to go into battle exhausted. The nights were cold in February and, "Captain Prentiss (who) slept outside was half frozen," Doubleday said.[138] In the morning they resumed the march through the mile-high mountains.

The march was a test of a man's strength (both physical and mental), a test of man against the enemy, and of man against nature. During daylight, the weather was unbelievably hot, bone drying hot. Sweat poured off the men, and there was no water to drink or wipe across a hot face. There was no water other than what they could carry with them, and they were moving as fast as possible in the burning sand and dust.

The march didn't go smoothly; five miles from Rinconda the axletree of the other eighteen-pounder gave way. The men couldn't give up the mission, too much was at stake. A few men were left with the huge piece and plans called for a new axletree to be made at Rinconda and then delivered to the waiting detachment. However, the men didn't wait for a new axletree. They struggled with the cannon using levers and jackscrews until they got it back on the wagon.

Once in Rinconda, Doubleday and his fellow soldiers made good use of a little creek. After the hot trek across the sands, Doubleday said he waded into the stream, "up to my knees" and "enjoyed a drink which was perfect nectar." [139]

Rinconda had suffered the ravages of war. Dead horses laid in the yards and the homes had been used as stables. While there the Americans received orders to stay at Rinconda until further notice. They were to place the guns in position and "hold to the last." The orders included the message that 3,000 Mexican soldiers were between Rinconda and Taylor's forces at Buena Vista leaving Taylor cut off from the rest of the army. Evaluating the ground around them, Doubleday and his comrades would hold the road; the mountains were too much of a challenge for heavy artillery pieces. They had about 150 men total, including thirty cavalry and twenty infantrymen, and were deep in unfamiliar enemy territory with no anticipated reinforcements.

Thinking they would be attacked at night, many men were detailed for guard duty once the sun went down. Several hours after dark, Doubleday went out to inspect the guards on duty. The night was so still, the only sounds were the rush of wind and the quiet, almost whispered, chatter of the guards. The inspection completed, he returned with the intention of sleeping the remainder of the night; however, new orders arrived. Doubleday and the troops were to pack up and immediately go to the aid of Taylor. The few cavalrymen they had would be sent to the front to intercept any approaching enemy soldiers. They were to use their forty wagons for protection, if needed. Would there be a route for possible retreat or would they be caught in a trap? If so, there was a danger to the entire army. The situation looked difficult with only 150 men available to hold the area. Skirmishing had begun at Buena Vista and the big guns were needed. The problems seemed enormous. The roads were too narrow for two wagons to pass at a time, and the heavy guns were hard to manage in the wagons. If the guns had been loaded it would be even more difficult to move forward fast enough in the unfamiliar country. Somewhere out there in the night, were 3,000 of Santa Anna's finest. The odds of the Americans being successful were overwhelmingly against them.

It was February 23, 1847, and the battle for Buena Vista was underway. One of the more experienced soldiers told Doubleday to put his ear to the ground. The rumbling of cannon could be distinctly heard. The men were eager to take part in the fight, but orders said they had to wait until 5 p.m. to begin their march. They left as ordered and pushed up the hills by bright moonlight. There was no way they could defend themselves if the enemy attacked them at night on the hillside. The men pushed onward and had to climb hills before they could then descend into Los Mueintos. As they traveled, they were fully aware the enemy could be anywhere close by. As the night got deeper, Doubleday found his eyelids growing heavier and heavier. The lack of sleep from the night before was beginning to tell. It was the thought of getting accidentally off the trail that kept Doubleday aware of his movements. The cold night dragged on as they moved forward mile after mile. All the men fought off fatigue as they put one foot ahead of the other. Doubleday was so sleepy that he could no longer sit on his horse and as he walked, "I felt as if I were walking in my sleep." [140]

Five more miles into the darkness, and a rider came with a message from Taylor. The men excitedly gathered around the horseman and learned that Taylor's men had been fighting all day. The man was "incoherent enough. It could not be well be otherwise. A soldier, who has been fighting all day in one locality in the midst of smoke and noise, is not a very good judge of what has been going on over a field of many miles."[141] Once the rider calmed down, he told them Taylor had held his ground, but the battle was expected to begin again at daylight. It was 2 a.m. and they had already marched twenty miles.

The men pushed ahead as fast as possible considering how exhausted they and their animals were. It wasn't long before their presence was noticed by a Mexican who fired on them before being chased away by American cavalry. At that point, one of the eighteen-pounders got stuck in a ditch. The men reacted quickly and using the mules got the piece back on the road.

Despite the situation, Doubleday was losing his fight to keep his eyes open. Still unable to stay upright on his horse or even to keep walking, he crawled into a wagon. As they entered Los Mueintos, Doubleday heard a familiar voice in the dark; it was Lieutenant William Shover who was preparing his battery for action. The two men greeted each other briefly, as they both had hard work ahead. Doubleday continued forward, and as he pushed through the village, he noticed lights in the church. Asking why, he was informed the church was filled with wounded and dying Americans. Doubleday knew many of the men inside. At once, he was filled with sadness, "as if the Angel of Death was singing a slow and solemn dirge."[142] Asking a few more questions, he was told nearly a thousand men were killed or wounded in the battle that day. As this information was being passed, a rider with new orders rode up. Doubleday's company was to push to Buena Vista.

It didn't matter how tired man or beast was, they had to move forward again. The tired men whipped the exhausted mules in an effort to make the poor animals gallop. Enemy cavalry came up behind them; fortunately the Mexican lancers left them alone. As they drew closer to the battlefield, they had to navigate around dead bodies and broken wagons in their path. By the time they arrived, reveille was sounding. They had marched all night covering forty-two miles and overcoming huge obstacles in delivering the heavy guns. By then, the battle had ended.

With the mission completed, Doubleday headed to a tent for much contemplated sleep. After an hour of tossing and turning, he gave up trying to sleep and left the tent. He got a horse from Shover who was commanding a light artillery battery. Shover and Doubleday took a six-mile ride to look at the battlefield. When the two men returned, they passed by a battery of artillery. Doubleday described the scene:

> I suddenly came upon [John F.] Reynolds in the early gray of the morning, in the pass of Buena Vista, on the high table-land of Mexico, at the foot of the great range of the Sierra Nevada. The scene was indelibly impressed on my boyish memory. There stood

[George H.] Thomas and Reynolds, each leaning upon a gun of Bragg's Battery, surrounded by dead Mexicans and the debris of battle, waiting for the signal to recommence the action. I asked Reynolds afterwards how he felt when he saw the well-appointed army of Santa Anna, 25,000 strong, confronting our little force of 5,000 men. He replied, 'I did not allow myself to think on that subject, for I might have thought wrongly.' It is not too much to say that the victory we gained that day was due to the admirable manner in which those guns were served.[143]

After hours of staring at dead men and animals, Doubleday had had enough. He spurred his horse for Saltillo. Once there, he got a meal and finally got some sleep. Although there was some skirmishing in the days to come, the battle of Buena Vista had ended.

With the battles of Monterrey and Buena Vista behind him, Doubleday returned to the everyday duties of the army in Mexico. The following month at Saltillo, he received news of a promotion. He was now a first lieutenant and a member of Co. H, First United States Artillery, but was serving on detached service with Co. E. His career was about to take an unexpected turn.

Fighting the Mexicans had been difficult, but Doubleday soon had another type of fight on his hands. Enticed by an offer that would increase his pay by $10 a month, Doubleday accepted the position of assistant commissary/quartermaster. He signed a receipt for the property placed in his care. "I thought I had made a good bargain, but soon changed my mind," he said of his new duties. Taking responsibility for the commissary, made him uneasy. There was only an old man and a dog to guard it and its contents from unsavory characters. Orders were given to sell the goods at public auction. Through some lack of communication, the goods were sent to the home of the winning bidder before payment had been made. The man who had bid on the items, turned out to have a reputation for bad business dealings. Doubleday was sure he was going to be stuck for the amount of money owed the army. Surprisingly, the man paid his bill and Doubleday was off the hook. When he tried to settle his financial matters, however, he had to go to the Board of Officers, present his evidence and was exonerated.[144]

A shipment of flour was due and when it reached its destination, no one was available to stand guard until it could be taken to the commissary store. Doubleday was in the proverbial hard place. Neither the store nor the goods should be left without guard. After several days, he finally found someone to stand watch over the flour.

Major Thomas W. Sherman had arrested the former quartermaster, Captain Chapman, September 20, 1848.[145] When Chapman was arrested, he declared he was no longer responsible for the army's property. Even as Doubleday began his new duties, the situation became worse under Sherman's command. Doubleday was ordered to supply meals for the civilian prisoners taken in Matamoras, even though such a move was against regulations. Then Sherman issued another order; all Texans on public grounds after lights out were to be arrested. It didn't make sense to Doubleday since peace had been declared. This newest order by Sherman caused several good officers to be placed in the guardhouse simply because they disagreed with their commander, Doubleday said later.[146]

Sherman apparently seized Chapman's funds, totaling about $80,000. Sherman then required Doubleday to take responsibility for the funds as well as other property. Six days after the new appointment, Sherman charged Doubleday with disobedience of orders, mutinous conduct and disputing authority.[147] Doubleday lost no time and ten days after becoming a quartermaster, he charged Sherman with numerous infractions: Not protecting civilians, changing the punishment meted out during a court martial, keeping a soldier in hard labor without benefit of a speedy trial, placing civilians in confinement if out after Taps, and converting the guard house into a county jail.[148]

Doubleday named witnesses in his action: Brevet Captain Wooster, Fourth United States Artillery; First Lieutenant Brown, First United States Artillery; [John F.] Reynolds, Third United States Artillery; Captain Hunt, Fourth United States Artillery; himself, and several non-commissioned men of Co. E, First United States Artillery. Sherman's witnesses included: Captain Hunt, Fourth United States Artillery; [John F.] Reynolds, Third United States Artillery; Lieutenant Brown, Fourth United States Artillery; Lance Corporal Douglas of Co. K, Fourth United States Artillery and himself.[149]

Still under a cloud of suspicion, Doubleday headed to his new assignment at Fort Columbus, in New York Harbor. From there on December 11, 1848, Doubleday wrote to Major W. G. Freeman, Assistant Adjutant General of the United States Army in New York City:

> I cannot ascertain whether these charges have ever been forwarded
> to higher authority. I am extremely desirous of having an
> opportunity of vindicating my military character and as I have

now been in arrest for nearly three months, and as the witnesses are all stationed upon the Rio Grande frontier I most respectfully request that the subject be acted upon as soon as possible.

Doubleday requested Major Freeman, and the top commander himself, General Winfield Scott, that he (Doubleday) should be immediately brought to trail or released from arrest and returned to duty.

Doubleday also contacted his father. On October 26, Ulysses Freeman, writing from New York City, wrote former New York congressman and governor, and current Secretary of State William Marcy. The father's letter said he had been expecting to see his son "after a very long absence" only to find his son was under arrest. Stating he was not sure he was "transcending the bounds of necessity if not of propriety" he continued his pleas for justice on his son's behalf. Doubleday's father stated that a fair hearing or court martial should be held, "or a full investigation by the War Department. Knowing the amiability of his disposition, I can hardly fear he had made himself liable to just censure."[150]

The wheels of military justice turned slowly, but Taylor relieved Sherman of command and sent him to the Eastern division where the charges could be reviewed. The charges were eventually dropped because the witnesses were on the front lines in Mexico. By December 16, Doubleday was on the other side of the judge's bench, once again sitting on a court martial panel. As 1849 began, he was in command of Co. E at Fort Columbus, New York.[151] Although the charges had been dropped, Doubleday's good name had been sullied.

The war with Mexico continued with battles at Vera Cruz, Cerro Gordo, Churubusco, and Chapultepec before the Americans would take Mexico City. The treaty of Guadalupe Hidalgo formally ended the war in early February 1848. Doubleday had spent three years and three months in Mexico. Of that time, he spent five days in actual combat. The remaining time was spent guarding supplies, drilling, and taking in the culture of Mexico. While there he learned the language, and that would put him a unique spot in the future.

During the years Doubleday had been in Mexico, changes were taking place in the East. In Rochester, New York [about sixty miles from his hometown of Auburn], former slave Frederick Douglass living as a free man, began his newspaper, *The North Star*. The country would soon hear about another former slave, Harriet Tubman [who would later live in Auburn] and her activities helping slaves escape to the North through the Underground

Railroad. Women in American met for the first time in Seneca Falls, New York (between Auburn and Rochester) to begin their fight for the right to vote, own property and to speak publicly about issues of the times. The country was undergoing "growing pains" as it dealt with territories becoming states and social and political changes.

The year 1849 would see Doubleday in many military courtroom settings, but not as either a defendant or a plaintiff. He would take his place among other officers sitting as judges. Perhaps one of the more notable cases he presided over occurred in March 1849. In either sublime irony or mistaken humor, poor Sergeant William Neal was brought before Doubleday and fellow jurists, Second Lieutenant S. F. Chalpro and Second Lieutenant D. M. Beltzhoover at Fort Columbus.

Neal was acting as the sergeant of police on March 21 and reported in mid-afternoon to Doubleday's friend and Officer of the Day Lieutenant James B. Ricketts. When asked if his duties were carried out, Neal stated the entire garrison had received its supply of coal to keep officers and soldiers warm. However, upon the complaint of one officer, Neal was found guilty of not doing his duty. The complaining officer was none other then the president of his court martial, Doubleday. Neal was reduced in rank for laxness in his duty.[152]

The following year, on July 16, 1850, Doubleday's twenty-six year-old brother, Ulysses, married Mary Stewart at Trinity Church Parish, New York City. Doubleday was thirty-one and still a bachelor. In August, he was apparently living at No. 40, John Street (possibly with his parents) in the city, received orders to take a company of recruits from Fort Columbus to Tampa, Florida[153]

As Doubleday endured the hot, miserable swamps of Florida, politicians in Washington passed the Fugitive Slave Act. The new law mandated all citizens were to assist officials in returning property—runaway slaves—to the owners. If a citizen did not obey this new law, a person found to be guilty would face a fine of up to $1,000 and a six-month jail sentence. Provisions were made in the law to pay officials for the retrieval of the slaves. The issue of slavery was like a pot of water placed over a hot flame and left to bubble away.

About the same time the Fugitive Slave Act was passed in September of 1850, Doubleday was back at Fort Columbus, but not for long. Company E was at sea, and Doubleday transferred to Co. K at Fort McHenry. Doubleday and Thomas Jonathan Jackson were assigned there at the same time. The two men exchanged their company positions with Jackson joining Co. E as Doubleday took Jackson's place with Co. K.[154]

Jackson was a memorable man for many reasons. He struggled his way through West Point, was known for his toughness, his religious fervor and unusual personal habits. Doubleday remembered the man as one "who never seemed to joke or enjoy anything of a humorous nature. At the same time he was cheerful and pleasant in his demeanor but somewhat reticent."[155]

Doubleday talked about Jackson's illness:

> He did not know the cause of it himself and he had some strange symptoms. For instance, he would walk a certain length of time, accurately by the watch. Then he would sit motionless for fifteen minutes. Then he would rise and pound and kick a bag of sand with his left hand under the impression that side of his body was dwindling.

Doubleday was impressed with Jackson's honesty and attention to duty. The two men had many exchanges before they each headed for new duties in opposite directions.

Endnotes

136 A. D., n. p.

137 Ibid

138 Ibid

139 Ibid

140 Ibid

141 Ibid

142 Ibid

143 Alexander A. Chamberlin, Thomas Chamberlin scrapbook of the 150th Pennsylvania Volunteers, speeches, 1890-1899, USAMHI

144 A. D., n. p.

145 Ulysses Freeman Doubleday, letter, October. 26, 1848 to Secretary of State William Marcy, Letters Received by the Adjutant General 1822-1860 (Main Series), RG 94, M567, Roll 375, NARA

146 A. D., n. p.

147 Ibid

148 Letters Received by the Adjutant General 1822-1860, (Main Series), RG 94, M567, Roll 21, NARA,

149 Ibid

150 Letters Received by the Adjutant General 1822-1860, (Main Series), RG 94, M567, Roll 375, NARA

151 Registers of Letters Received, Office of the Adjutant General, 1812-1889, RG 94, M711, Roll 2, NARA

152 Records of the U.S. Regular Mobile Units, Artillery Regiments, First U.S. Artillery, Orders Issued, RG 391, Vol. 1, March 22, 1849 Ft. Columbus, and General Court Martial Orders, 10, First and Third Military District, Feb. 22, 1849, NARA

153 Letters Received by the Office of the Adjutant General (Main Series), 1822-1860, RG 94, M567 Roll 416, letter 487, NARA

154 Records of the U.S. Regular Army Mobile Units, orders issued 1840-41 First U.S. Artillery, RG 391, NARA

155 A.D., n.p.

CHAPTER 9

"A soldier's daughter"

Doubleday found himself gazing into the eyes of a lovely lady. Soon after, he pulled out pen and paper. The transfer to Fort McHenry put him in Baltimore, and he soon found a very special lady. He had finally met the woman who claimed his heart. Thirty-one year old Doubleday was head-over-heels in love. The long-time bachelor was smitten and writing romantic verse:

> "Thy name, dear lady, is a spell,
> Which has the instant power to start
> A thousand thoughts which upward well
> From the deep fountain of the heart,
> Where memory's court is open wide
> And history speaks in tones of pride."

A few verses later, he refers to his new love as:
> "A soldier's daughter;—thou hast dwelt
> Beneath our starry banner's belt
> The cannon's threatening thunder rolled,
> And ever to shine e'er would come
> Like household tones, the rolling drum."[156]

Doubleday was wooing Washington belle, Mary Hewitt. It was not the first time he had shown interest in a female. When stationed in South Carolina in 1845 he made a comment that "he had not married a wealthy woman because he did not love her."[157] He had not given up dancing when he was stationed at Fort Preble. While there, he wrote to a Boston tailor requesting a "citizens dress coat" for "small dancing parties." He told the tailor that only a few changes in the size were needed. He asked for a slightly longer coat and roomier chest measurement since his coat was tight "under the arms." [158]

Seven years after leaving Fort Preble, in 1851, it was Mary Hewitt's "beautiful eyes" that cast a spell on him and caused Doubleday to relinquish his bachelor days. She was the daughter of Baltimore attorney, Robert Hewitt. Her mother died when she was only eight months old. The devastated new father took baby Mary to her grandmother's for care. Her grandmother was none other than Mrs. Francis Hopkinson, "whose husband was the son of Francis Hopkinson (1737-1791), one of the signers of the Declaration of Independence."[159] Grandfather Hopkinson was born in Philadelphia, and counted Benjamin Franklin a close friend and wrote frequently to George Washington and Thomas Jefferson. The Philadelphian represented New Jersey when he added his signature to the document declaring America to be free from England. Hopkinson is also claimed to have designed the first American flag.[160]

After the death of Mrs. Hopkinson, Mary was once again shuffled to a new home. She was sent to live with her aunt who was married to Colonel Charles R. Broom. Broom was a member of the Marine Corps and commanded the barracks at the nation's capital. Mary and Doubleday met while she was living there.[161] Doubleday and his lady with the beautiful eyes exchanged their marital vows January 16, 1852. It was also the year Harriet Beecher Stowe published her book, *Uncle Tom's Cabin*. Mary Hewitt Doubleday would not only prove to be the perfect Army wife, but also a plucky woman who endured the hardships her husband faced and was at his side whenever possible. They were not blessed with children, but married life agreed with Doubleday. However, duty called Doubleday the following October and the newlyweds were separated as a result of the new orders. Doubleday received a summons; he was asked to meet with a congressional committee.

The committee was investigating the claims of Americans who had suffered losses during the war with Mexico. George A. Gardiner and John H. Mears claimed substantial losses and Doubleday soon found himself returning to Mexico. The treaty that ended the war with Mexico had a provision "to liquidate the claims of American citizens against Mexico."[162] The document set aside considerable funds for the purpose of reimbursing Americans for any losses.

Gardiner was a man with a plan. He claimed damages to his mining operations in Mexico. The American government awarded Gardiner $428,750 toward his $500,000 claim for damages to mines in the Mexican state of San Luis Potosi. Officials became suspicious of Gardiner's claim so President Pierce and a congressional committee appointed several men to investigate: Henry May, James K. Partridge, Buckingham Smith (former Secretary of Legation to Mexico), Lieutenant W.W. Hunter of the U.S. Navy and Doubleday.[163] Originally commissioners included Samuel F. Dupont, instead of Henry May, and Captain Samuel G. French, instead of Doubleday, but May and French were unable to serve.[164] As the commission evolved, Smith believed he, not May, should have headed the expedition, and consequently he did not act in concert with fellow committee members during the work ahead.

Transportation to Mexico had not significantly improved from when Doubleday went to war only a few years before he and the commissioners headed southwest. They left Washington, went to New Orleans and then set sail for Mexico. Told that he would need to supply his own equipment, Doubleday packed double barrel guns, India rubber blankets and ammunition for his pistols and other arms. The evening before leaving the Crescent City Doubleday and Partridge sat on the hotel piazza discussing the architecture of buildings near them and ones seen by Partridge in other places. Doubleday said he was feeling ill, excused himself and went to bed. That night he had nightmares in which he was drowning at sea and he hoped it was not a bad omen. His nightmare didn't come true, and the group reached Mexico in early November 1852 without any major incidents. Once there, Doubleday found he related to his war experiences so intensely that he found it difficult to deal with his war memories. He was surely reminded of his friends and acquaintances that had died in the battles he had fought in. However duty called and regardless of his memories, he had to return to Mexico which was then at peace with America.

On their arrival in San Luis Potosi, they gathered their baggage and headed for their place of lodging. They found it to be cramped, airless, and with little privacy. Groups shared quarters in small rooms containing several narrow beds. Doors and windows were left open to allow the flow of air to circulate throughout the building. The following morning they set out to begin their investigation. They used mules to haul supplies and the trip proved to be lengthy and difficult. Many Mexicans still hated Americans and shared that opinion freely with the commissioners. As the commissioners gathered information about the mines, it became apparent that things were not as Gardiner had represented them to be. The mines weren't located were they were supposed to be, and there was no steam engine working at one of the sites as claimed.

Not all the time was spent investigating the Gardiner claims. This son of a Universalist even went to a Catholic cathedral to hear Mass one

Sunday. Doubleday couldn't help but notice the gold railing and silver candlesticks inside a house of worship in a very poor country. During this Mexican experience, he also saw a chain gang, more Mexican troops and other buildings of interest. At each stop near where a mine was claimed to be, they encountered new scenes and new experiences. But nighttime was difficult. The commission members had to share their beds, not with each other, but with fleas. The group had supplied their own bedding; the fleas were an added bonus. The pesky insects were even evident when the group had to pitch tents for cover. They rarely stayed more than one night in any particular place. During one of the overnight stops, Doubleday couldn't get to sleep. A goat, likely a male with strong horns, kept butting the door until it pushed its way into his room. He probably chased the goat back outside and convinced it to leave.

The trip was far from being a delightful experience. Doubleday noted they were often given dirty forks, had to drink stagnant water and ride over hot, dusty roads. The scenery was the only thing of beauty they encountered as their wagon bumped and rocked up and down the mountainous roads. In one village they were treated to tangy oranges, sweet bananas and tart lemons; in other locations it was a new beverage, one of the gods, hot chocolate or the more familiar, coffee. If they found a river, they could stop to take a bath. The trip was lengthy, and by Christmas they were still seeking truth. As they continued this quest, they discovered that documents had been forged and Gardiner had indeed committed fraud with the help of his friends. Gardiner's attorney was Waddy Thompson, the South Carolinian who served in Congress with Doubleday's father and vehemently opposed anti-slavery petitioners and had formerly served as minister to Mexico. Thompson would have a hard time in presenting a defense for Gardiner against such overwhelming evidence.

Their mission completed, the commission returned to Vera Cruz and set sail for America by way of Cuba as there was no direct sailing line available. They arrived in the nation's capital January 1853, just in time for Doubleday and Mary to mark their first anniversary.

The commission made its report to Congress, and the country read about Gardiner and Mears in many newspapers. The findings were: Gardiner was not an American citizen; neither man was involved in San Luis Potosi mines; during the period the two men claimed to be in mining, Gardiner acted as a dentist, a peddler and a mine company manager in San Luis Potosi; and each document provided by the defense was forged. Mears somehow managed to walk away from the situation and Gardiner committed suicide in 1854, and is buried in the Congressional Cemetery in Washington, D.C. Mears seems to have disappeared from history.

After Doubleday reached Washington, he was out doing some errands one day when Mary decided to unpack her husband's bags. There must have been a question or two in Mary's mind when she saw the contents of one particular bag. To her astonishment, inside were six beautifully embroidered petticoats. When her husband returned, Mary teased him about going into the petticoat business. Doubleday explained that one of the commission members had purchased the underpinnings as gifts, but since that person's luggage was already on board, the petticoats were hastily stuffed into Doubleday's remaining piece of luggage and forgotten. Mary had considered giving all but one of the petticoats away, then upon hearing her husband's explanation changed her mind.[165] Whatever happened to the original petticoat owner, Doubleday did not say, and Mary likely donned one of the beautiful petticoats beneath her day dress.

Once the commission made its report, Doubleday received his commissioner's pay of $2,000 minus pay already received. He then had new orders to re-join his company stationed at Fort Duncan, Eagle Pass, Texas in August, 1854.[166] Mary, like many army wives, accompanied her husband and soon put together a home on the frontier. However before leaving Mrs. Spriggs' boarding house in Washington, Doubleday wrote a letter to the widow of his former colleague, Lieutenant William Shover who had died at West Point in 1850.

The letter to Felicia Shover, in Baltimore, indicates Doubleday was paying attention to the fad of the day, the spirit world. He writes about a young girl being trained as a "medium." Doubleday said the girl was convincing, and that he was "watching this case with much interest."[167]

Doubleday informed Mrs. Shover he would soon be leaving Washington for Texas. He and Mary were on their way to west Texas. The fort itself had been built in 1849 opposite Piedras Negras, Mexico, a year before the Fugitive Slave Law. When gold was discovered in California, the "Forty-Niners" often chose the Fort Duncan area as a place to camp and to cross the Rio Grande. Later, during the Civil War, it became the only place for the Confederacy to export cotton in order to finance its army.[168]

On their journey to the fort, the couple was delayed in San Antonio. It was a time when a pistol and Bowie knife were essentials carried by most men. There were robbers and thugs in the area, and one day while the Doubledays were out dining, two or three of the thugs broke into every room of the hotel where they were staying. "Had I been at home," said

Doubleday, "there would in all probability have been one or two dead roughs for I was well armed."[169]

The fort had a reputation for being a most social place to do military duty, but at the same time it was not a pleasant setting. Robert E. Lee had chosen the site (as a captain of engineers) about 1850. Writing his memories of service in Texas then-Brevet Second Lieutenant Zenas Bliss, an 1854 West Point graduate, and officer in the First United States Infantry, said the fort was "the wildest post I have ever served at." It was also the year that yellow fever struck the post hard.

There were many wild horses, no railroads, no telegraph, and more than enough rattlesnakes. Bliss remembered the continuing problems along the border between Texas and Mexico. Stopping cattle rustlers, Indians, and bandits were all part of the daily duty in trying to keep peace. Add to that the activity of slave catchers, dealers in slavery (some of whom were Creek Indians[170]) and kidnappers and it is obvious that Fort Duncan was a place of seemingly never-ending activity.[171] Only five years earlier General William Belknap had rescued three blacks and their Seminole owner, Jim Bowlegs, from the Creeks.[172] The Comanches also attacked the Black Seminoles (African Americans mixed with Native Americans) as they went through Texas, headed for Mexico and freedom.[173] It was a large post with ten companies of men, including one of artillery and one of rifles. Men of the First United States Artillery were used as infantry at the post where daytime temperatures could hit one hundred and four degrees daily.

The post had three stone houses used for the hospital, ammunition storage and equipment. Some of the housing was nothing more than tents, others had small houses and the officers' homes totally made of thatch. It was a thatch house that Doubleday and his wife called home. But the thatch houses were easily caught on fire and the couple lost their home to a blaze. Bliss said the house was nothing but ashes in only a few minutes. The Doubledays lost several hundred dollars worth of valuables.[174]

Bliss also remembered Fort Duncan as the "gayest" and "largest" of the Army's forts. Several young married couples held parties, hayrides and dances to relieve the otherwise boring life at the outpost. Members of the post bonded with each other as members in a larger family, one where all those who lived there also suffered together.[175] Bliss said that the higher ranking officers would gather on muster days at the home of Colonel Bainbridge for lunch. Bliss even remembered bull-fighting taking place as an entertainment at the fort.

Mary Doubleday was as brave as any woman faced with Indians and living so far from civilization. One of the wives, Lydia Lane, described Mary as not even being afraid of rattlesnakes, but a mouse was a different story. Mary, "a pretty, refined woman," was terrified of mice. So much so, she had a special frame "fixed all around her bed and covered with netting" to keep the mice at bay. Lane said the fort was "a wretched place to live in."[176] It gave rise to an old Texas saying that Bliss remembered years later: Texas was a good enough place for men, "but awfully rough on women and oxen." It was hard on dogs too. Second Lieutenant Philip Sheridan shared quarters with Bliss. Bliss noted Sheridan had a pointer, but the dog got screw worms and had to be put down. Today, the fort is not visible; several floods since then have deposited silt or washed away all evidence of its existence.[177]

In spring of 1855, Doubleday sent a thank-you letter to New York's United States Senator William H. Seward, of Auburn. Seward had pushed for Doubleday's new promotion as a captain. The promotion meant Doubleday would now receive $40 a month and four rations a day. The couple had remained on the Texas frontier until May 1855, when in true army fashion they had to relocate again. This time Doubleday was assigned to Fort Monroe, Virginia where life in comparison seemed more civilized.

Virginia was a slave state and very focused on related events. Only the year before, Anthony Burns, a slave who had been living free in the North, was returned as a slave to the South. The action created a riot in Boston where the trial took place. The event put the issue of slavery squarely on tongue of many, like Bostonian conservative George S. Hillard, who joined the anti-slavery movement following the riot. This event did not escape the eyes of Southerners and it would add one more step on the way to the Civil War.

Endnotes

[156] This poem is in the Doubleday family and was copied with permission from the late Betty Doubleday Frost. The poem was transcribed at some point in the family and a date of 1842 attached. However, this date may be incorrect.

[157] Edward M. Coffman, *The Old Army*, (New York: Oxford University Press, 1986), 107

[158] Abner Doubleday letter, July 28, 1845 from Fort Preble, Maine, New York Public Library Archives, New York City

[159] McCalmont

[160] Marc Leepson, *Flag*, (New York: Thomas Dunne Books, St. Martin's Press, 2005), 33-34

[161] McCalmont

[162] Congressional record for the Thirty-third Congress, 1st Session, Senate, Report of Mr. Brodhead, Oct. 7, 1852, 184, NARA

[163] Records of the U.S. Senate, Thirty-third Congress, 1st Session, Report of the Select Committee of the Senate in Relation to the Proceedings of the Board of Commissioners on the Claims Against Mexico, March 28, 1854, RG 46, NARA

[164] Congressional record for the Thirty-third Congress, 1st Session, Senate report, report of Mr. Brodhead, Oct. 7, 1852, 184, NARA. The following day the appointments for May and Abner were announced.

[165] A. D., n. p.

[166] Thirty-third Session of the Senate, Feb. 23, 1853; Abner Doubleday, "*From the Mexican War to the Rebellion, First Rough Draft*"

[167] Abner Doubleday to Felicia Shover, letter from Washington, D.C., May 29, 1854, Virginia Historical Society, Richmond, VA

[168] Viento Fronterizo, "Fort Duncan, Eagle Pass, Texas", *Border Wind*, Piedras Negras, Coahuila, Mexico, Vol. 1, No. 3, December 1994

[169] A. D., n. p.

[170] Kevin Mulroy, *Freedom on the border: the Seminole Maroons in Florida, the Indian Territory, Coahuila, and Texas*, (Lubbock, Tex: Texas Tech University Press, 1993), 61

[171] Mulroy, 87

[172] Mulroy, 61

[173] Mulroy, 62

[174] A. D., n. p.

[175] Zenas Bliss, papers, Vo. 1, 34-95, USAMHI

[176] Lydia Spencer Lane, *I Married A Soldier*, (Albuquerque, New Mexico, Horn and Wallace, Publishers, Inc., 1964), 28-29

[177] William T. Field, "Fort Duncan and Old Eagle Pass," *Texas Military History*, Vol. 6, Summer 1967, National Guard Association of Texas, 1961-1970, 160-171

CHAPTER 10

"Not one foot of the United States"

"I take the liberty of writing you a few lines," Doubleday scrawled across the page. The letter was addressed to fellow Auburn resident and United States Senator William H. Seward. Events in Virginia were very much on Doubleday's mind. The pen kept moving as Doubleday described the situation. "The partisans of Gov. Wise" were at it again. Doubleday knew many Virginians were talking wildly. John C. Fremont was running for president on an anti-slavery platform. Slave owners were sure Fremont would free the slaves nearly as soon as he won the election. "There are not wanting of men of influence to counsel acts of open treason," Doubleday told Seward. The 1855 political climate and the news that much of the military presence would soon be going to Florida would leave Fort Monroe "without a single soldier to defend it. The same men also talk of seizing the navy yard at Portsmouth. The importance of this place cannot be overestimated," Doubleday continued. He put his pen down, tucked the letter in an envelope and sent it on its way.[178]

Fort Monroe was an artillery training post at Old Point Comfort on the eastern coast of Virginia. Although Doubleday and his wife were there for only a short time, Doubleday noted the political climate and wrote Seward that politics there were ready to boil over in reaction to the first Republican candidate, Fremont.

The country was shocked in mid-May 1856, when its citizens learned that Massachusetts Senator Charles Sumner had been assaulted with a cane held by Representative Preston Brooks of South Carolina. The assault followed a speech against slavery in Kansas in which Sumner compared the state of South Carolina to that of the Kansas Territory. At that time, Kansas was known as "Bleeding Kansas" for the many acts of violence regarding the slavery issue. Virginia was not alone in its struggle with slavery and the shouting voices that were leading the country down a dangerous path.

The stay in Virginia came to an end and Doubleday had new orders. He and Mary were headed for Fort Dallas, Florida, along with many other garrison members. Fort Dallas was situated near the Everglades and eventually became present-day Miami. For the next two years, Doubleday and his fellow soldiers battled yellow fever and mosquitoes, Seminoles and the land itself to build a road from Fort Dallas to New River in Broward County. The men had to cut their way through trees and swampland, no easy task in 1857. Then with a new set of orders, Doubleday was assigned to command Fort Moultrie, South Carolina. The Doubledays must have looked forward to leaving Florida, the spiders and other insects, snakes and alligators.

After their arrival at Fort Moultrie, Doubleday's wife wrote to a friend, "I quite envy you the pleasure of arranging your new home, for that's to me is always a pleasant occupation." She continued by discussing an impending court martial of a doctor ordered by the president, and ending with, "We were quite gay here for two or three weeks about Christmas in the way of dinners & supper parties & little dances."[179]

Word came in 1857 the Supreme Court ruled Dred Scott, a slave who lived in free states for many years, would remain a slave. Chief Justice Roger Taney, a slaveholder himself, handed down his decision and added fuel to the anti-slavery movement.

The country was continuing to grow with Minnesota gaining statehood in 1858 and Oregon the following year. Citizens were reading a "*Tale of Two Cities*" by Charles Dickens and the first baseball club was formed in the nation's capital. As the country lurched toward a division over slavery, the nation lost its simplistic way of life. The coming split divided people as little else since the decision was made to separate from Great Britain that ignited the American Revolution. Could anyone safely talk to their neighbor, to a merchant, to a brother? Would their views on the peculiar institution (meaning slavery) lead to being branded a traitor to their country?

In the autumn of 1859, a disturbing message arrived at the fort. Doubleday's mother was seriously ill. He hastily turned the command over to Brevet Colonel John Gardner. Then Doubleday and his wife hurried to Hester's bedside in Bloomington, Illinois. While the couple hurried to Bloomington to see Doubleday's dying mother, an event took place that shocked the country. John Brown and his followers raided Harpers Ferry, Virginia (West Virginia was not yet a state) on October 16. Except for the growing army of abolitionists, the nation was outraged by the event. Brown's act would lead to a public perception that if a person supported the end of slavery, he or she would be labeled with several unflattering names including "Black Republican" and viewed as a trouble-maker like old John Brown. In 1861 the song "John Brown's Body," set to an old musical piece, would be heard in Boston for the first time. The song made its way across the land.

Hester Donnelly Doubleday died on November 14, 1859, at the age of 71. Her funeral was held at the Baptist Church in Bloomington where the service was conducted at the local Presbyterian Church. She was buried in what is now called the Old City Cemetery in Bloomington.[180]

After the funeral, Doubleday and his wife went to New York City to visit his brother, Ulysses and his family. There, on December 5, Doubleday, referring to his mother's death and Mary's poor health from living in the south, requested an additional four months leave. (At that time there were many diseases encountered in the South.) Knowing of the events following Brown's raid, Doubleday said he would be in New York City or Washington and could easily be reached if needed. With the John Brown episode on the minds of many, the answer was cautiously worded stating that Doubleday could only have until the end of January.[181] However, he continued to ask for and receive extensions on his leave until the spring of 1860.

National elections were around the corner, and the results would soon split the country. Issues of the coming elections received great notice when Lincoln gave a speech at Cooper Union in New York City on February 27, 1860. It is likely Doubleday, and his brother Ulysses, were two of the 1,500 who listened to Lincoln as he made the argument that the Federal government had the right to enter the slavery issue.

As the politicians verbally thrust and parried, they took the old disagreement over states' rights and slavery to new heights. In faraway Detroit, Michigan, serving in an army engineer unit and conducting a lake survey while working toward building and keeping the nation's lighthouses operating, Captain George G. Meade was one of several officers refusing to take on oath of allegiance to the United States at a public meeting. Their stated reasons ranged from action unbecoming an officer to stating since they had already taken an oath, there was no reason to take it again. During a time of public suspicion of military officers, the refusal was met with an outcry from abolitionists' quarters.[182] One can only imagine how the news affected Doubleday and the few other officers who were regarded as Black Republicans. Indeed, such a refusal may have contributed to a difficult future relationship between the two men. Meanwhile, there were those who believed that diplomacy would settle the old question but some men, including Doubleday, realized the pot was about to boil over and tried to prepare. Only four years earlier, he had written to Seward telling him that those who supported former congressman and then-Virginia Governor Henry A. Wise were telling Virginians that if Fremont won the

1856 election, all their slaves would be taken away and they should seize Fort Monroe. "There are not wanting of men of influence to counsel acts of open treason," wrote Doubleday. He told Seward the Virginia citizens were looking to capture Fort Monroe and the arsenal at Harpers Ferry. Four years later, Brown and his little band of followers tried to take the arsenal, and all were hanged for treason.[183]

Major Robert Anderson was stationed at Fort Monroe, and sent circulars to his artillery captains. Even though Doubleday was on furlough, he soon received his copy. Anderson was seeking suggestions on how to improve the training of the soldiers. Doubleday, in an unusually short letter for him, answered in a two-page letter from Washington, D. C. He suggested the course of training be "simplified." He suggested using a new technology: Photography. Doubleday told Anderson that since not every post had the same cannons, models should be at Fort Monroe and when that would not be possible, to use photos of the others! Doubleday explained, "A very small photograph can have all its minutiae brought out with a magnifying glass to any extent and it will give a far clearer idea that any plan or section in many cases." Doubleday also took the opportunity to complain that the drilling of the infantry "keeps the artillery officers from perfecting themselves in their own arm." Doubleday didn't criticize without offering a suggestion; a new weapon was on the horizon. It could help. "If we could substitute the Volcanic gun (which is now being perfected in New York) for our own musket it would be a great advantage as this gun contains the entire charge in the copper cylinder." This new method would eliminate "belts, cap pouches or cartridge boxes." With the threat of disunion, the effectiveness of this new gun could change the army.[184]

However, the new weapon would not evolve into an army owned piece for some time, but when it did, it would become known as the gun "you loaded on Sunday and could shoot all week:" the Henry rifle.[185] On April 26, 1860, two days after writing to Anderson, Doubleday wrote to Adjutant General Colonel Samuel Cooper. He stated:

> common soldiers have almost insufferable difficulty in estimating distances, which renders the long range of the new arms almost useless. I am desirous of experimenting two or three weeks at the arsenal upon a glass which I think will do much to obviate the difficulty. It consists of two lenses upon a slide with a micrometer either between the glasses or marked upon them.

Trying to push his plea forward, Doubleday said the new "glass" could be made inexpensively and "furnished at the rate of one to a company."[186] Although he was on leave, his mind was obviously still with the army; his body would soon follow. He returned to duty at Fort Moultrie the first week of May.[187]

Doubleday wrote to his brother, Ulysses, in September, and he, in turn, forwarded the letters to then-candidate Lincoln. The letters pointed out that people in Charleston were preparing to take over the fort and that the men in the fort, were taking steps to make the fort stronger.

Concerned Doubleday's letters were being opened before Ulysses received them, the two brothers worked out a secret code to use if needed. Each had an identical dictionary and would assign numbers to words and pages. However, the September 23, 1860, letter from Doubleday to his brother, Ulysses, is not in code. Doubleday said he doubted the necessity at that time. "I have along been puzzled by the way the people or rather the leaders of the people talk Secession with (every) one I meet to be as a foregone conclusion." Doubleday believed William Henry Trescott, the assistant secretary of state, to be a secessionist. Trescott, a diplomat, visited the fort and told commander Brevet Colonel John L. Gardner the Buchanan administration would give the forts to South Carolina after withdrawing troops, cutting off the harbor, mail and telegraph services. Doubleday in his characteristic manner bluntly stated: "I do not believe the Administration has the right to give up one foot of the United States to the state of South Carolina." Along with the two letters of Doubleday's, Ulysses sent a map his brother had drawn. Stating he supported Lincoln, Ulysses finished his letter with: "I shall never have any favor to ask of you as President."[188]

Doubleday also wrote Ulysses that there was a great deal of the dreaded fever that fall in the Charleston area. Letters about secession began to appear in newspapers in the North and were reprinted in the South, including the *Charleston Mercury*. Doubleday later claimed a correspondent for the *New York Times* wrote the letters, but Southerners were positive that "Black Republican" Doubleday had written them. Consequently, correctly or not, he became the target of their growing anger.[189]

In Charleston, both St. Phillip's and St. Michael's churches took out ads in the *Mercury* supporting candidates in the coming elections. The ad called Lincoln and the Republican Party "fanatical" and "diabolical."[190] In Norfolk, Virginia, Governor Wise told a crowd that should Lincoln be elected, the South would consider it "an open declaration of war."[191]

On Tuesday, November 6, 1860, 39.8 percent of Americans chose Lincoln, the self-made man from Illinois, as president-elect of a nation soon to be at war. Presidential candidates Stephen A. Douglas, also of Illinois received 29.5 percent; Kentuckian John C. Breckinridge took 18.1 percent leaving John Bell, of Tennessee, with 12.6 percent of the vote. The day after Lincoln won South Carolina's Palmetto flag was raised in Charleston above the offices of the *Charleston Mercury* in defiance of Lincoln's election. Charlestonians also reacted to the news by arresting a United States officer for attempting to take federally owned supplies from the Charleston Arsenal to Fort Moultrie, as he was supposed to do.[192] Only three days later, an editorial appeared in the *New York Evening Post* detailing the poor conditions of forts Moultrie and Sumter. It stated so much "sand has drifted against the walls in such a manner that at some places the cows come in." The piece went on to accuse the sitting president of shipping arms to the arsenal at Charleston.[193]

Five days after the election, in a report to Adjutant General S. Cooper, Assistant General Fitz-John Porter, who had visited Charleston Harbor, described Fort Moultrie in detail. He wrote that Companies E and H of the First United States Artillery were "capable of enduring the fatigues incident to any duty that may be demanded of them." The report made no mention of the fever and its effect on the troops. Porter said Fort Moultrie's condition invited an attack and the work could have been done easily over the past few months; now it would require doing the work without arousing Charlestonians. Porter continued by stating Fort Sumter was not ready to fight off an attack. One hundred and ten men were working on the fort to prepare it for whatever might happen. Porter noted the magazine contained 39,400 pounds of gunpowder. Nearby Castle Pickney held the gunpowder formerly stored in Charleston, but Castle Pickney's magazine and quarters also needed work, said Porter. In all, the three important Federal holdings in Charleston Harbor, Fort Moultrie, Fort Sumter and Castle Pickney, were not battle ready.[194] The city of Charleston was built on the tip of a peninsula created by the Ashley River to the south and the Cooper River to the north of the city. The land between the rivers provided a place for Charleston to grow. At the tip of the peninsula, the waterways meet and empty into a harbor leading to the Atlantic Ocean. Fort Sumter sits at the entrance to the harbor. The day after the report was written, Major Robert Anderson was ordered to report to Washington, D.C., by General Winfield F. Scott. Three days later Anderson was assigned to Fort Moultrie and Colonel John Gardner, who had been filling in for Doubleday, was sent to Texas.

Fifty-five year old Kentuckian Anderson had graduated from West Point in 1825 and had seen action in the Black Hawk War and in Florida against the Seminole Indians. Anderson had also served with Scott in the Mexican War. Only the year before Anderson had been honored as a Master Mason at Lodge 50 in New Jersey where he dined on salmon, mutton, lobster, ice cream and champagne.[195] In contrast, he would find the fare at Charleston Harbor very sparse. It was said that during the Revolutionary War, Anderson's ancestor served at Fort Moultrie, so Anderson must have felt honored to be assigned there.[196] Doubleday, who acknowledged Anderson's bravery in Mexico, however, accused Anderson of being a pro-slavery man.[197] In his first report to the adjutant general, Anderson recommended more men, ordinance and supplies be furnished as soon as possible. While he prepared for the worst, Anderson hoped to "avoid collision."[198] It is perhaps this stance that caused Doubleday to think his new southern-born commander was pro-slavery. It was a time when suspicion touched many.

As the officials on both sides tried to stop the "irrepressible conflict," as Seward had called the situation, work on the forts continued. However, the sending of more reinforcement troops remained undecided. If troops were sent, the touchy Charlestonians would assume they would be under attack any minute; to not send men could be a death sentence for the small band of men under Anderson's command, and in the White House sat a lame duck president who didn't want to go down in history as the president who began an internal war.

Government in Washington was in turmoil. Equally loud voices on both sides were raised, yet nothing of lasting value was accomplished. The lines were being drawn. Pick your side. Words would soon be exchanged for cold steel and hot iron. Foolishly, each believed God would be on his side and therefore the "right" side would win the contest in short fashion. As daylight grew shorter each succeeding day, the small band of men, with a few women and children, sat like sitting ducks in Charleston Harbor praying their President Buchanan would do something, anything, to save them. Southern leaders such as the rabble-rousing Wise continued to ignite the emotions of the people against the North. In the North, people could not believe the South would really withdraw from the Union. It was a time of monumental blindness on both sides, and those like Doubleday, who had warned of coming strife, were quickly dismissed. The collective heads of citizens and leaders were way down deep in the sand.

December arrived along with more workmen at Fort Moultrie. They went about the business of fortifying the structure. In Charleston, volunteers put on red sashes, picked up guns and began drilling; preparations were being made for an attack on the forts in the harbor. Doubleday contributed something that puzzled many on shore. He designed "a sloping picket fence, technically called a *fraise*, to be projected over the parapet." This stout fence would certainly delay an attacking party armed with ladders. The *Mercury* took note this way, "Make ready your sharpened stakes, but you will not intimidate freemen.'"[199]

With such a small number of soldiers to do guard duty, volunteers offered their assistance. Mary Doubleday and the wife of the First United States Artillery's Captain Truman Seymour took turns "walking the paparpet, two hours at a time."[200] For this and other acts of bravery, Mary would receive special recognition in 1896.

The situation was looking pretty bleak to the people in the harbor. The North was slowly beginning to grasp the seriousness, yet some were concerned about losing trade with the unruly sister states of the South. President Buchanan sat still and waited for his long, lanky successor to take the burden off his shoulders. Buchanan, a Democrat, was a native of Pennsylvania, and had been the target of House of Representative's "Honest John" Covode, a Republican, in early 1860 for everything from abuse of presidential power and favoring slavery, to bribing newspaper editors in return for favorable press articles and influencing the passage of the Lecompton Bill. More than 100 witnesses testified before a special committee. While Covode was unsuccessful in his efforts, it took a toll on Buchanan and the Democratic Party that became evident when "Honest Abe" won the election.[201]

Doubleday became disgusted with northern attempts to save business trade with the south. The world as it was known was falling apart. Many people didn't know how, or if, the country would ever reunite. On December 17, 1860, a convention gathered at Columbia, South Carolina. By evening convention members had passed an ordinance to secede. Three days later, it was official. The United States was no longer united. As the nation moved closer to war, on the front page of the *New York Evening Post* and in the pages of the *Atlantic Monthly* a poem made its first public appearance. Henry Wadsworth Longfellow reminded the public of the "The Midnight Ride of Paul Revere" and the war that turned thirteen colonies into a united country.

In the nation's capital, Buchanan watched his cabinet unravel. He appointed Attorney General Jeremiah S. Black as the replacement for resigning Lewis Cass. Cass had resigned because Buchanan would not send help to the forts in Charleston Harbor. Secretary of War John B. Floyd, Secretary of Treasury Howell Cobb, Secretary of Navy Isaac Toucey and Secretary of Interior Jacob Thompson were sympathetic to the south.[202] When word of the official secession move by South Carolina reached Buchanan, he was attending a wedding reception; he quickly left.[203]

At Fort Moultrie several of the officers including Doubleday, approached Anderson about their precarious situation, but Anderson said his orders warned against doing anything that might worsen the situation.[204] However, Anderson was secretly making plans to abandon Fort Moultrie. Work continued so nothing would look suspicious to the people of Charleston. Anderson kept his plans to himself until nearly the last moment. Doubleday became suspicious when Anderson asked him how to make the gun carriages unserviceable. Not realizing what Anderson had in mind, Doubleday suggested burning them, but the smoke would tell the people of the city something was happening within Fort Moultrie. Doubleday became even more certain of Anderson's plans when he requested permission to buy a substantial amount of wire. Doubleday was going to create a barrier in front of his assigned area for defense. Giving approval for the purchase, Anderson, upon hearing Doubleday's wish to start immediately objected in such a way that made him certain that reinforcing Fort Moultrie was no longer a top priority. This took place only the day before they actually left Moultrie, yet nothing had been said by Anderson to his men.

Quartermaster Lieutenant Norman J. Hall had been told by Anderson to get three ships and barges to take the families of the men to Fort Johnson on the other side of the harbor where buildings owned by the government sat. With all that was going on, it certainly made sense to get the women and children out of danger and would not arouse suspicion. In reality, the ships and barges would be loaded with supplies for Fort Sumter and the men once the civilian transfer had been completed. Hall was to approach Fort Johnson, appear as if preparing to land, and wait for a gun to be fired, a signal the move to Sumter was underway. Christmas came and went without much notice by those in the harbor. Assistant Surgeon Samuel Wylie Crawford (who would purchase the land near Devil's Den on the Gettysburg battlefield for the first preservation of that site) thought Anderson had planned to move the troops on Christmas when it would be less likely to be noticed, but a rain changed the timing.[205] One more night would be spent at Fort Moultrie. The day after Christmas, Doubleday strode up to Anderson to invite him for tea with he and Mary as the rays of the sun slipped over the western horizon. Anderson was with a group of officers, including Crawford.

Doubleday greeted Crawford, but Crawford seemed to be preoccupied. As Doubleday strode closer to the group, all conversation halted. Anderson walked over to Doubleday and told him they would be leaving for Sumter as soon as possible. Anderson told Doubleday he had only twenty minutes to prepare. Surprised and concerned they would be discovered and fired upon; Doubleday first assembled his company for inspection. Then with only ten minutes left, he hurried to his quarters where he told Mary. The only woman remaining at Fort Moultrie, she would now have to leave her husband behind and flee for her own safety. Tea was forgotten as his wife threw her clothing into trunks. Doubleday called two men to carry the trunks outside the main gate. One can only imagine a few quick, sad hugs and kisses, maybe a few tears, as the couple separated without knowing when or even if they would ever see each other again. Doubleday told his wife to go to a friendly family outside the fort and "get behind the sandhills as quickly as possible" in case firing began. Mary surely must have been frightened as she hurried toward an uncertain future. With Mary's departure, Doubleday strapped on his revolver and blanket, then hurried to report to Anderson and to board his men in the waiting boats.

While the Doubledays were saying their goodbyes, his men under the direction of Lieutenant Jefferson C. Davis prepared for the transfer. Davis, an Indiana man, fought in the Mexican War and at the battle of Buena Vista with the Third Indiana Volunteers.[206] Davis was now detailed to the rear guard along with Captain John G. Foster and Crawford. The men formed up, knowing the guns aimed at Fort Sumter would be used if they were detected as they moved the command. Doubleday and Mary had to leave personal belongings behind. Doubleday said they did not lose much as it had been sent to New York (probably to brother Ulysses), but others did. Foster, who had been living outside the fort, lost nearly all of his personal items. Anderson's secrecy caused some important supplies to be left behind, including some of Crawford's medical supplies.

Crawford, Foster and two sergeants were ready to use all of the five Columbiads if needed. Boats from Charleston had been, in effect, guarding the fort for several days and if they interfered with the secret move, the Union troops would be sunk. However, with all the activity, two people had not yet been informed, but Reverend Matthias Harris, and Surgeon Simons could see what was happening and they quickly left the island too. Shortly after dusk, the troops began the move across the harbor. The waters were still and the moon lit up the night sky. The men crept toward the boats that were well hidden from prying eyes.

Endnotes

[178] Abner Doubleday to Seward, Oct. 7, 1856, William Henry Seward Letters, University of Rochester, Rochester, NY

[179] Mary Doubleday, letter dated Fort Moultrie, January 16, 1859, Abner Doubleday folder, miscellaneous papers, New York Public Library, New York, NY

[180] Hester Doubleday obituary, *Daily Pantagraph*, Bloomington, Ill. Nov. 16, 1859; also *New York Tribune*, Nov.19, 1859. The burial place is listed in the Illinois, *McLean County Cemeteries book*, Vol. XIII-I, Old City, 42

[181] Letters Received by the Adjutant General, M567, roll 599, NARA

[182] Meade, Vol. 1, 214-215

[183] William Henry Seward letters, letter from Abner Doubleday to Seward Oct. 7, 1856, University of Rochester

[184] Robert Anderson papers, Apr. 24, 1860, Library of Congress (hereafter LOC).

[185] *Flayderman's Guide to Antique American Firearms*, Seventh edition, Norm Flayderman, Krause Pub., 1998, 262 states a volcanic gun in 1998 has a value range of $2,000 to $14,000 depending on model and condition.

[186] Letters sent/rec'd Adjutant Gen Office Apr. 26, 1860, M567, Roll 622, NARA

[187] Returns from Regular Army Artillery Regiments, June 1821-1901, M727, Roll 4, May 6, 1860, NARA

[188] Abraham Lincoln papers, M567, Roll 599, LOC

[189] Abner Doubleday, *Reminiscences of Forts Sumter and Moultrie in 1860-61*, (New York: Harper and Brothers Publishers, 1876), 25-26

[190] *Charleston Mercury*, October 2, 1860

[191] *Charleston Mercury*, October 2, 1860

[192] E. B. Long, *The Civil War Day by Day*, (New York: Doubleday and Co., 1971), 3

[193] *New York Evening Post*, Nov. 9, 1860, pg 2

[194] OR, Vol. I, 70-72

[195] Robert Anderson papers, Vol. 8, Nov.15, 1859, LOC

[196] Abner Doubleday, *Reminiscences*, 41

[197] Abner Doubleday, *Reminiscences*, 42

[198] OR, Vol. 1, 74-76

[199] Abner Doubleday, *Reminiscences*, 49

[200] Abner Doubleday, *Reminiscences*, 50

[201] Arthur M. Schlesinger Jr., and Roger Burns, eds., *Congress Investigates A Documented History 1792-1974*; Vol. II, 1071-1086, (New York: Chelsea House Publishers, 1975), Roger A. Burns, *The Covode Committee 1860*

[202] Abner Doubleday, *Reminiscences,* 55

[203] Long, 10-13

[204] OR, Vol. 1, 94

[205] Samuel Wylie Crawford, *The Genesis of the Civil War, The Story of Sumter,* (New York: C. L. Webster & Co., 1887) 102

[206] Ezra J. Warner, *Generals in Blue;* lives of the Union commanders, (Baton Rouge: Louisiana State University Press, 1964), 115

CHAPTER 11

"An insolent request"

Doubleday was careful not to upset the small boat as he removed his coat and folded it inside out. Quietly he issued an order, "Men, do as I have. Remove your coats and fold them so the buttons aren't seen." He could barely see a steamboat approaching his position, but doffed his hat, too.

Doubleday and his command had hidden behind a rocky sea wall waiting to begin their dangerous mission. His boat pointed outward, Doubleday and his men had just pushed off to Sumter, a mile away. The steamboat was performing guard duty in the harbor. Because the men rowing had little experience, progress was slow. The men followed his orders and then wrapped their muskets in their coats too. Now nothing would reflect the moonlight. Quietly the paddles dipped into the water as the boats glided along. While the transfer of troops was taking place, South Carolina representatives were arriving in Washington, D.C. to request the forts and other federal property be surrendered to the state.

The chugging of the steamboat told the soldiers it was getting even closer. It stopped about a hundred yards away so the crew on board could get a better look. The boat paused for a moment, and then moved on. Letting out a collective quiet sigh of relief, the men dipped the oars in the dark water even faster. When they reached Fort Sumter, the soldiers were met by workmen who were less than enthusiastic about their midnight visitors; many of the workers where wearing secession badges. They were angry at this new development and seemed very threatening. Doubleday ordered his men to form up and conduct a bayonet charge. The angry workmen beat a hasty retreat into the fort. Once Doubleday and his men were safely inside the fort, the boats were sent back for Seymour's men at Moultrie. Anderson arrived and soon all the men including the rear guard had made the transfer safely. The signal gun was fired and the ships landed with the families and supplies under Hall's watchful eyes. With the successful move, the still angry secessionist workmen were then put on the boats and sent across the river to Charleston. On shore Mary hurried to the home of post sutler, Dan Sinclair, but she didn't stay long. When it was evident the people of Charleston had not seen the movement, once again exhibiting bravery, Mary went back to Moultrie to get the rest of the couple's belongings and returned to shore where she located Chaplain Harris' residence and safety. Unable to sleep, Mary walked out to the beach where she paced and peered into the night looking for any signs of trouble at Sumter. It would be a very long night. When morning came, an exhausted Mary went to the Harris home where she would stay for the next few weeks.

As the soldiers left Moultrie, Foster made sure the guns there were spiked, the gun carriages burned, and no ammunition was left behind. He then cut the flagstaff down and took it to Sumter. With little left to do and taking whatever might be useful with them, the remaining men headed to Sumter. The next day at noon, with the troops in attendance, Anderson held a flag-raising ceremony at Fort Sumter. The ceremony featured a prayer by Reverend Matthias. As the Amens were said, Sergeant James E. Galway's regimental band struck up "The Star Spangled Banner" to three cheers of all the men. The American flag was hoisted up the flagpole where it quickly caught a breeze and fluttered above them.

The men settled down and began putting their baggage and equipment away. Chaos was soon replaced with order inside the fort; quarters for the men were designated, as well as for camp women. Furniture that was hastily thrown in a heap when unloaded was distributed to different rooms. Doubleday said he chose a room and "made it so comfortable that Anderson and Seymour came there temporarily to live with me."[207]

Doubleday was hoping Anderson would do more than just watch the shoreline for a threatened attack. Other than threatening to shoot out the light of a lighthouse, Anderson just watched the opposite shore. By waiting for the South Carolinians to attack first, Anderson would win Northern approval in the coming months and gain an important advantage in the court of public opinion.

Curiously, the move from Moultrie to Sumter would be laid at Doubleday's feet years later through, *The Diary of a Public Man.* The diary states Stephen Douglas told the anonymous diarist that Doubleday had been in contact with powerful anti-slavery Ohio Senator Benjamin Wade prior to the move and Doubleday and Wade were reportedly attempting to keep Seward out of Lincoln's cabinet.[208] Considering the relationship between Doubleday and Seward, it seems preposterous that Doubleday would try to keep a personal supporter from becoming a cabinet member under Lincoln. Modern authors who refer to the "*Diary*" indicate its contents while making interesting reading, must not be taken too seriously, as is obvious in this case.[209]

The news of Anderson's move swept through the northern states and the citizens at last had something to celebrate. Many communities fired a hundred-gun salute in their honor.[210] Yet as Anderson and his men raised the flag over Sumter, secessionists, without the knowledge of South Carolina's Governor Francis W. Pickens, took Castle Pickney, another piece of Federal real estate in the harbor. Charleston troops took over what was left of Moultrie. The circle of safe territory was growing smaller around Sumter, and the fort still needed to be made a strong defensively. Men could have easily breached the walls of Fort Sumter with ladders considering its condition at that time. Numerous openings created another concern. Sumter was a pentagon in design; sixty feet high with three foot thick walls and regarded as "impregnable." Anderson and the men inside knew better. They were certainly hoping the Confederates wouldn't realize the fort's weaknesses.

It was a good thing they were making preparations to defend the fort for they soon had visitors. Colonel James L. Petigru and Major Elison Capers, from the volunteer rifle regiment in Charleston, arrived in full uniform. They were paying a call on Major Anderson. Doubleday attended the meeting, and although he didn't take notes, he said the two told Anderson that Buchanan had agreed not to reinforce the fort and that the move from Moultrie to Sumter violated that agreement. The two men said the violation meant Anderson and his men should vacate Fort Sumter immediately. Anderson said such an agreement did not exist and that he had a duty to defend the fort; he could not comply with their request. Petigru and Capers left unsuccessful in their mission. Such a request made Doubleday angry, for he considered their request, "insolent."[211]

As the Southerners prepared to take their boat back to shore, Doubleday took the opportunity to tell the boatmen that shells had been prepared to greet any attack. The information was given with the knowledge it would be repeated in town. Long before the phrase, "psychological war" was coined, Doubleday used this technique often to deter the enemy. After Anderson refused to comply with the demand to give up the fort, Anderson expected an attack, but nothing happened. Rumors and speculation ruled the days that followed. Banks refused payments on bills; talk of a naval attack by the federal government was on the lips of many in Charleston. Work to make the illegally seized Moultrie and Pickney secure continued, as did the work at Sumter. Each side was lining up and preparing for a battle that would surely come.

The seizure of Castle Pickney and Fort Moultrie were only the first of several other federally-owned properties to be taken by the Southerners. The new legislature of the Confederate States of America was struggling to identify itself. Many suggestions were made and they ranged from kidnapping Lincoln to only admitting slave states and expelling any state that freed its slaves. The pot was truly at a feverish boil. As William C. Davis writes in his book, *Look Away*, "Even in 1832 there were those in the South who confessed that the tariff was only a battlefield, not the war. If they did not fight their ground and win on the tariff, soon enough they would be fighting for something even closer to their hearts, slavery itself."[212] That time had arrived.

It wasn't long before all civilians were ordered to leave Moultrieville where Mary had been staying. She had been sending candles to her husband by passing them through the lines with some of Sumter's workmen. No mail was delivered to Sumter and negotiations had temporarily ended. The men in the fort were now down to an extremely limited menu: Pork, beans and hard tack.[213] Each day brought new difficulties. A short-handed command meant duties had to be divided among the few. "Captain Seymour and myself were the only officers for duty as Officers of the Day, Lieutenant Davis and Lieutenant Hall were serving under us as officers of the guard," Doubleday said.[214] Surgeon Crawford volunteered to take on the additional duties as Officer of the Day. As the days dragged on, the men did what they could to make the fort stronger. Yet a week after the move, on New Year's Day an inventory showed they only had provisions for a short time. The South Carolinians had taken possession of Castle Pickney and Fort Moultrie, the local customhouse and all its funds and other federal properties in the city. Ships could no longer enter the harbor since the lights of the lighthouse had been destroyed. With no mail, little fuel and food, how long could the men expect to hold out? The clock was ticking, and through it all the soldiers could do little except become frustrated with the lack of support from their government.

With the New Year there were new hopes of resolving the crisis. But even as the last toasts of holiday cheer were made on both sides, President Buchanan finally took steps to provide assistance to the United States soldiers in Charleston Harbor. Three hundred men at Fort Monroe were ordered to reinforce Fort Sumter. The order didn't remain active for long. General Winfield Scott applied pressure to the president to change orders that were sending supplies and only 250 men on board the *Star of the West*. At a cost of $1,500 per day for ten days, the ship was prepared and sent on its journey on the fifth day of the New Year.

A short time later South Carolina's sister to the north saw citizens seizing Fort Johnston, at Smithville, North Carolina, the very first post Doubleday had been assigned to as a young soldier right out of West Point. On January 9, Fort Johnston fell, and the next day the Smithville citizens emboldened by their success, also took Fort Caswell.

Endnotes

[207] Abner Doubleday, *Reminiscences,* 79

[208] Anonymous, *Diary of a Public Man,* originally appeared as a series in The North American Review, 1879.

[209] J. G. Randall, *Lincoln the President,* (New York: Dodd, Mead, 1945), 295 and Hans Louis Trefousse, *The Radical Republicans; Lincoln's Vanguard for Racial Justice,* New York: Knopf, 1969), 146 footnote

[210] *New York Tribune,* Jan. 3, 1961, The firing of one hundred guns was done in Seneca Falls and Waverly, both in New York state.

[211] Abner Doubleday, *Reminiscences,* 80

[212] William C. Davis, *Look Away! A History of the Confederate States of America,* (New York: The Free Press, New York, 2002), 10

[213] Abner Doubleday, *Reminiscences,* 86

[214] Ibid

CHAPTER 12

"Let the people rise in their might"

Doubleday said the men inside Fort Sumter were good, reliable soldiers. He continued, "We were quite fortunate: the habits of the officers were good, and there was no dissipation or drunkenness in the garrison. They were full of zeal, intelligence, and energy."[215] The officers would need all of these qualities and more as the days slid toward the inevitable.

Many of the officers had served in the Mexican War. Among those were Captain John G. Foster, of the army's engineer branch. Foster was from New Hampshire and had graduated in 1846 from West Point. Vermont born Captain Truman Seymour, First United States Artillery, was another 1846 graduate of West Point, and would later gain fame for his part in the assault on Battery Wagner in July 1863, the battle that won fame for the black troops of the Fifty-fourth Massachusetts Infantry. Seymour had served in the Seminole War in Florida. First Lieutenant Jefferson C. Davis, First United States Artillery, had served at the Battle of Buena Vista in the Mexican War. A Kentuckian, he was not a West Pointer. Also serving at Sumter was Dr. Samuel Wiley Crawford, an assistant surgeon in the regular army. Crawford grew up at "Allandale" in the hamlet of Fayetteville located between Gettysburg and Chambersburg in Franklin County, Pennsylvania. At genteel "Allandale" peacocks glided across the spacious lawn.[216] In all, the garrison had nine officers, seventy-three enlisted and about forty laborers to stave off those who would claim Sumter. Their commander, Major Robert Anderson, had been born in Kentucky and married a woman from Georgia. He was known as a good soldier, but his pro-slavery view put him in a personal dilemma. He would do his duty at Fort Sumter, but his heart wasn't in it. Anderson's allegiance to the country would be called into question.

Doubleday was among some of the best men in the regular Army, but he was the only officer at the fort to favor the election of Lincoln. Not only that, but he was an outspoken opponent of slavery and wanted Anderson to be more bold in defense of the fort. These issues alone made him a marked man in the opinion of not only his fellow officers, but made him an evil, dangerous man in the eyes of the secessionists.[217]

In early January, Major Anderson's wife, Eliza, arrived at the fort to visit her husband. Rumors said she brought "dispatches from Washington" for evacuation of Sumter, but time proved the rumors to be wrong.[218] She would not be the only woman at the fort. Mary Doubleday and a few other women had rejoined their husbands.

A correspondent for the *New York Tribune* sat down to a meal with the men in the harbor. He reported to his readers an unidentified officer stated, "We will fire the magazine, and be buried in one common ruin, before we will surrender." Even though the reporter didn't say which officer, it seems plausible that Doubleday made the statement, for all the officers mentioned in the article were said to be popular except, "Captain Doubleday."[219] The newspaper, noting Ulysses Freeman lived in Brooklyn, described Doubleday as "a capable officer and particularly obnoxious to the Rebels."[220]

In early January of 1861, Doubleday wrote to General Jesse Segoine of the local militia in Auburn, who at the age of fifty-eight would later become the colonel of the 111th New York Infantry. Doubleday voiced his happiness about the move from Moultrie to Sumter saying, the move had "been approved by my former townsmen. We have been so long surrounded with trimmers and traitors that I began to fear the love of the national flag was dying out in our country." He described conditions in the harbor, "The light in the harbor [has] been out, the buoys taken up, all communication has been cut off with us except such as the governor chooses to authorize and yet we hesitate to fire on them." He continued, "If war must come, let the people rise in their might, and maintain the integrity of the Union."[221]

Doubleday also implied that Moultrie's commander, John Gardner, was replaced by Buchanan with Anderson for political reasons favorable to the South.[222] The appointment was even questioned in the South; the famous Charleston diarist Mary Chesnut wrote, "Why did that green goose Anderson go into Fort Sumter? Then everything began to go wrong."[223] It was as though having a particular person in command would solve the festering, wounded Southern pride.

By the end of January, the country had a new state: Kansas, the site of so much violence regarding the slave question.

The soldiers of Sumter were tense; they had rations for only a few weeks. Time was running out for them all as they continued to fortify Sumter. Doubleday ordered "iron-plated bullet-proof galleries over the angles of the parapet."[224] In the bottom of the galleries, he left trap-doors for the dropping of shells on the enemy. As the preparations for battle took place, it wasn't long before many of the officer's wives who were in the Charleston area, headed for the safety of New York City.

Shortly after Lincoln had taken the oath as president, Doubleday wrote to Felicia Shover again. Doubleday called his situation a "peculiar position" and said, "I do not see how even the Secessionists can blame us for adhering to our oaths or for defending ourselves against attack." Doubleday went on to present his views on how two countries could not live together easily. He pointed out how much it would cost to guard and maintain a boundary between North and South. He also said he was unhappy to see some of his private letters had been printed in newspapers, "I have no fancy for seeing myself in print." He described life at Sumter, saying that he and his fellow soldiers "have been cooped up so long in our island prison that we shall enjoy our liberty when it arrives."[225]

Not all Charleston citizens were Secessionists. Doubleday had seen and heard how torn James Louis Petigru, of Charleston, was at the idea of a war. "The tears rolled down his cheeks as he deplored the folly and madness of the time." Petigru described his home state as, "too small for a republic and too large for a lunatic asylum," when asked if he would join the rebels in his city.[226]

In mid-March Mary, who had sought safety in Washington, received a surprise visitor—the lanky, bearded man who lived at the White House. Lincoln was on a fact-finding mission and asked to see the letters Doubleday had sent to Mary, so he might learn more about the resources of the fort in the harbor.[227] Lincoln had already received Doubleday's letters home via Doubleday's brother, Ulysses.

As Lincoln settled down in Mary Doubleday's parlor (probably at The Willard Hotel which became **her** headquarters throughout the war when not visiting her husband in the field), the *Star of the West* steamed down the coast. At Sumter, Anderson sent a memo to the adjutant general's office. Anderson detailed the fortifications made by the people in Charleston, and said, "It would be dangerous and difficult for a vessel to enter the harbor." The *Star of the West* arrived in the harbor soon after the men had transferred to Sumter. Proving Anderson correct in his analysis of the situation, the citizens in Charleston fired on the ship. No reserve supplies were delivered. The ship turned around and began the journey home.[228] Captain Foster wrote to Washington, D.C., a few days later: "The temper of the people of this state is becoming every day more bitter, and I do not see how we can avoid a bloody conflict."[229]

Not long after the *Star of the West* began its return trip north, a group of Charleston citizens visited the fort. Their purpose? To tell the soldiers that one way or another, they would take Sumter. United States District Judge Andrew Gordon Magrath gave an impassioned speech that was effective on Anderson, but not on Doubleday. In the ensuing conversation Anderson trying to be diplomatic, suggested sending opposing views to Washington and let the government sort it all out. Doubleday opposed the suggestion on the grounds it would allow more time for the secessionists to fortify and make preparations to take the fort. Doubleday knew that Anderson was a popular man in Washington, so the suggestion would be "sustained." Lieutenant Theodore Talbot would be sent to represent the men of Sumter in the nation's capital as the discussions continued.[230] As the days passed, the supplies inside of Sumter whittled away. Across the waters of Charleston Harbor, Southern troops continued to add to their supplies and fortifications.

When Talbot returned, he brought Doubleday some interesting news. In Charleston, "the mob were howling for my head," since he was the only Black Republican in the fort.[231] It was a time when anyone in favor of Abolition for thousands of Black slaves was labeled with the vilest name and lumped in with the category of persons who joined in John Brown's beliefs. By the last day of January, Doubleday had been sent a letter from the not-so-friendly citizens of Charleston. If he entered their fair city, and if he was caught, he would wear tar and feathers as an Abolitionist![232] Southern hospitality was only a memory for Doubleday.

The day after Lincoln was inaugurated, Anderson wrote to the new commander-in-chief and said no reinforcements were necessary. Anderson did not want to go down in history as the man who began a civil war. By mid-March the soldiers inside the walls of Sumter were surviving on pork and hardtack. Inside the fort, the army's stomach was growling with hunger pangs. Later that month Colonel Ward C. Lamon, the former law partner of Lincoln, paid a visit to Sumter. When he left, he took with him the knowledge that the food at the fort would run out by mid-April.

Just ten days before the inevitable, Doubleday wrote to his wife Mary and confided that life at Fort Sumter was not going well. Many of the men had dysentery and they were bored with nothing to do but guard duty, "eating and sleeping. I cannot see how this national quarrel is going to end. Everything looks dark and yet I feel as if it would all come out right at last."[233]

Negotiations between all parties involved failed. By April 12th, everyone knew something would have to happen soon. The stand-off couldn't continue forever. That night in Charleston, Mary Chesnut tossed and turned in her bed as she tried to fall asleep. Her husband, Colonel James Chesnut, had been to the fort and tried to negotiate with Anderson to no avail. She tossed and turned. She listened to the bells of St. Michael's Episcopal Church at the corner of Broad and Meeting Streets as they pealed the hour. One . . . . Two . . . . Three . . . . Four . . . . A half an hour later, cannons boomed from shore. Her husband had given the order to fire on Sumter.

As Mary Chesnut lay awake counting the bells in the early morning of April 12, Doubleday was awakened by a noise in his room. Anderson was there and shared a message he had just received. The recently resigned superintendent of West Point was preparing to open fire on his former artillery instructor. Pierre Gustave Toutant Beauregard, an 1838 graduate of West Point with the nickname; "The Little Napoleon" was on the opposite shore and warned Anderson, he would open fire on Sumter shortly after 4 a.m. In the dark, Anderson and men inside Sumter couldn't prepare for the attack and it was decided to wait for daylight.

Doubleday went back to bed and waited. It didn't take long. A cannon ball soon buried "itself in the masonry about a foot from my head, in very unpleasant proximity to my right ear." Considering the walls of Sumter were about five feet thick, a cannon ball that close to his bed had to be unnerving. The sounds of shelling became more rapid and the fort began to literally crumble with each shot from shore. Doubleday laid there thinking about the loose powder in his quarters catching a spark from the cannon shot. It didn't take much imagination to picture his fate. The attack didn't stop the soldiers from grabbing some hardtack for a hasty breakfast. By sunrise, the men were ready for action and they were soon at their posts to answer the guns on shore. Doubleday and his company headed for the casemates. The honor of firing the first gun against the attack went to Doubleday. For years historians have debated whether or not Doubleday really did aim and/or fire the first answering shot. Doubleday himself says he aimed and shot the cannon, and his brother, Ulysses, wrote in his diary that his brother aimed and fired the gun. Given his artillery background, the letter threatening tar and feathers, and his anti-slavery views, why would it be doubted? Doubleday was not afraid to give or back up his views with action, a stance that would cause him problems later in the war.

His first shot bounced off a roof over the attackers' batteries on the opposite shore. He then shot a forty-two pounder into the center of a group of Southern troops watching the attack. The thunder of cannon was heard on all sides and acrid smoke billowed up. Men were trying to breathe in the foul air. Yet each side was determined to win and the firing became very regular. Shells of many sizes rained on Sumter. Fragments of shells filled the air. Parts of Sumter's masonry flew as it was hit by cannon balls. As they hit their targets, the ground shook. To Doubleday, it felt like an earthquake rumbling beneath his feet. Across the water at Cummings Point, opposite of Fort Moultrie on Morris Island, the attackers had a Blakely twelve pound rifled gun. It was a very effective gun with enough force to send a ball crashing through a wall where Doubleday and his company were working their guns. Brick fragments went flying in all directions, slightly wounding a few men. This firefight continued for three hours.

Seymour stopped at Doubleday's guns and using his sense of humor to lighten the moment asked, "Doubleday, what in the world is the matter here, and what is all this uproar about?"

"There is a trifling difference of opinion between us and our neighbors opposite, and we are trying to settle it," Doubleday retorted.

Seymour relieved Doubleday who needed some rest. For another three hours the firing continued with Seymour, before Doubleday returned to his guns. Orders came from Anderson to concentrate the fire on the Blakely gun that was doing so much damage, but with little effect. The fight went on all day and only stopped when it became too dark to see targets.

The battle began again the next morning about four. By 7 a.m. the air was filled with shot and fragments flying about again. It wasn't long before the officers' quarters caught fire. The area was entirely constructed of wood and burned well. The men now had to contend with not only the smoke of the cannon, but also smoke from the fire. Other dangers abounded. Loose gunpowder had been spilled here and there. A spark from the shelling could cause an explosion that none of the men inside wanted to experience. The magazine itself had more than 300 barrels of powder. A spark could cause more damage than the Confederates. Coughing and choking from the smoke-filled air, the men managed to move about a third of the barrels before a shot hit the lock and bent it so the men could no longer remove the remaining barrels. By noon, the men were exhausted and suffering from the effects of the smoke. Handkerchiefs were placed over their mouths, some tried to find a less smoke-filled place to stand. The troops inside Sumter were crawling through the smoke and debris in search of breathable air. As flames crackled and sizzled, shells dropped from the sky, and the sounds of masonry falling, it must have seemed like the fires of hell had opened on Sumter. The Stars and Stripes had been shot down and nailed to a temporary pole as the battle continued. [234] At his guns, Doubleday set his sights on the Moultrie House on Sullivan's Island. It was an upscale place for the wealthy planters who visited the area. The state flag that flew above the hotel had been taken down. Doubleday aimed two of the forty-two pounders and fired at the upper story. The Southern troops, who had taken over the building, came flying out as Doubleday's shot hit its mark and went through the length of the building.

The fighting continued until Beauregard sent a small boat with Colonel James Chesnut to Sumter. A white flag was hoisted and Chesnut and his few companions began their diplomatic mission. They arrived at the smoking fort in the harbor and delivered a message from Beauregard requesting a cease-fire. Anderson was ready to call a halt to the fight. The shelling had taken its toll on Sumter's walls; it was a no win situation. The Secessionists had won the first battle of the Civil War. The soldiers inside the fort would leave in the morning.

April 14th, the men rose early, gathered their belongings and made ready to leave the still smoking fort. As part of their surrender, Anderson requested that the Confederates allow him to keep and salute the American flag as it was lowered. Fifty rounds later (originally there was to have been 100 rounds) the flag that had endured the opening battle of the Civil War was gently lowered. Surprisingly, only one man, federal soldier Private Daniel Hough, was killed during the ceremony to surrender. A pile of cartridges were under the muzzle of a cannon, and when it was fired as part of the gun salute, his arm was ripped off killing him instantly.[235] As the smoke curled up from the cannons, Confederate troops marched into Sumter. Doubleday formed up the men on the parade ground. With the American flag flying and drums beating *Yankee Doodle*, the men left Fort Sumter. Once the men had marched out of Sumter, Anderson tucked the flag tucked under his arm and left the fort. The men took the tattered American flag and flew it on the steamship *Baltic* all the way to New York City.[236] Little did the brave Union soldiers know that as the flag was lowered at Sumter, ordinary citizens throughout the north raised the Stars and Stripes above their homes, stores and wherever a flag could appropriately fly or hang.

Two months after the fall of Sumter, Doubleday wrote Anderson and accused Anderson of trying to embarrass him with comments about the losses suffered at Moultrie at the time they had left the fort for Sumter. Doubleday also told Anderson that a list of men who had suffered the loss of clothing could not be found. The letter refers to a fund raised and distributed among the brave Sumter men then in New York. Doubleday solicited Anderson saying that if Anderson had any money for that purpose, it should go to the families of the "maimed men." Doubleday said his company had suffered five injured and that Company H had six injured men. Yet in spite of their differing opinions regarding slavery, Doubleday ends his letter on a friendlier note, saying he wished Anderson good health and stated, "The whole country looks to you with a depth of affection which has not had its parallel since the days of Washington."[237] Fifteen years after the fall of Sumter, in 1876, Doubleday commented on the leadership of Major Anderson. Doubleday said Anderson's private life was conducted in a manner that won respect, but that's where Doubleday stopped. Because of his own devotion to the elimination of slavery, an unpopular stance, Doubleday saw Anderson as a man who wanted to save the union, but without harming slavery.[238]

Endnotes

[215] Abner Doubleday, *Reminiscences,* 23

[216] Warner, 157, 432, (Note: The Crawford home was visited by the author in 1995, and it was in nearly perfect pre-Civil War condition.)

[217] Abner Doubleday, *Reminiscences,* 2, 32

[218] *New York Tribune,* Jan. 9, 1861

[219] Ibid, Jan.23, 1861

[220] Ibid, March 5, 1861

[221] *New York Tribune,* Jan. 6, 1861. Abner to Gen. Segoine. This line could have been inspired by the last line of Lincoln's Cooper Union speech made February 27, 1860 "Let us have faith that right makes might, and in that faith, let us, to the end, dare to do our duty as we understand it."

[222] *Charleston Mercury,* Jan. 19, 1861. The letter Abner wrote found its way into the *Mercury.*

[223] Mary Chesnut, Mary Boykin Miller, and C. Vann Woodward, ed. *Mary Chesnut's Civil War,* (New Haven: Yale University Press, 1981)., 45.

[224] A. D., n.p.

[225] Abner Doubleday, letter to Felicia Shover, from Fort Sumter, March 13, 1861, Virginia Historical Society, Richmond, VA

[226] Carl Sandburg, *Abraham Lincoln; The War Years,* (New York: Harcourt, Brace & Co, 1939), Vol. 2, 528-529

[227] Sandburg, Vol. 1, 189

[228] OR, Vol. 1, 134

[229] OR, Vol. 1, 138

[230] Abner Doubleday, *Reminiscences,* 109-112

[231] Ibid, 113

[232] Ibid, 119

[233] David C. Mearns, *The Lincoln Papers,* (Garden City, New York: Doubleday and Company, Inc., 1948), Vol. 1, 513-514

[234] Abner Doubleday, *Reminiscences,* 159

[235] Ibid, 172

[236] *New York Tribune,* April 19, 1861

[237] Robert Anderson papers, Vol. 13, Abner Doubleday to Anderson, June 22, 1861, LOC

[238] Abner Doubleday, *Reminiscences,* 90

CHAPTER 13

"Modest, unassuming man"

The boats in New York harbor whistled and tooted loudly. Sailors cheered. Doubleday stared as he looked all around him. He was being called the hero of Fort Sumter! He and his fellow soldiers and the few remaining civilians from Fort Sumter had sailed to New York, arriving on April 19. In the South the of Hero of Fort Sumter title went to Beauregard. In the North, Old Glory was seen flying above homes, shops and other buildings, much as it did following a terrorist attack on September 11, 2001. Most of the defenders of Sumter were given leave, however Doubleday was given command of Fort Hamilton in the absence of Anderson.

In Washington, Lincoln was seeking someone to command an army that would defeat the Confederates and save the Union from dissolving into two countries. On the short list was a man who was wounded in the Mexican War and had served as superintendent at West Point. United States Army Colonel Robert E. Lee was approached by Francis P. Blair on behalf of Lincoln and on the recommendation of General Winfield Scott. Blair offered Lee command of the entire federal army and Lee left the meeting a troubled man. He had taken an oath to serve the United States, so how could he take up arms against his homeland—Virginia? It is claimed Lee spent much of that night pacing in the rose garden of his home, Arlington House, just a stone's throw across the Potomac River from the White House. After a restless night, Lee made the decision to remain true to Virginia. Three days after the fall of Fort Sumter, Virginia joined its southern sisters, South Carolina, Mississippi, Florida, Alabama, Georgia, Louisiana and Texas in secession. Arkansas, Tennessee and North Carolina would soon follow.

After Sumter fell, Lincoln called for 75,000 men from the Northern states to volunteer for duty. In early May, Lincoln issued a second call for an additional 42,000 men. In Northern states, regiments were forming and men were lining up for what some viewed as a great adventure that would end quickly.

The organization of the army in 1861 was very different from today's military. At that time, there were about 14,000 United States Army military men, called "regulars," and the majority were stationed in the West where they would receive orders to head east. The states would individually send troops to fight this new war. Many of the regulars would return to their home states to recruit civilian-soldiers. About a week after Sumter fell, Doubleday wrote to Colonel Lorenzo Thomas, adjutant general of the army, and requested a leave of absence to organize a regiment of volunteers from his home town of Auburn. He also asked that he not be forced to resign his commission as an artillery officer in order to organize a regiment. His requests were denied. The army had other plans for Doubleday. On May 14, 1861 Doubleday was promoted to major of the newly created regular army regiment, the Seventeenth United States Infantry.[239]

The month of May also found Doubleday at a dinner with other soon-to-be military luminaries. He was invited to dinner at the home of prominent Republican Alexander Kelly McClure, in Chambersburg, Pennsylvania. Also attending the dinner were: George H. Thomas, a colonel at Carlisle Barracks who had been at West Point with Doubleday (Thomas graduated two years before Doubleday.); sixty-nine year old veteran of the War of 1812, Major General Robert Patterson; Philadelphian and attorney-turned-military man, Major General George Cadwalader who had fought in the Mexican War and former Reading, Pennsylvania, mayor, Major General William Keim, New Hampshire born and 1845 West Point graduate, Colonel (soon to be Brigadier General) Fitz John Porter (West Point 1845); and the local militia's John Sherman. Interestingly, Thomas was born in Southampton County, Virginia where he taught fifteen slaves to read. He and his family hid in nearby woods during the uprising by slave, Nat Turner. Following the firing on Sumter, Thomas is said to have renewed his oath to the United States as he made his way to Carlisle, but not all officers would take that step.[240]

During the evening, the talk inevitably turned to the war. McClure noted that all except Doubleday and Thomas were positive the war would quickly end. Doubleday, one of the more knowledgeable officers in the gathering, quite forcefully disagreed with that view and told his companions the war would be long and bloody. After all, hadn't he been a live target only the month before? Doubleday, who left the dinner early, was dismissed for his remarks, because he "was a Spiritualist and a little gone in the head."[241] Unfortunately, Doubleday's words would prove to be sadly accurate.

During the weeks following the fall of Fort Sumter, Patterson of the Pennsylvania Militia, was appointed to command the military activities of Delaware, Pennsylvania, Maryland and the District of Columbia. In the Confederacy, General Robert E. Lee accepted command of troops in Virginia.

On June 1, Doubleday, who was on detached service from the Seventeenth United States Infantry, was serving with Company E of the First United States Artillery which had been stationed in New York before being ordered to join Patterson at Chambersburg. Two days later members of the artillery regiment boarded a New York Central Railroad train and headed for Harrisburg, Pennsylvania. The following day, Doubleday reported to Patterson and was assigned to Thomas' brigade. The men of Company E were joined by William McMullen's Philadelphia Rangers, and on June 7, they marched eight miles before camping at Brown's Mills, between Chambersburg, Pennsylvania and Williamsport, Maryland. Meanwhile, Lieutenant Elder of Doubleday's battery was sent from Chambersburg back to Governor's Island, New York, to get four siege guns, ammunition and other equipment. More men arrived in the Chambersburg area and Doubleday's command was increased with Captain R. I. Dodge's regular army recruits of the Eighth United States Infantry.

During that time, the country received startling news. The "Little Giant" and Lincoln's opponent, Stephen A. Douglas, died in Chicago after contracting typhoid.

As the new Union volunteers gathered and marched toward Hagerstown, Maryland, Confederate Joseph Johnston began to evacuate Harpers Ferry. Patterson's army, including Doubleday and his command, reached Hagerstown, Maryland and continued southward to rural Williamsport, Maryland where the infantry soldiers were detached and reassigned. Then Doubleday received orders to keep two companies of artillery and prepare to man a siege gun battery consisting of heavy guns and howitzers. Doubleday headed back to Hagerstown to wait for the big guns, but the aging General Winfield Scott, believed Washington was being threatened by the Rebels and ordered Patterson to forget Johnston and head quickly to the nation's capital. Doubleday and his men boarded a train and started for Washington. At Harrisburg, they saw their siege guns going in the opposite direction, toward Hagerstown. By the time Doubleday reached York, Pennsylvania, at two in the morning on June 18, he received a telegram countermanding his orders, sending him back to Hagerstown at once. There had been a report the enemy was headed toward Hagerstown. However, the report was false. As nearly any veteran can attest, this type of misinformation and the delays that follow are common in any action. The see-saw of information, commands and counter commands would continue for a few more days. Scott was trying to keep the capital safe and the whereabouts of the enemy known.

The ever growing army of Patterson gathered in the area of Hagerstown and Williamsport. Local citizens were curious and visited the camps. Many of the locals had heard about Doubleday at Fort Sumter, and flocked to see his camp located near the Franklin Rail line at Williamsport, a community once discussed as a possible site for the nation's capital. In the crowd was Angela Kirkham Davis, a native of Batavia, New York, and her husband, Joseph Davis. Following their wedding they had moved to his native state of Maryland. They lived a few miles from Hagerstown where they owned a country store. They too, wanted to see the "Fort Sumter Garrison," just beyond the western edge of Hagerstown. The couple was introduced to Doubleday and Angela describes Doubleday as a "fine, modest, unassuming looking man." She observed his tent had flowers and books in it.[242]

Seemingly overnight, Williamsport had become a hub of military activity. Still mounted on the rail cars used to transport them, Doubleday's siege guns had arrived. They quickly became the center of attention for many men and boys.[243] On June 19, army regulars who had been at Harpers Ferry arrived at Williamsport after destroying all arms and goods that could benefit the rebels just before the Southerners took over the arsenal. The next day Doubleday's battery moved to a Williamsport cemetery located on a hill overlooking the Potomac River.[244]

In early June a heavy summer rain had washed out some of the area roads making travel even more difficult than usual. The delivery of mail stopped when Confederates destroyed bridges that crossed the Potomac River dividing Maryland and Virginia.[245] By early July, Patterson's Army crossed the Potomac and headed for Martinsburg, Virginia. (now West Virginia). Once the high waters of the Potomac had receded, the army could cross to the other side, a crossing that took twelve hours. The water at that point is normally low and one man said it could be crossed without even getting wet above the waist. The men took off their shoes, socks, underwear and pants to make the crossing. Whole regiments of men with shoes tied together, encircling and dangling from their necks with shirttails flapping or damply clinging to them must have been quite a sight.[246]

Following the placement of his guns at the high point of the cemetery, Doubleday's battery fired several rounds at a small toll house along the Martinsburg Pike a few yards from the river. The toll house, usually operated by an old woman, had been taken over by the Confederates who had forced the old lady to leave. The Confederates destroyed her dishes and furniture, and one of the cannonballs from Doubleday's battery smashed the front porch and chimney. In spite of the damage, the old woman was glad to see the Union troops as she peered from behind her spectacles and they were rewarded with a "toothless grin" as they hiked up the river bank on the opposite shore from Williamsport.[247]

The Confederates had long since taken off for the woods nearby. Doubleday and his battery were detailed to guard the river crossing at the ford, as the rest of Patterson's Army made its way toward Martinsburg.[248] Not sure of their reception, the troops found the Virginians friendly, some of the women even waving handkerchiefs.[249] However, the calm was short-lived. The soldiers were soon fired on by the Confederates. The Confederates, under Jackson and Lieutenant Colonel James Ewell Brown (J.E.B.) Stuart were serving under Johnston, and greeted the Northerners with deadly fire. Stuart tried to turn the flank of Company B, First Wisconsin Volunteer Infantry, commanded by Colonel John C. Starkweather. His company had been sent out in advance on each side of the road along with Companies A, B and C of the Eleventh Pennsylvania Volunteer Infantry under Colonel Jarrett.[250]

It was, as battles go, a small conflict, but it would not be the only time federal troops would face Jackson and Stuart during the coming months and years. Once the main body of Union soldiers entered Martinsburg, Doubleday and his battery soon followed. It was at this time Doubleday received his official commission as major of the Seventeenth United States Infantry. Other orders soon followed: Doubleday and his battery were sent to Williamsport July 6, but once again, his orders were countermanded the following day. His quick return saved the battery from possible capture by Stuart's cavalry which was still roving the countryside. Patterson's Army was soon joined by more volunteers. A war council was held and it was decided to hold Charlestown, near Harpers Ferry. However, events not far from Washington would soon require movement of the federal forces. Confederate forces were gathering near Manassas, Virginia. Patterson was ordered to keep Johnston from joining Beauregard at Manassas. General Irvin McDowell set about defending Washington, and Patterson stayed near Harpers Ferry. In commenting on the events, Doubleday said that although the three-month volunteers had served their terms, he thought Patterson should have been ordered to join McDowell since it was not that far away. So with fighting taking place July 21 near Manassas in what would become known as the First Battle of Manassas just outside the nation's capital, Doubleday and the troops under Patterson were left on the sidelines. Three days later, Patterson was relieved and Major General Nathaniel Prentiss Banks, a political general from Massachusetts, took command.

In late July Lincoln placed West Point graduate George Brinton McClellan in command of the Army of the Potomac. McClellan was a major general of Ohio volunteers when Lincoln tapped him for his new command and McClellan was outranked only by Scott himself as the second choice for the position Lee had refused.

On the very day that McClellan took command of the Division of the Potomac, Saturday, July 27, Doubleday went riding with Banks and was severely injured as he rode through a gateway at full speed when a six-mule team unexpectedly swerved and blocked the way. Doubleday's left leg was badly gashed. The following day Doubleday moved with his battery to Sandy Hook, Maryland, where they camped, but by August 8 his leg was in no condition to stay in the field. He received a week's leave and went to Washington to heal. The leg grew worse by the middle of August, but anxious to return to his command Doubleday left the city and located his men at Buckeystown, Maryland. In his absence, his guns had been turned over to Lieutenant Hall of Company E, First United States Artillery in Baltimore.[251] Doubleday's time in the field was short. Banks soon ordered Doubleday and Companies E and H of the First U.S. Artillery to Washington where they would report to General McClellan on August 30. Duty now placed Doubleday in command of all heavy artillery from Long Bridge to Fort Corcoran[252]

Endnotes

239   Abner Doubleday to Lorenzo Thomas, letters received by the Office of the Adjutant General (Main series), 1861-1870, RG 94, M649, Roll 15 letter 115, NARA

240   Cleaves, Freeman, *Rock of Chickamauga*, (Westport. Connecticut: Greenwood Press Publishers, 1948), 68. Thomas was a Virginian by birth.

241   Alexander Kelly McClure, *Abraham Lincoln and Men of War-Times*, (Philadelphia: The Times Publishing Company, 1892), 369 and Freeman Cleaves, *Rock of Chickamauga*, (Westport, Connecticut: Greenwood Press, Publishers, 1974 reprint), 71

242   S. Roger Keller, *Events of the Civil War in Washington County, Maryland*, (Shippensburg, PA: White Mane Pub. Co., Inc., 1995), 21: Angela Kirkham Davis diary, 14, Western Maryland Room, Washington County Library, Hagerstown, MD

243   Keller, *pg. 21*

244   Ibid

245   Ibid, pg 8

246   Ibid, 24; and Frank Moore, "*The Rebellion Record; A Diary of American Events,*" (New York: G.P. Putnam, 1864,) Vol. 2, 1862, 242-243

247   Keller, 25; Moore, 243

248   Abner Doubleday, U.S. Army Generals Report of Civil War Service 1864-1887, (hereafter GR), Roll 8, NARA

249   Moore, 243

250   OR, Vol. 2, 182, 183, 185

251   Abner Doubleday, GR

252   Abner Doubleday, GR

CHAPTER 14

"I was glad to be relieved"

It seems plausible to believe the injured leg was the cause of the shift in duties for Doubleday. He was only a major, but was assigned to oversee the forts defending Washington. Doubleday was responsible for preparing the forts (many were still under construction) surrounding Washington, the majority at the southern end of the city, for defense. Doubleday noted that he was outranked by many other officers who commanded many of the forts. That seemed unusual to him since as all military men, he was always conscience of rank and one's place within the chain of command, but ever the good soldier when duty called, he answered. Doubleday, and many others over the next few years, would make Robert E. Lee's beautiful Arlington House their headquarters. With only one orderly to assist him, Doubleday put all his energy into his assignment and set about the task of making the forts battle ready.

Doubleday focused on outfitting them with artillery, hardly a surprise since he was an artillery man, and cannon have the necessary long firing ranges. Doubleday worked on the forts until early 1862. He was called to testify before Congress' Joint Committee on the Conduct of the War. Two notable senators lead the committee, Benjamin F. Wade of Ohio and Zachariah Chandler of Michigan. Both men had a reputation as "Radicals," meaning they favored ending slavery. Doubleday testified about the events of the previous summer at Hagerstown, Maryland and the Battle of Falling Waters, south of Hagerstown, near the border of what would become West Virginia. Doubleday said that his men "behaved very well" in this initial engagement.[253] Doubleday also testified that the forts did not have enough artillerists and new recruits would need two or three months' drill to be proficient with cannon.[254]

McClellan was under fire for not moving the army, a situation that would frustrate many, including Lincoln. In his defense, "Little Mac" had been sick since early January, but an impatient Lincoln tried to set a fire under McClellan by demanding the army should move by Washington's Birthday, but the fire didn't catch for several more weeks. Chandler had even tried to pass a resolution in the Senate to have McClellan removed from military service.[255]

With a shiny new silver star on each shoulder strap denoting a brigadier general, Doubleday began the task of recruiting and organizing his staff. As a brigadier general, Doubleday was entitled to the following staff: one assistant adjutant general to handle all the necessary paperwork; an assistant quartermaster to oversee equipment, clothing and tools; a commissary of substance who was in charge of obtaining and distribution of food—each of these three were captains with their own supporting staffs; then two aides (first lieutenants) to personally assist their general. Also on staff was a major, a surgeon and a brigade guard at Doubleday's headquarters. Then there were the various orderlies and dispatch riders. As a man rose in rank, so did the number of staff personnel.

Doubleday's first appointment as an aide-de-camp was Benjamin T. Marten,[256] a brown-haired, gray-eyed twenty-two year old first lieutenant with Company E of the Forty-seventh New York Infantry. Calling New Jersey home, Marten had been with the Forty-seventh New York for six months before he was tapped for his new position. He remained on Doubleday's staff until April 1864, when he handed in his resignation a month after being separated from his general. Marten never married nor had children. He died in New York City in 1908.[257] For his second aide-de-camp, Doubleday appointed William Cullen Bryant Gray. Gray was serving with the Fourth New York Heavy Artillery, commanded by Doubleday's older brother, Thomas. Gray, who preferred books to sports and had a reputation for being faithful to his God, kept a small diary during his short time with Doubleday. Gray resigned as a staff officer in mid-summer. He became ill and died January 1, 1863.[258]

The position of adjutant general was filled by Oneida County, New York, native, attorney Eminel P. Halstead of Company H, Second New York Heavy Artillery. Halstead had joined the artillery regiment the previous September at the age of twenty-eight. Once the war ended he moved around the country and married twice before he died in 1912. After the war, Halstead wrote several articles about his service.[259]

Doubleday's next appointment was a person definitely not a stranger to him. His blue-eyed brother Ulysses, who would be labeled a "*vade mecuem*" (In this case, it refers to the ability of Ulysses to pass on his knowledge of artillery without using a manual.) by the men who served under him,[260] was a major in the Fourth New York Heavy Artillery. Ulysses became Doubleday's ordinance officer and right-hand man. Ulysses' diary, still in the family, begins with a detailed listing of ordinance, elevations and the technical information needed for a successful artilleryman.

Next, Doubleday selected George F. Noyes, a lawyer from Portland, Maine, and California. Noyes was chosen to be the captain of the Commissary Department and wrote a year-long diary of his activities.[261] For brigade surgeon, Daniel Holmes was selected. Holmes had been born in the small village of Oxford, New York and attended Oxford Academy there.[262]

Not all appointments of staff officers were made easily. In a letter to abolitionist F. W. Ballard, Ulysses noted Doubleday was facing "more red tape" regarding a person recorded only as Benny. Ulysses told Ballard that Doubleday had sent a letter and spoken to Adjutant General Lorenzo Thomas, but Benny was too far away to serve on Doubleday's staff, thus orders had not been issued. Ulysses described Doubleday's choices for staff officers as all being "emancipationists, and good men in every way." The ongoing selection of staff officers took a small portion of Doubleday's time. He had larger challenges to resolve. In the same letter to Ballard, Ulysses says there is "utter confusion in which things were before the army moved [and] has since intensified. None but a military man however can appreciate it." Ulysses says the situation "would be laughable if the food and health of thousands of brave men were not in consideration." Ulysses even takes McClellan to task, "But McC. has to fight or resign, and accordingly today is moving his headquarters staff to the front. Everything is in a state of shameful confusion; no one knows where to go, or how to stay." [263]

Among the many problems facing Doubleday was sorting out a problem involving the commander of the Seventy-sixth New York Infantry. This unit was raised in Cortland County and Cherry Valley, both in New York state, and was one of the two regiments assigned to Doubleday. The regiment's Colonel Nelson W. Green, who had been at West Point at the same time as Doubleday, had a dispute with Captain Andrew J. McNett regarding command of the regiment as the unit was being organized. Green ordered McNett to remain in his own tent. Green passed by and saw McNett standing outside his tent. After a brief exchange, with McNett refusing Green's orders, Green shot McNett in the chin with the ball lodging in the neck of McNett on December 16, 1861, before the regiment even left for Washington.[264] New York's Governor Seymour reassigned McNett to serve with the Ninety-Third New York Infantry. Even so, the bad blood continued between the two men even when they reached Washington.

The same day Doubleday officially began his command as brigadier general, he had Green arrested and held in confinement.[265] Immediately Green began a letter writing campaign to Doubleday. In early March, Doubleday wrote again to the adjutant general stating Green was considered insane and requested a prompt resolution in the case. However, the case dragged on for weeks. Green, who had attended West Point in 1839 but was injured and left before graduating, was eventually ordered released and told in April to return to his home in Cortland County, New York.[266] Unfortunately, this would not be the only problem within a regiment Doubleday would have to face. Soon enough his second regiment, the Ninety-fifth New York Infantry, would present its own set of problems.

In spite of the many challenges, Doubleday's top priority was preparing the fortifications ringing the nation's capital for possible attack. He now had to inspect the very forts he had outfitted the previous summer and fall. Getting the forts armed and manned would be an enormous task. Doubleday had again gone before the Joint Committee on the Conduct of the War in early January and testified that 60,000 men would be needed to protect the nation's capital. He said most of the forts had enough ammunition, but there weren't enough men to fire the ammunition if an attack began. He had requested more artillerists, but testified he had not been provided with them. In a list of problems, he said the infantry was receiving more training than the artillery branch, the forts should have been manned long before his appearance before the committee, and that the men garrisoned at the forts were spending more time working as laborers than soldiers. It was a grim condemnation of the country's readiness to protect the seat of its government[267]

As the work continued at all the forts, more regiments arrived in the Washington area. Among the thousands of men to reach the capital were the members of the Doubleday Regiment, the Fourth New York Heavy Artillery, in February 1862.[268] The regiment received its nickname not only because Doubleday's older brother, Thomas, had been selected at colonel, but because several Doubledays and their relatives were members. However, Thomas would not remain its colonel for the duration of the war. The men of the Fourth New York Heavy Artillery found time to write home and their letters were filled not only with bits of army life, but hinted at what would happen to Thomas. The situation with Doubleday's older brother would be all too evident in the coming months. Thomas had a serious problem with alcohol. James W. Hildreth, of Company F, said men in the regiment were divided in their opinions regarding Thomas and some were determined to get rid of every Doubleday man before another colonel of the regiment could be appointed. Hildreth anticipated Ulysses Doubleday would be the next commander.[269] Thomas' problem with alcohol had to be a hard cross to bear for the general who would forbid drinking and had a reputation as a non-drinker. Doubleday had even ordered the confiscation of all liquor sold to soldiers.[270] Thomas was court martialed in December of 1862. He was charged with drunkenness on duty, conduct unbecoming an officer and a gentleman and neglect of duty. The final straw had come on October 12, 1842 at Fort Ethan Allen, Virginia when he appeared "grossly intoxicated" for evening parade and fell from his horse while talking to a guard at Aqueduct Bridge. As the court martial records show, Thomas had failed to provide instruction to his officers and troops, had not drilled his men, nor issued an order to instruct his officers. Thomas' military career was over and he would be cashiered officially from the army March 17, 1863. Doubleday's writings are silent regarding his older brother's problems. In spite of Thomas' faults, he was remembered as having "great courage and great energy." The regimental historian noted Thomas' "kindness of heart was perhaps his greatest fault. He hated to say no to anyone." Thomas' life ended May 10, 1864 when he was trying to get on a carriage in New York City. He slipped and fell into the path of another coach heading in the opposite direction.[271] Thomas Doubleday was 48 years old.

In letters home, one of the new soldiers told of a parade review in which the men showed off their "new coats and white gloves" in hopes of impressing their new brigadier general.[272] Not all expressed delight with their new lives. Fifty-sixth Pennsylvania Infantryman Samuel Healy wrote in his diary his battery had drill for the "edification of General Doubleday." If Doubleday approved their drill, they would become part of his brigade. Healy went on to say, "If the truth was known he was glad to get us good or bad." Doubleday must have liked what he saw for they became the third regiment in Doubleday's command.[273]

Assigned to defend the capital, train raw recruits, hold parade reviews, and prepare the forts made for an endless list of tasks to be done for Doubleday and his, as yet, incomplete staff. Added to this they would soon find yet another issue to settle: what to do with the Negroes came into camp looking for protection as they were fleeing north. Many slaves who were heading north, were hoping they would find shelter and safety within the Union army camps and forts. Former hop grower turned military man Lieutenant Colonel John D. Shaul, from Herkimer County, New York,[274] was commanding the Seventy-sixth New York after Green had been arrested. Shaul wrote to Doubleday and asked the question that was already reverberating throughout the military. The controversy surrounding slaves in the District of Columbia was an old, old argument by the time of the Civil War. Doubleday's father, Ulysses Freeman, spent his days in Congress listening to the heated debates and heard the elder statesman, John Quincy Adams claim slavery *could* be controlled by the government, all within Constitutional bounds, if the country was at war. The general reception to Adams' idea was chilly to say the least a thing in 1836.[275] No, the slavery issue wasn't new.

Twelve years earlier, in 1850, the Fugitive Slave Act had been passed by Congress, but two Union generals took it upon themselves to create national policy regarding the troublesome question. While stationed at Fort Monroe, Virginia, after the beginning of the war Major General Benjamin F. Butler, a New Englander by birth and influence, was the first to declare slaves fleeing the South as contrabands of war. Naturally, slave owners who considered the slaves as property, weren't happy with Butler. In fact, they were furious. The next month, May 1862, the same month Shaul asked his question, would find Major General David Hunter, a native of the federal capital, setting national policy when he abolished slavery as commander of the Department of the South in Georgia[276] The country wasn't ready for it yet. Hunter seemed to have momentarily forgotten President Lincoln and Congress were in charge of national policy, not himself. Lincoln was forced to officially overturn what Hunter had done which certainly didn't set well with abolitionists.

In answering Shaul's question, Doubleday said the Negroes who sought safety behind the lines of the army should not be treated as property, but as people who could perform valuable service. The Negroes knew the area, roads, landmarks, and the politics of the people who lived there.[277] In mid-April 1862, Lincoln signed the legislation that outlawed slavery in the District of Columbia. In early May Doubleday issued an order stating his subordinate commanders had authority to arrest anyone trying to kidnap Negroes; an order that violated the Fugitive Slave Act.[278] One can almost hear the howl that must have risen from slave owners. After all, they had wanted Doubleday's head while he was at Fort Sumter, long before he made this decision.[279] This order by Doubleday became the target of discussion, and the order itself was in direct violation of an order issued by Major General Henry W. Halleck. Doubleday believed his stance on slavery caused Halleck to be hostile toward him. Halleck, born in Westernville, Oneida County, New York, was an upperclassman when Doubleday began his studies at West

Point. Halleck would certainly have a say in Doubleday's army career, and in all probability it would not be favorable.

The slave question pervaded the army as much as it did those in civilian life. When General Christopher Augur took Fredericksburg, he promised that fugitive slaves coming into Federal camps "would be sheltered and held against reclamation." Yet a few days later, General Ambrose Burnside announced he would refuse to keep and protect run away slaves.[280]

As Doubleday wrestled with his new duties, Lincoln and his wife sat vigil with their sons, Willie and Tad, who had typhoid fever. Willie died February 20, 1862, sending his parents into deep mourning. It was a harbinger of the many deaths to come during the years ahead as the nation's youth marched off to war. Mary Lincoln would lose a brother during the second day of the battle of Shiloh on April 7, 1862; Samuel B. Todd fought for the Confederacy. *The Richmond Whig* was quick to say that her brother's death was "taken at the hands of her husband's mercenaries."[281]

Nevertheless spring was on its way, and regardless of controversial issues within the army, the troops must soon be moved to meet the enemy. McClellan was preparing the Army of the Potomac for his Peninsula campaign. He had graduated second in his 1846 class at West Point and stayed in the army until he left in 1857. He quickly rejoined after the war began. He had won a couple of small, early battles when Lincoln tapped him for duty as commander of the Army of the Potomac. McClellan began the long process of building an army following his defeat at the First Battle of Manassas and in the process created an aura that in turn created an undying devotion by many of the soldiers who loved "Little Mac." However, his arrogance and continued requests for more manpower along with his inability to push the army forward would create many problems. Although McClellan saw himself as the Union's savior, the Lincoln administration and even Lincoln himself would eventually see that the Union army needed an extraordinary leader.

Doubleday's brigade was assigned to the division commanded by Rufus King, a native of New York City, who's Third Division was part of the First Corps' commander General Irvin McDowell. Ohioan McDowell had graduated from West Point just as Doubleday was finalizing his application to the military academy in June 1838. McDowell had served as a staff officer for Brigadier General John Wool, another New Yorker,[282] during the war with Mexico.[283] Rufus King, forty-eight years old in 1862, graduated from West Point in 1833. After only three years of army life as an engineer following graduation, he resigned and became a civil engineer for the New

York & Erie Railroad where he could presumably earn more money. He later entered the field of print journalism for a time in New York and later moved to Wisconsin. Once the war began, he re-entered the army and became a brigadier general in May 1861. It was King who began the recruitment and organization of what would eventually be known as the Iron Brigade. King was not without his problems; he had a reputation for nipping at the bottle. King was an epileptic and with his consumption of alcohol, it was a bad combination that would ultimately place his military career in serious trouble following the Second Battle of Manassas.[284]

Early in May a New York State Chamber of Commerce ceremony was held in New York City to honor the defenders of Fort Sumter. The bronze medals featured a bust of Anderson, who was presented with the one of a kind medal—six inches in diameter. Other medals were given to the men who defended Sumter the previous year. The remaining two types of medals were similar in design, but in smaller sizes. As a commissioned officer, Doubleday received a bronze medal that was four and a half inches and slightly lighter in weight than Anderson's. The smallest Sumter medals went to the non-commissioned officers. However, only Anderson and Sergeant Hart, who was depicted on the medals as the man who climbed the flagpole to reattach the Stars and Stripes during the shelling of the fort, were able to attend the May 2 presentation.[285] Duties called the others elsewhere and they had to miss the event.

In Washington, Doubleday and his men were waiting for orders to move. It was frustrating for Doubleday and his men who craved action. Someone else was even more frustrated: Lincoln, as he watched the buildup of an army going nowhere. In April Lincoln had even called the army McClellan's bodyguard and continued by saying, "If McClellan is not using the army, I should like to borrow it."

Finally in mid-May, Doubleday received orders to take two infantry regiments, the 102 New York Volunteer Infantry and the Seventy-sixth New York Volunteer Infantry to meet General Irvin McDowell in enemy territory, at Fredericksburg, Virginia. Doubleday held a review of his men and then took the Seventy-sixth New York, under the temporary command of Shaul, and began its march down Seventh Street toward Pennsylvania Avenue in Washington. Colors flying, the men, tired of garrison duty and eager for action, stepped smartly forward. However, action came a lot sooner than anticipated when the march was interrupted near the present day site of the National Archives. Slavecatchers had spotted John and Charles Burch, two fugitive slaves who were now part of the regiment performing a variety of duties including carrying baggage belonging to officers. The slavecatchers wanted to claim the two men and got a policeman to assist them in their efforts. The brothers Burch were marching with Company D when an attempt to arrest them was made. A Washington policeman tried grabbing one of the brothers by the collar, when infantryman Corporal Jay Webster, a farm boy from Marathon, New York,[286] barked the order to "Charge." Within seconds the policeman was knocked out and hit the ground; it seems his head and the butt of Webster's gun had a sudden collision. Of course, this scuffle did not go without notice. While some officials cried "Foul," the officers of the Seventy-sixth New York and "true hearted" Doubleday stood behind his troops. The incident made the newspapers, even in London.[287] The rest of their march was without incident and they boarded a steamer headed for Virginia where they hoped to see a different kind but equally successful action. With the soldiers on deck, Doubleday and his staff in a cabin, they made their way south along the Potomac River, past the home of George Washington, Mount Vernon, Virginia. As the day came to an end, the officers of the Seventy-sixth New York entered the cabin for supper. Following their meal, many went to the upper deck for a look at the passing landscape. Doubleday wrapped himself in his coat and rested on a settee in the cabin.[288] At midnight, they reached their destination. The men camped for the night at Acquia Creek while Doubleday and his staff took a train to Fredericksburg and reported for duty to McDowell.[289] The same day Doubleday and the Seventy-sixth New York left for Fredericksburg, Lincoln boarded another vessel with Secretary of War Edwin M. Stanton and headed for the same destination where they planned to discuss plans with McClellan.[290]

The Ninety-fifth New York Infantry had already been at Acquia (sometimes spelled Aquia) Creek for a month. The regiment was under the command of Lieutenant Colonel James B. Post who frequently wrote to his wife, Carrie. The regiment was supposed to be commanded by New Yorker Colonel George H. Biddle. Post told his wife Biddle wasn't suited to the position. "He may be a fair military man, but he has no administrative powers and is very dull in comprehension in regards to orders and he disgusts a good many of us."[291]

In addition to the problem of command in the Seventy-sixth New York, Doubleday now had to deal with the Ninety-fifth New York's commander. One could easily wonder if the enemy was not only on the fields of Virginia, but within the army itself as men complained about nearly everything at one time or another. The problem of leadership within the Ninety-fifth

New York would continue to plague the regiment and Doubleday well into summer. Post wrote his wife that Biddle "don't want to leave and quietly uses his influence to remain." Post continued to relieve his frustration in letters to his wife and said Biddle "has not been with the regiment an hour." Post paints Biddle as "jealous and tenacious of his authority, and frequently makes himself very ridiculous." Post even noted, "The Colonel's conduct is known at Washington and I very much fear if he gets into a tantrum sometime he may get into trouble, particularly as Gen. Doubleday is a regular army officer and won't stand for any nonsense."[292]

The problems with Biddle apparently even involved Doubleday (at least on paper). Post wrote home again and hinted a replacement for Biddle might be waiting to take over. Post said Biddle's behavior was even more "ridiculous" and that Biddle didn't like Doubleday because if Doubleday got the regiment under his command, Biddle would lose his "comfortable and independent position." Post said Biddle even thought the officers of the regiment were conspiring against him.[293] However, Post seemed to like Doubleday, and that relationship would grow during the coming months, in spite of differing views about the abolition of slavery. Post wrote to his wife the issue of slavery was too prevalent in the war, and "if it comes to be a abolition war as it daily grows to be, I fear; I will have nothing to do with it anyway.[294]

Fredericksburg, Virginia, was an old town at the time of the Civil War having been officially established in 1728. It was a tobacco town, and two years later it was officially named as a licensing and inspection station for the broad-leaved crop. By 1835, the town boasted 1,797 whites, 1,124 slaves and 387 free blacks. By the time the war began, Fredericksburg had "730 households."[295] The city sits along the Rappahannock River which eventually flows to the Potomac before it empties into the Chesapeake Bay. Located about fifty miles south of Washington, D.C., the Union army needed Fredericksburg to launch its operations and the river gave them a place where goods could be transported with ease. The community had a rich heritage even then: George Washington had lived nearby as a boy and courted his bride-to-be at the beautiful estate, Lacy Mansion, (now known as Chatham), high above the river. The one-time plantation with 100 slaves was used by several Union generals during the war, visited by Lincoln, and descriptions of it are found in many of the soldiers' diaries. Post described the property to his wife: "[It has] a lawn of say five or six acres perfectly gorgeous in its green and clover mantel." He went on to describe the rose bushes and tulips "in bloom." [296] Fredericksburg was also home to James

Monroe, the fifth president, who had lived in Fredericksburg as a young lawyer. Washington's mother chose a home there in her later years.

Doubleday would soon have new orders. Upon Doubleday's arrival at Fredericksburg, McDowell ordered Doubleday to relieve General Marsena Rudolph Patrick as military governor of Fredericksburg. Patrick, a native of Watertown, New York, was now fifty-one years old and had studied medicine before entering West Point. He graduated in 1835 but left the army in 1850 to become president of a state agricultural college in his native county. When the war began he offered his services to the Union.[297] By the time Doubleday arrived, Patrick had been military governor of Fredericksburg for several weeks and the citizens there at least tolerated him. The Fredericksburg people had been told by General Augur when he took the town that they and their property would be protected, but that would not include contraband (slaves). The loyal Confederate citizens would suffer "humiliation and distress of Yankee domination," shouted *The Richmond Whig*.[298]

With his new orders, Doubleday left immediately for Patrick's headquarters at the Farmer's Bank on Princess Anne Street, where later that day Lincoln would address Fredericksburg citizens.[299] Since Doubleday's own baggage had not yet arrived and Patrick still occupied the building, Doubleday sought shelter in an unoccupied house owned by Dr. Carmichael who was serving in the Southern army.[300]

Without elaborating Patrick claimed Doubleday, "made a fool of himself within an hour of his arrival." In his diary Patrick said the community of Fredericksburg was sad that he was reassigned and Patrick himself felt sorry the Fredericksburg families would be left to Doubleday, "an Abolitionist."[301]

The following day Patrick noted the arrival of not only Doubleday, but Lincoln and Stanton. Brigadier General John Gibbon and many other officers met with Lincoln at the Lacy Mansion.[302] The president upon hearing Gibbon's name asked, "Is this the man who wrote *The Decline and Fall of the Roman Empire*?" Since the book was written by Edward Gibbon in the 1700s, the question embarrassed the general, but Lincoln put him at ease saying that if Gibbon would "write the decline and fall of this rebellion, I will let you off." [303]

As Lincoln visited Fredericksburg, in Charleston, South Carolina, *The Mercury* printed the following: "Some woman in Georgetown (now part of Washington, D.C.) has threatened to shoot Lincoln if her son in the rebel army shall be killed."[304] The notice was a reminder of the many threats against the president.

In Fredericksburg, the news of the slavecatchers, fleeing slaves and the scuffle in the streets of Washington, as the Seventy-sixth New York headed for the steamer that took them to Fredericksburg, was spreading rapidly. The Fredericksburg citizens were outraged that Doubleday would protect escaped slaves by allowing them to march with one of his infantry units, as was Patrick. There was plenty of outrage in Fredericksburg. Doubleday was outraged that he had to order men to protect "Rebel" property. He put it this way:

> Union men were refused a guard while the rebels had a sentinel over their cherry trees, privies & etc. A rebel mayor was left in power and he was in the habit of constantly sending Union men to jail for alleged violations of city ordinances. Union men were seized, their hands were tied behind their backs and they were sent off on horseback to Libby prison and there were not hostages held for their return and no action of any kind taken. It soon became evident that I could not be relied upon to carry out any measures, which in my opinion amounted to persecuting the loyalists and I was glad to be relieved. The rebel citizens of the town seemed to expect that I would devote myself to preventing the escape of fugitive slaves, and that I would stop all the colored men from passing the river into our lines. In this they were disappointed and they complained bitterly to Gen. McDowell.[305]

Sixteen year old Lizzie Maxwell Alsop, of Fredericksburg, wrote about Doubleday in her diary. "Doubleday or Doubledevil as some call him, it suiting his character better than his real name," said the local citizens complained to McDowell and requested the return of Patrick. "So old Doubledevil did not stay in this charming Southern Town but two days,"[306] Upon hearing about the letter requesting the change of military governor, a gleeful Patrick asked for a copy to send his wife.

Doubleday described his two days as military governor, (he was replaced by John F. Reynolds) as being "impossible" because the policy of the army at that time favored the Rebel citizens, rather than the Union army. [307] By late spring Fredericksburg, according to the teenager Alsop, had all its grain and chickens taken, sixty citizens had been arrested, and there were no more than "two dozen colored persons left in town."

"Doubledevil" Doubleday wasn't afraid to say the army's policy protecting Confederate property was, in his opinion, wrong. The following month, he went before the Joint Committee on the Conduct of the War and testified that

McDowell had talked about keeping rebel property safe. Doubleday told the committee when he tried to use Dr. Carmichael's residence, he was ordered by King, under orders from McDowell, [308] to give up the use of the house due to the pressure the secessionists placed on the Union commanders. Doubleday said the Union soldiers were "utterly worn out" guarding property of the enemy even while the citizens insulted them as they went about their duties. Patrick, King and McDowell—all were attempting to appease the enemy and in Doubleday's mind that was inconceivable during war time. Doubleday fully believed in loyalty to the Union and stated the military should encourage such a stance.[309]

The Fredericksburg citizens were happy with Reynolds as their new military governor. *The Christian Banner*, a local newspaper, noted the delight of the citizens with Patrick and Reynolds this way: "Truly the citizens of Fredericksburg have abundant reason for gratulation at having had two such accomplished Generals to preside over them, taking care of their interests, and saving them from insult and injury, from any and all sources."[310] It was an obvious slap to Doubleday.

Two more regiments of Doubleday's infantry regiments arrived in Fredericksburg: the Ninety-fifth New York and the Fifty-sixth Pennsylvania. With the addition of Captain McMahon's light battery the brigade was growing in strength, but Doubleday noted because of the duties performed by the troops as guards of railroads and bridges and rebel property, regular drills were nonexistent.[311]

Many times Doubleday would see to the care and comfort of his men. Lieutenant Colonel Post said when his regiment arrived at Fredericksburg, Doubleday was pleased with the promptness of the Ninety-fifth New York's march and because it was very hot, tents would not be required. He allowed the men to be "comfortable in the grove."[312]

He also expected things to be done correctly. Doubleday took McMahan of Battery B, of the Second New York Light Artillery, to task by sending him a notice that administering "saber blows to enforce discipline in your battery (is) unnecessary and subversive." Doubleday said, "punishable offences should be reported in a proper manner so courts martial may be held and the offender duly tried." [313]

In early June, Major General George McCall's division left Fredericksburg to join McDowell leaving Doubleday in temporary command. It was also the time Doubleday's staff officer, Major Charles E. Livingston, was appointed military governor of Fredericksburg. However, the appointment did not take place without incident. A short time after the appointment Livingston went for his evening meal at Planters Hotel. He became violently ill, giving rise to the possibility he had been poisoned. Livingston was so ill Doubleday worried the major might even die. Aide-de-camp Gray went to visit his sick friend and was also anxious for Livingston's well-being.[314] Livingston was a very sick man, but he survived and eventually returned to duty.

The same day Livingston became violently ill, Major Lacy owner of the Lacy House, was captured. The following day, Gibbon arrived with his brigade at Falmouth and was quickly followed by the return of Patrick's brigade. Gibbon, born in Philadelphia, and raised in North Carolina, graduated from West Point in 1847.

At the age of forty, Major General John Pope took command of the Army of Virginia. Pope, a native of Kentucky, had graduated with Doubleday from West Point in 1842. Pope, like Doubleday, Gibbon and others, was a veteran of the Mexican and Seminole wars. Pope had a reputation as a man who knew how to handle horses and ride well. As a captain, he had accompanied Lincoln from Illinois to Washington, D.C., for Lincoln's inaugural. Pope was known as a braggart and could be obnoxious at times. He advanced in the army, not only because he had claimed Island Number Ten in the Mississippi for the north, but he also had influence in high places. When he took over the Army of Virginia, Pope ordered King's Division, including Doubleday and his command, to stay in Fredericksburg.[315]

Pope would become the butt of jokes when he announced his "headquarters would be in the saddle." This would lead to the remark that Pope's "headquarters are where his hindquarters ought to be."

At last the case against Nelson W. Green had been resolved. Green was discharged and sent home. In early July, Colonel William P. Wainwright, a native of New York City and a non-practicing doctor, took command of the beleaguered Seventy-sixth New York. Doubleday continued his practice of hiring fugitive slaves as laborers as more and more of the blacks streamed northward. The month of July rolled by with the mayor of Fredericksburg and other rebel citizens arrested. They were sent to Fort McHenry in exchange for prisoners who had been sent to Richmond.[316] In Congress, the Confiscation Act of 1862 was approved. It gave a measure of protection and freedom to the slaves who entered army camps, but would not always be obeyed.

We get a glimpse of everyday life in Fredericksburg and a more personal look at Doubleday through the eyes of Gray, his young aide-de-camp. Gray soon found himself following Doubleday's directives and issuing passes for "Negroes and others to various places."

During the second week of June, Doubleday received reports of enemy activity, and sent out cavalry to scout the area. The Fourth Pennsylvania

Cavalry was assigned to accompany Doubleday and his staff when needed. Gray's duties included copying maps for his general. There were other changes in the wind. Dr. Holmes went to Washington to obtain another surgical position, as his position at brigade level was one of many abolished. Once King was on site, Doubleday's duties changed again.

Gray and Noyes took time to visit the, "Picture Gallery," in Fredericksburg, as well as a tailor. The change of duties for Doubleday also made less work for his staff. Gray and Noyes went for a ride in the countryside, and then sat in a cherry tree to watch the Seventy-sixth New York in a dress parade. Doubleday even found time to tell Gray about events in the area of Fredericksburg. Gray wrote:

"Gen. Doubleday gave me a full account of the Secession outrages in Fredericksburg and in this vicinity—of the persecution of Union men by aristocrats, and of the careful guarding of Secession property while loyalists are unprotected—Much indignation is felt by the Staff at these proceedings, and we truly wonder if the War will ever end with such a policy in force."

As Doubleday and his brigade stood guard over the rails and bridges in early summer, the sounds of gunfire were heard in the Shenandoah Valley and in front of Richmond as the main bodies of the Union army fought the rebels. Ulysses and the artillery practiced with howitzers. There was even time for a photograph of Doubleday and his staff on the front porch of headquarters and another one the following day, this time with a negro, said Gray.

The first day of July found Gray traveling by steamboat the fifty miles to Washington. The trip took four hours. Once there, he went to Willard's Hotel where Mary Doubleday was staying. He had messages from Doubleday for her. The messages may have been in the code Doubleday had devised with Ulysses at the beginning of the war, for Gray took time to explain the code to Mary during his visit. He was not the only visitor Mary had. New York Senator Ira Harris was also in the parlor. Gray was introduced and proceeded to inform Harris of events at Fredericksburg. It was a late night for the small group before each went his own way.

Refreshed after a night's sleep in a real bed with sheets, Gray returned to The Willard Hotel and met with Mary Doubleday again to complete his mission there and then left for business with the army's paymaster. He received pay for himself, Halstead, Dr. Holmes and Lieutenant Marten, but lacked paperwork for Ulysses and one other man, so could not collect their pay. Gray completed several more errands before returning to Willard's. During this time, Mary wrote letters to Doubleday for Gray to take with him. The following day, Mary and the young lieutenant met at a bank to exchange pay vouchers for cash. He presented her with $150 of Ulysses' back pay he had finally received, and told Mary the money was for Ulysses' wife. While in Washington, Gray ran into an old friend, Doubleday's nephew, Lieutenant Ulysses D. Eddy, of General Whipple's staff. Eddy had been a member of the Fourth New York Heavy Artillery. He would be captured at the Battle of Fredericksburg in December, and then held as a prisoner at Camp Parole, Maryland. He was released in a prisoner exchange the following April.

With much of his business completed, Gray began the return trip to Fredericksburg, on July 4. He missed the Fourth of July celebration when Doubleday's brother Ulysses gave the oration. However, Gray brought news about battles near Richmond. Mary Doubleday had sent the news with Gray to the camp, where the news was welcomed by all.

Many of the men in Doubleday's brigade were ill for days after the celebration. Both Ulysses and Doubleday were in Gray's words, "quite ill." In spite of the illness, Gray and Doubleday still found time to discuss poetry. However, the illness persisted and as McDowell sent orders to prepare for a march, Doubleday and Halstead were still fighting to return to good health. From July 7-12, all were sick, and with Halstead sick, Gray took over his duties and rode to local farms seeking meat and vegetables. In late July, Mary Doubleday visited the camp to see if her husband and the troops were feeling better.[317]

Though Doubleday and his brigade had not yet seen serious fighting, August would bring a change of scenery and activity. Early in August Pope ordered King's Division to cross the Rapidan River. Doubleday's brigade with Gibbon, Patrick and Phelps were all assigned to King's Division. [318]

It was an exhausting march for men who had been ill and had done little more strenuous duty than guard bridges and railroads. Drill had been held, but because of their duties they had not the same amount of drill as other brigades. Meanwhile, Jackson was doing his Shenandoah two-step of push and retreat and push again as he tested the mettle of men in both armies before vanishing on the other side of the mountains from Gordonsville to regroup again with Longstreet. By the middle of the month, Pope learned Lee's army was preparing to move forward. So Pope decided to fall back and wait for McClellan to reinforce him. As the retreat began, Doubleday said the roads were so blocked with men and equipment he couldn't move until the next day. For the next several days the two armies played cat and mouse as they prepare for a general engagement. Skirmishing and firing was heard as they headed to the area around Manassas, Virginia.

Endnotes

[253] United States, B. F. Wade, and Daniel Wheelwright Gooch. *Report of the Joint Committee on the Conduct of the War*, (Hereafter CCW) (Washington: Govt. Print Off., 1865), Part II, 67

[254] CCW, Vol. 1, 209-210

[255] *The Richmond Whig*, January 2, 1862, (*The Whig* had picked up the story from the *Cincinnati Enquirer*)

[256] Often spelled Martin

[257] Benjamin T. Marten, military and pension records, NARA

[258] Joseph Parrish Thompson, Bryant Gray: The Student, The Christian, The Soldier, (new York: A.D. F. Randolph, 1864) 13

[259] Eminel P. Halstead, military and pension records, NARA. (Halstead's article about the first day's battle of Gettysburg names Archer as a West Point graduate meeting Abner at Gettysburg. Archer was never at West Point. It is also interesting to note Abner's cousin Abner D. Doubleday served in the same regiment as Halstead.)

[260] George F. Noyes, *The Bivouac and the Battlefield: Or, Campaign Sketches in Virginia and Maryland,* (New York: Harper & Bros, 1864), 18. A physical description of Ulysses is found at the New York State Archives war service records

[261] Abner Doubleday, GR

[262] Clay W. Holmes, *A Genealogy of the Lineal Descendants of William Wood,* (Elmira, New York) 269; Army of the Potomac, Brigade Surgeon to General Doubleday, Defenses of the Potomac, Special Order No. 99, Washington, D.C. May 5, 1862, NARA

[263] Ulysses Doubleday to F.W. Ballard, March 14, 1862, Duke University

[264] Smith, 23-25

[265] Abner Doubleday, GR; RG 393, Army of the Potomac, Orders Book, Part 2, Entry 3718, Vol. 7, NARA

[266] Smith, 345-348

[267] CCW, Part XX, 209-213

[268] Kirk, 30. The Seventy-sixth New York Infantry, the Ninety-fifth New York Infantry and the Fifty-sixth Pennsylvania Infantry, who would all serve under Abner, were assigned to various forts around the city.

[269] James W. Hildreth to mother March 14, 1862, Harrisburg Civil War Round Table, Dawson Flinchbaugh collection, USAMHI

[270] Abner Doubleday, April 2, 1862, and May 6, 1862, letters sent, Army of the Potomac, RG 393, NARA. Abner ordered liquors destroyed except for medical needs.

271 Thomas D. Doubleday papers, Records of Courts Martial, New York State Archives; Kirk, 435-436; *New York Times*, May 12, 1864

272 George Lacey to mother, March 30, 1862, Civil War Miscellaneous Collection, USAMHI

273 Samuel Healy, diary, May 28, 1862, Gettysburg National Military Park, Gettysburg, Pennsylvania (hereafter GNMP)

274 John D. Shaul, papers, New York State Historical Society, Cooperstown, N.Y.

275 Miller, 208

276 Long, 209

277 Edward McPherson, *The Political History of the United States of America during the Great Rebellion,* (Washington, DC, second edition, 1865), 250, McPherson was a citizen of Gettysburg, PA. and served in the House of Representatives.

278 Abner Doubleday, letters sent, May 11, 1862, RG 393 Army of the Potomac, RG 393, part 2 entry 3714, NARA

279 Charles Sumner, and Beverly Wilson Palmer, *The Selected Letters of Charles Sumner.* (Boston: Northeastern University Press, 1990), Vol. 2, 112. In a letter to Massachusetts Governor Andrew, Mass Senator Charles Sumner (a protégée of that elder statesman, John Quincy Adams) inquired if Abner had contacted Andrew regarding the slavery issue.

280 *The Richmond Whig,* April 24, 1862; April 30, 1862.

281 *The Richmond Whig,* April 25, 1862

282 Warner, 573

283 Patricia L. Faust, and Norman C. Delaney. *Historical Times Illustrated Encyclopedia of the Civil Wa,* (New York: Harper & Row, 1986), 459

284 Faust, 418

285 *New York Times,* May 2, 1862

286 Jay Webster, pension records, NARA. He served in Company D, 76th New York Volunteer Infantry. He later moved to Troopsburg, Steuben County, New York.

287 Smith, 58; *New York Times,* May 23, 1862

288 Noyes, 20

289 Abner Doubleday, GR

290 Earl Schenck Meirs, *Lincoln Day by Day A Chronology 1809-1865,* (Dayton, OH: Morningside, 1991), 114

291 James B. Post letter to wife, April 26, 1862, Ninety-Fifth New York volunteer Regiment papers, letters file, USAMHI

292 Ibid, July 25, 1862

293 Ibid, Aug. 8, 1862

[294] Ibid, Aug. 21, 1962

[295] Barbara Pratt Wills and Paula S. Felder, *Handbook of Historic Fredericksburg*, Historic Fredericksburg Foundation Inc., 1993, 6, 8

[296] Post letters, May 25, 1862, USAMHI

[297] Faust, 561

[298] *The Richmond Whig*, April 24, 1862

[299] Wills, and Felder, 26; the bank was also home to escaped slave John Washington: David W. Blight, *A slave no more: two men who escaped to freedom : including their own narratives of emancipation*, (Orlando: Harcourt, 2007) 198

[300] CCW, 31

[301] Marsena Rudolph Patrick, and David S. Sparks, *Inside Lincoln's Army; the diary of Marsena Rudolph Patrick, Provost Marshall General, Army of the Potomac*, (New York: T. Yoseloff, 1964), 82

[302] John Gibbon, *Personal recollections of the civil war*, (New York: G.P. Putnam's Sons, 1928), 32

[303] Emanuel Hertz, *Lincoln talks: an oral biography*, (New York: Bramhall House, 1986), 416

[304] *The Charleston Mercury*, May 23, 1862

[305] Abner Doubleday, GR

[306] Lizzie Maxwell Alsop journal, Fredericksburg National Military Park (hereafter FNMP)

[307] Abner Doubleday, GR

[308] Abner Doubleday, GR

[309] Abner Doubleday testimony, June 1862, Report of the Joint Committee on the Conduct of War, Washington, (hereafter CCW)

[310] *The Christian Banner*, June 7, 1862

[311] Abner Doubleday, GR

[312] Post letters, Aug. 8, 1862, USAMHI

[313] Abner Doubleday, Army of the Potomac, June 5, 1862, Letters sent, RG 393, Part 2, Entry 3714, Vol. 1, NARA

[314] Abner Doubleday, Army of the Potomac, July 20, 1862, Letters sent, RG 393, Vol. 1, Entry 3714, NARA

[315] Abner Doubleday, GR

[316] Abner Doubleday, GR

[317] William C. B. Gray, diary, The City College, CUNY, New York City

[318] OR, Vol. 12, (III): 532

[319] Abraham Lincoln, Roy P. Basler, ed., *The Collected Works of Abraham Lincoln*, (New Jersey, Rutgers University Press, 1953) Vol. IV, 209

**Abner Doubleday and the lady with the beautiful eyes,
Mary Hewitt Doubleday**
(Library of Congress)

**This is Abner Doubleday in
his later years.**
(USAMHI)

**Thomas D. Doubleday,
the general's older brother.**
(Kirk)

**Ulysses Doubleday, a younger
brother, and the general's right
hand man.**
(Kirk)

Stephen Ward Doubleday, son of
Thomas; nephew of the general.
(Kirk)

Adelbert S. Eddy,
son of Herman J. Eddy.
(Kirk)

Herman J. Eddy, brother-in-law
to the general.
(Kirk)

Ulysses D. Eddy, one of General
Abner Doubleday's nephews.
(Kirk)

General Abner Doubleday's shoulder boards.
They are at The National Baseball Hall of Fame.
(Lew Warner)

This is a folding chess set that belonged to General Abner Doubleday.
It is at Gettysburg National Military Park.
(Dan Bartlett)

General Abner Doubleday's wooden trunk. The trunk is at
The National Baseball Hall of Fame.
(Lew Warner)

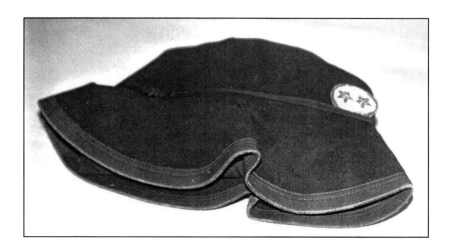

This hat is claimed to be the hat Doubleday was wearing when he
was hit by a shell fragment during the Battle of Gettysburg. It is at
Gettysburg National Military Park.
(Dan Bartlett)

This long, black metal tube is Doubleday's document case, used for carrying important papers and possibly small maps. It is at Gettysburg National Military Park.
(Dan Bartlett)

This statue of General Doubleday is at Gettysburg National Military Park where he keeps a vigilant eye for Confederates.
(by the author)

This is a Doubleday family headstone for Capt. Abner Doubleday at a cemetery in Cooperstown, N.Y.
(by the author)

Eminel P. Halstead
(Photo by permission of Donald Wisnoski)

Henry T. Lee
(Kirk)

William C. B. Grey
(Kirk)

CHAPTER 15

"My men held their ground"

Doubleday was riding with his troops along the dusty roads; the dust was so bad that man and horse took on a gray-brown appearance. With each step they were closer to the unseen enemy. Doubleday was considering how the next battle would begin and how he and his soldiers would react. All at once, a heavy fire began scattering men in all directions. "Take cover, take cover," he shouted.

Manassas, Virginia, had already seen both armies clash during the First Battle of Manassas in July 1861. A year later it was about to repeat with differing details, yet similar results. The two opposing armies began their convergence on Manassas with the hope, as before all battles, the win would be decisive and the carnage would end. Groveton was no more than a crossroads along the Warrenton Turnpike between Warrenton to the west and Centreville and Washington D.C. to the east.

Pope issued a statement meant to motivate his troops but the wording was so condescending, it was one more example of Pope's inability to be silent. He would have done well to remember Lincoln's words: "I am rather inclined to silence, and whether that be wise or not, it is at least more unusual nowadays to find a man who can hold his tongue than to find one who cannot."[319]

The Army of Virginia, as it was known in the summer of 1862, was under the command of Pope, a man who had a good, although not brilliant, military record. He also had good connections in Washington in spite of his reputation for the exaggeration of facts for his own benefit. Pope was selected by Lincoln in late June. When Lincoln's choice became known within the army, Major General John C. Fremont, a man of note, resigned rather than serve under the new commanding general. One can only guess at how Doubleday must have felt to see his former West Point classmate, Pope, in this new command.

It didn't take Pope long to incur the wrath of the Confederacy; he ordered his army to use the provisions of the countryside to sustain it. In a second order, Pope announced that civilians who caused problems for the Army of Virginia would not escape his notice. Pope ordered the arrest of all disloyal male citizens. These orders were as revolutionary as the thought of the United States becoming two countries.

The army's Third Corps was under the command of Irvin McDowell. The Third Corps' First Division was commanded by Rufus King. Within that division, Doubleday commanded the Second Brigade. Brigadier General John P. Hatch commanded the First Brigade, Marsena Patrick commanded the Third Brigade leaving the Fourth Brigade to the command of John Gibbon. Hatch was another New Yorker, born along the shores of Lake Ontario in Oswego. Like so many of his colleagues, Hatch had seen action in the Mexican War shortly after his graduation from West Point in 1845.

All of these men were filling posts of high command and had egos to match their ranks. Many of Lincoln's generals were stubborn, self-assured with more than a hint of self-interest. Some were quietly going about doing their duty; some were brash and rubbed each other the wrong way. Pope and McClellan were in the latter category which certainly made for difficulties and it didn't stop there. Many didn't like Doubleday for his abolitionist stance, others because he was outspoken and not concerned with what others thought; and he was

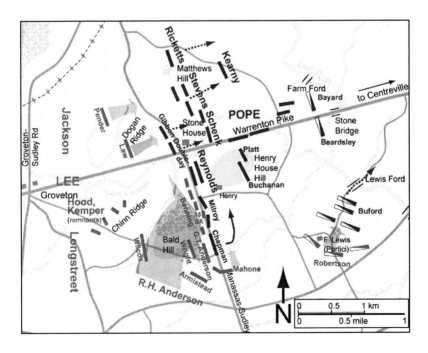

This map of Second Bull Run depicts troop placement. You can see Doubleday's troops were close to the Warrenton Pike.
(Map courtesy of Hal Jespersen)

known for dabbling in the spirit world. Cohesive would not be a word used to describe these individuals within the leadership of a central command.

McClellan built a grand army but always believed the opposing force had superior numbers, and had not been able to defeat the Confederates near Richmond that spring in his Peninsula Campaign. As Pope stated in his report, the object was to connect the Army of the Potomac and the Army of Virginia to protect Washington and continue attacking the enemy.[320] It would prove to be a task much more difficult than it looked on paper.

In early July, Pope ordered King to send out the cavalry. Their mission was to knock out all communications between Richmond and the Shenandoah Valley along the Virginia Central Railroad. Jackson, however, was equally determined to protect the railroad from the Union troops. A clash between the two armies was inevitable. The timing and the location were the only real questions to be answered.

By mid-July, Lincoln was showing his cabinet members a new proclamation he was drafting. In its final form it would set slaves free in the rebellious states and allow them to participate within the United States Army. It was not a legislative proposal needing debate and a vote of approval to become law; it was a presidential ruling. It would be known ever after as the Emancipation Proclamation and it was due to become law on New Year's Day 1863. The only question remaining was when would Lincoln unveil it?

On the battle front, Jackson was still doing his back-and-forth movement keeping Federal troops chasing after him in the Shenandoah Valley. Pope didn't have enough men to send reinforcements to McClellan who was outside Richmond. From late June to early July, the two armies pounded each other until McClellan received orders August 4 to pull back. Being McClellan, he waited to move, and when he finally got underway, he did not reach Pope's Army of Virginia, located in the Culpeper area of Virginia, until August 22.

When Jackson turned his attention to Pope's Army of Virginia, Pope needed reinforcements from McClellan. What would Lee do then, send the hunted to look for the hunter? So on August 23, Jackson's men prepared for yet another move. Their objective was to get past the Union lines and through Thoroughfare Gap.

Meanwhile, King's Division was retracing its steps after the battle of Cedar Mountain with Jackson. Jackson's men valiantly marched around Union troops and without any warning pounced on Federal supplies at Manassas Junction. Confederates who needed clothing, shoes and food found plenty there. Taking what they could, Jackson's men destroyed the rest. It was quite a prize for the Southern general and his men. Pope tried to make the best of a bad situation. He didn't need Jackson dogging him from the rear so Pope headed toward Manassas and that forced Jackson to move north too.

As King's Division marched along toward a coming battle, a different kind of battle was taking place among the army's leaders. After all, promotions meant accompanying pay raises, and reputations were as much at stake for officers as the war itself. Men of lower rank were continually jockeying for greater rank and its benefits of more money, more staff, more rations and even more servants. There were those who thought Pope was not the best man for the job. For all his bluster, it would soon be discovered that Pope was sadly unequal to the task ahead of him.

This was the situation as King's men were marching along the Warrenton Turnpike, not knowing they would become caught in Jackson's carefully placed trap. Doubleday and his troops, along with the rest of King's Division, were headed east along the Warrenton Turnpike. About noon they stopped for lunch and rested for several hours before resuming their march toward Centreville.[321] Doubleday was in a good mood.

A few miles after resuming the march, Doubleday stood on a hill waiting for Gibbon's and Patrick's men to pass when he heard cannon fire in the distance. Since he had not received any information to the contrary, Doubleday assumed it was the enemy's advance including the horse artillery of the Confederate cavalryman, and sometime rogue, James Ewell Brown Stuart.[322] The Union troops pressed forward. In the late afternoon of August 28, King's Division turned north toward the turnpike and Centreville. King's 10,000 man division, with Hatch's brigade in the lead, were marching right under Jackson's well-hidden troops. Behind Hatch, were the divisions of Gibbon, Doubleday, and Patrick.

The men marched on, with a ridge to their left. On the ridge was the Brawner family farm. It was a typical farm, with open fields and a small orchard. Nothing about the scene caused the men to suspect the presence of Jackson. However, Captain Amos Swan of the Seventy-sixth New York claimed, "The very air seemed to whisper, danger! danger!" [323] And unseen danger there was. Doubleday said he stopped to talk with Patrick and during their short conversation, he noticed, "a large man on horseback suddenly appear on a hill about 200 yards" north.[324]

Although neither Patrick nor Doubleday recognized the man at that distance, they later learned from captured enemy prisoners it was none other than Jackson himself surveying the area. Doubleday and Patrick discussed the rider, but concluded they didn't need to worry as scouts had reported only a half hour before that no enemy was seen. (This conversation is not mentioned by Patrick in his *Inside Lincoln's Army: The Diary of General Patrick.)* The rider wheeled about and could be seen motioning to someone behind him. Gibbon said he observed horses coming from the woods. As an artillery officer, Gibbon recognized danger as soon as the horses turned "their flanks" to prepare for the placement of cannon.[325] Much to the surprise of Doubleday and Patrick, artillery was moved out from the wooded area to their left, and began firing on them.[326] Soon the shouts of, "Take cover men, take cover," were heard all along the lines. [327]

The soldiers of Gibbon and Doubleday had been just quietly moving in that monotonous way of putting one foot in front of the other down the dusty road when shells burst in their midst. The Confederates, who had been able to line up their sights perfectly and without detection, now had the Union troops in their sights as if the invisible circles of a Bull's Eye target surrounded them. Within seconds shelter was found by some of Doubleday's brigade—trees, fences, anything big enough to hide a man; it was time to see how small and flat you could make yourself. Hatch was ahead by two miles or more and already engaged with the enemy. For whatever reason, Hatch had not sent word of the enemy's presence to the troops following him. With Patrick's men behind and King even further back, orders would not be received in time to give direction. It was up to Gibbon, Doubleday and Patrick to decide on a course of action. To complicate matters, King was ill. Only five days before, King had suffered an epileptic seizure and had been hospitalized.[328] Gibbon and Doubleday held a hurried conference. As they discussed the situation, the commander of the Fifty-sixth Pennsylvania, Lieutenant Colonel J. William Hofmann, requested orders for his men. "My men are eager for the fray," he told the generals.[329]

For Doubleday this would be his first time as brigade commander; for the regiments in his brigades it would be the first time to "see the elephant," a nineteenth century expression for overcoming hardships that also was used to mean that a man would find his courage in battle. Would they be up to it? Gibbon had long drilled his men, and put them in distinctive clothing and the famous black Hardee hats. It was a measure designed to create a cohesive unit, one the members could identify with and be proud of. It worked. These Midwest regiments would soon be known as the Iron Brigade—the "black-hatted fellows" before the battle ended.

Doubleday, still thinking they were being shot at by the battery of Stuart, said the enemy guns should be taken. Gibbon quickly said, "By Heavens,

I'll do it." and sent the Second Wisconsin men off into the fields with orders to take the guns. Doubleday ordered the Fifty-sixth Pennsylvania and Seventy-sixth New York under Wainwright, to support Gibbon. The troops hurried off the road and into the nearby woods. Trained as a doctor, Wainwright had gone to Europe and studied in Berlin; not medicine, but the art of war. His only experience was with the militia before he was appointed to lead the Twenty-ninth New York Volunteers early in the Civil War. Now he would discover if he had truly acquired the art of leading men into combat for the first time.[330]

Little did the two commanders know they were taking two brigades up against two-thirds of Jackson's entire army, including Virginian and West Pointer (Class of 1840) Richard Ewell who had fought at the First Battle of Bull Run. Fellow Virginian and Harvard educated William B. Taliaferro fought in the Mexican War and was at Harpers Ferry when John Brown tried to capture the arsenal there. Taliaferro would be wounded three times in this action and Ewell would be hit in the knee causing him to lose a leg.[331] These two leaders would keep the Union soldiers busy.

As the battle progressed, the Second Wisconsin pushed ahead and fired upon enemy skirmishers who fell back into their own lines and the large force waiting to join the battle. The Second Wisconsin men pushed forward. Gibbon ordered the Nineteenth Indiana forward to assist the Wisconsin men, then the Sixth and Seventh Wisconsin regiments. By this time, Gibbon was facing overwhelming odds and "begging me for God's sake, to come to his assistance," Doubleday reported. With no direct orders from King, Doubleday took the initiative and ordered two of his three infantry regiments forward.[332] The Seventy-sixth New York and Fifty-sixth Pennsylvania rushed forward to support Gibbon, with the Ninety-fifth New York held in reserve.

The battle continued, yet no orders from King arrived. Doubleday said he saw King only once, and that was when King rode at full speed past Doubleday, up the turnpike and out of sight. Campbell's Battery (Battery B, Fourth United States) was positioned on the right; the Seventh New York Infantry was placed between the Sixth and Seventh Wisconsin regiments. These regiments were only fifty yards from the Confederates.[333] The Fifty-sixth Pennsylvania took up its position on the right of the Seventy-sixth New York with the Sixth Wisconsin on the right of the New Yorkers. The Union line was too short and easily flanked by the rebels who outnumbered the Federals. Doubleday now had to send in his reserve, the Ninety-fifth New York to support Campbell's battery. The Confederates turned all their firepower on the Union line; right, left and center were pounded. In places, Doubleday noted, the men stood not more than fifty to seventy-five yards from each other; hard to miss at that range. The fighting was fierce with neither side backing down. Brawner's peaceful farm field was now covered with shells, bullets and bloodied men in blue and gray. As it became twilight, Captain Andrew J. Grover of Co. A, Seventy-sixth New York Infantry, lead eight skirmishers toward the rebel lines. When they got within fifty feet they could hear the orders being given by Confederate officers. One of the men took the information back to Doubleday. Then Grover and the six other brave men "laid upon the ground firing" in an attempt to get the enemy's focus on them and not the men behind them who were maneuvering. Grover was hit in the back and leg, but he stayed on the field for an hour and a half before he withdrew. Grover's story became a common one. William H. Miller of the Company H of the same regiment was wounded in the foot; he too refused to leave. Miller lay on the ground and kept firing until it was too dark to see the enemy. "The approaching darkness and the uncertainty of the enemy as to the position of the remainder of Pope's army is all that saved us from destruction," noted Doubleday.[334]

As a exhausting day came to an end, Doubleday sent for Hatch to return with his brigade. As the brigade arrived, Doubleday asked for and got cheers to encourage the men who had fought so hard in an impossible situation. About the same time Hatch arrived, the enemy ceased fire.[335]

When battle reports were written, Gibbon, who commanded the Sixth Wisconsin, Second Wisconsin, Seventh Wisconsin, Nineteenth Indiana and Campbell's battery, stated two of the enemy's cannon were firing on Doubleday's brigade behind Gibbon. Gibbon also stated Hatch had not sent word of enemy presence even though he was only a short distance in front of Gibbon and Doubleday.[336] Gibbon continued, "Two of General Doubleday's regiments finally got into line and the fight was kept up vigorously until after dark." Doubleday reported he had halted his column to wait for orders, yet none came, so he took it upon himself to order the Fifty-sixth Pennsylvania and Seventy-sixth New York forward to aid Gibbon. Gibbon would later say he didn't know Doubleday's men had taken place in battle line. The "fog of war" enveloped officers and enlisted men alike more often than any of them would want to admit.

Hatch, commander of the First Division, Third Corps, stated Gibbon's command "had been detached to support some batteries."[337] Hatch continued, "Doubleday's brigade moved to the front under a very heavy fire, which they gallantly sustained; but the firing" was too hot and his own brigade under Colonel Sullivan moved to support Doubleday and his regiments. The fight lasted about forty-five minutes and involved hand-to-hand combat said Hatch. Hatch praised Doubleday's "gallantry" in leading his brigade under such a heavy fire and extended that praise to Doubleday's brother, Ulysses, and Doubleday's staff member, Halstead. Lieutenant Marten's horse was shot twice from under him. In the darkness after the battle, Ulysses went to within thirty yards of the Confederates to rescue wounded men, dodging bullets all the way. He was lucky, but his horse was killed beneath him as he rode.

The losses were heavy. Ewell lost a leg and would not fight again until the following July. Colonel Edgar O'Connor of the Second Wisconsin was killed. Many on both sides fell to the earth and would not rise again. On the home front many would grieve.

With the battle of Brawner Farm ended, the generals had to plan their next move. King called a meeting of brigade commanders to determine the next course of action. Gibbon urged a retreat, thinking Jackson would probably attack at first light. When the meeting ended, the decision had been made. Much to the disgust of Doubleday, the commanders had agreed to retreat. It was about 1 a.m. when the retreat began toward Manassas Junction. However, Doubleday believed a retreat would allow Jackson to be joined by Longstreet, the very object the army had been seeking to stop. Doubleday said the retreat, "was worse than useless. It simply took us out of our position and we had to return the next day." [338]

Worn out from fighting, and with no possibility of sleep, the Union troops began a march in the dark toward to Manassas Junction. They did not arrive at there until 6 a.m., hardly a good beginning for the next battle. General McDowell, who was already at the Junction, allowed four hours of rest before returning them to the place they just left.

Breakfast was made from sharing rations and left little time to rest.[339] About 10 a.m. the brigade of Major General Fitz-John Porter began its march toward Gainesville. The First Corps, under Major General Franz Sigel, went looking for Jackson in an attempt to find the enemy's lines. Prussian-born Brigadier General Carl Schurz, under Sigel, sent his soldiers who were near the Manassas-Sudley Road to find the enemy and push it back into the woods north and west of the road. About noon on the August 30, General Samuel P. Heintzelman's troops arrived and took their position on Sigel's right flank. General Jesse Lee Reno's men were held in reserve near center of the Union lines and Reynolds was placed on the left of General Robert Cumming Schenck. Pope arrived about an hour later and rearranged some of the troop positions. As the Union troops took position, the men of Jackson's corps waited unseen behind the unfinished railroad; some taking advantage of the ridge there, others in the woods behind.[340] King's Division, now under the command of Hatch, King being too ill to continue, was quietly waiting to take its place. So Hatch's Division followed Porter's along the Manassas-Gainesville Road with Patrick taking the lead, followed by Sullivan, Doubleday and Gibbon.[341]

There they would stay until late afternoon. Sullivan, Doubleday and Patrick would remain near the road, with Patrick moving only a short distance. Gibbon's men moved closer to the front where they would support artillery. It was around 6 p.m. before the remainder of Hatch's Division saw combat. Shortly after that McDowell, on the orders of Pope, sent orders to Hatch to hurry forward west along Warrenton Turnpike. The Confederates were retreating. Hatch ordered Sullivan's Second United States Sharpshooters forward. The Sharpshooters "almost immediately became warmly engaged," reported Hatch. Doubleday then took his brigade to the front on the south side of the road where they were greeted with Confederate bullets.[342]

Doubleday said, "We marched forward in double time to attack, not a flying enemy but a fresh army." For the exhausted men who had fought so hard the night before, and had lost so many, this would be a sharp contest.[343]

Far from being a retreat, Longstreet had lengthened Jackson's line and the Union troops, believing a rout was underway, were not prepared for Longstreet's advance. Doubleday said McDowell was alongside the advancing troops and kept encouraging them to follow and take as many prisoners as possible from the "retreating" army. Doubleday said as the advance began "everything seemed quiet," but when they had gone about three-fourths of a mile ahead of Union lines, Confederate infantry appeared on the north side of the road headed for the Union troops. The Second United States Sharpshooters fell back and the First New Hampshire Artillery under Capt. George A. Gerrish opened fire. "Some 14,000" Confederates answered the call, Doubleday said. They had been hiding behind a fence and now returned fire from three sides.[344]

To meet this unforeseen and deadly development Doubleday tried to send his troops to the right of the Ninety-fifth New York. However, Hatch took two of Doubleday's companies to support a battery. By then, the Ninety-fifth New York was under tremendous fire. They had barely fought the day before, so this was a new experience for them. There was no opportunity to withdraw the Ninety-fifth New York to reform their lines, because the Seventy-sixth New York and Fifty-sixth Pennsylvania were in a desperate fight and Doubleday didn't have reserve troops to send into action. George Gordon Meade's men tried to provide assistance on Doubleday's left and Bayard on the right, but the Confederate advance was too strong. It was getting dark; the lines were getting leaner and nearly surrounded. Doubleday and his staff would have been captured except for the bravery of Captain Bloodgood of the Ninety-fifth New York. Bloodgood and his company got between the officers and the advancing rebels.[345]

As daylight faded into darkening skies the enemy could no longer see where Union troops were located. There was a deep ditch between the lines, creating enough shelter so Doubleday and his men could return to the main Union lines. Thanks to a cavalry charge by Kilpatrick and the arrival of Patrick's brigade, Doubleday and his men were able to escape the fire of the rebels. Doubleday said once the fighting had ceased, men of Patrick's brigade and some of the rebels actually slept on the ground only a short distance from one another without realizing their closeness.

Doubleday wrote his official report of the battle and praised his men: "Throughout the whole action my men held their ground unflinchingly, and in this their maiden fight covered themselves with glory." He also had a few words to say about Major Charles Livingston. Having regained his health after the possible poisoning episode in spring, he was trying to rally the men of the Seventy-sixth New York around its flag, when he discovered (in what had to be an embarrassing moment to talk about the rest of his life), the troops he was rallying weren't men of the Seventy-sixth. They were men from the Second Mississippi, and the Mississippians took Livingston prisoner. As the Mississippians discovered, it's one thing to take a prisoner who has been rallying you, and quite another to keep him. Livingston managed to escape, be recaptured and then escape again during the night posing as a doctor. When he returned to the Seventy-sixth, he was "warmly congratulated" for his efforts to rally the Mississippi men.[346]

The Union had met both Jackson and Longstreet and despite ferocious fighting could not hold their ground against overwhelming numbers. The Battle of Second Manassas ended with both armies becoming more experienced in the art of war. A lieutenant wrote home: "I will resign before I will fight again under Gen. McDowell. I do not care to risk my life under such a block head." The battle was over, but the assessment had just begun.[347]

Endnotes

[320] OR, Vol. 12, (2): 23

[321] Noyes, 114

[322] Abner Doubleday, GR

[323] Smith, 116

[324] Abner Doubleday, GR

[325] John Gibbon, *Personal Recollections of the Civil War*, (Dayton, Ohio: Morningside Press, 1988 reprint), 51

[326] Abner Doubleday, GR

[327] Patrick and Sparks, 131

[328] Jack D. Welsh, *Medical Histories of Union generals*, (Kent, Ohio: Kent State University Press, 1996) 195 Even looking across the years, it's difficult to determine if King was able to issue orders.

[329] Noyes, 116

[330] Smith, 348

[331] OR, Vol. 12, (2): 369; Faust, 740-741

[332] Abner Doubleday, GR

[333] Ibid

[334] Ibid

[335] Ibid

[336] OR, Vol. 12, (2): 377

[337] OR, Vol. 12, (2): 367

[338] Abner Doubleday, GR

[339] Ibid

[340] Ibid

[341] John Hennessy, *Second Manassas battlefield map study*, (The Virginia Civil War battles and leaders series. Lynchburg, Va: H.E. Howard, 1991), 97

[342] OR, Vol. 12, (2): 367

[343] Abner Doubleday, GR

[344] Ibid

[345] Ibid

[346] Noyes, 132-133

[347] Jeffery D. Marshall, ed., *A War of the People Vermont Civil War Letters*, (Hanover, NH, University Press of New England, 1999), 103

CHAPTER 16

"Out of Cartridges"

The saddle leather creaked as Doubleday shifted his weight and turned to look at the scene the army had just traveled through. They had made a long climb up a mountainside. Below them sat the city of Frederick, Maryland, farms, fields, and a scattering of houses and barns. "What a magnificent view," Doubleday exclaimed.[348]

The Second Battle of Manassas had ended and the Union troops had taken a beating. Pope was relieved of his command. Poor leadership, even when provided with significant information, caused the death of many men. Those left to grieve would be putting up black crepe on their doorways and wondering how much longer and how many more would pay the ultimate price in a fratricidal war. Leaving the dead and wounded behind, the Union army began another march in search of a victory.

Lee and Jackson were moving north, with an eye toward Harrisburg, Pennsylvania where they hoped to then head south and capture Washington. They would conquer "those people," as Lee referred to Northern troops and citizens.

Changes in command had taken place since the defeat at Manassas. McClellan had been returned to his former full command. Major General Hooker commanded the First Corps's three divisions. Hatch replaced Rufus King. The First Division's First Brigade was now comprised of Hatch's brigade now under the command of Colonel Walter Phelps. Doubleday had the Second Brigade plus one more regiment, the Seventh Indiana, under Major Ira G. Grover. Patrick had the Third Brigade and Gibbon the Fourth. Artillery was under the command of Captain J. Albert Monroe and included Battery B of the Fourth United States Artillery.

After a short stop in Washington, Doubleday and his men prepared to join the main army as it headed north toward Frederick, Maryland, with their tattered battle flags. It wanted what the South had already tasted, a win. Politically, the North was desperate for success. Lincoln was preparing to issue his Emancipation Proclamation to free the slaves in the rebellious states; but the timing had to be right, or the document would not be received enthusiastically. More troops joined the embattled Army of the Potomac and if numbers alone could win this miserable war, success was within sight. As they all knew, winning took more than tipping the scales of troop strength in their favor. The right combination of generals, information, planning, attitude and luck would make the difference. McClellan had been a great organizer of the army, but would not use it. Pope had his faults as a leader at Second Manassas, believing his subordinates read his mind and would move forward while he ignored valuable information regarding enemy movements and position. As the men marched north, they had to be wondering what they would be facing next. The attitude of many, both enlisted men and officers, is reflected in a letter by Alpheus S. Williams to his daughter in late 1861. Williams, a veteran of the Mexican War and a lawyer in private life, had been appointed as a brigadier general of Michigan volunteers before entering the Union army at the same rank. A graduate of Yale University, he scorned the prevailing belief that only West Point men possessed leadership qualities. Commenting on West Point and its graduates, Williams wrote, "I begin to think that all the prominent acquisition obtained there is superciliousness, arrogance, and insolence."[349] Such was the mood of many as they marched toward the next battle, whenever and wherever it would take place.

Doubleday's Commissary of Subsistence, George Noyes, wrote about their move from the nation's capital through the countryside of Maryland. Since Maryland had thus far escaped the ravages of war seen in Virginia, it was a far prettier place to be, Noyes wrote of the march. Although there were some citizens who supported the South, there were those who were glad to see Union soldiers. Crowds gathered to watch the army pass. Women waved their handkerchiefs and some offered flowers and water, Noyes said. The line of men was visible as far as the eye could see, both to the front and the rear. As the men passed by residents of the countryside, they were given information about Rebel movements and the condition of the Southern soldiers. If there had been any doubt about the enemy's ability to fight even though poorly dressed and equipped, the Yankees now knew they were in for a long war. Noyes was surprised that so many Southerners lacked the basic skills of writing and reading and concluded they had been lead to believe, unjustly, that the North wanted to take over the south and so were ready to take up arms.[350]

A.P. Smith, regimental historian for the Seventy-sixth New York, noted when they left Washington only a few months before, the regiment was 800 strong with full bellies and happy faces to meet the enemy. Four months later, as he looked around, Smith saw gaunt men; men with blistered feet, men who had seen death and their ranks thinned. The facts were the same for the other regiments in their brigade too. Marching from Washington, the troops endured heat, dust that was four inches deep and they weren't able to stop for food or coffee, said Private Uberto A. Burnham Company D of the same regiment.[351]

The march allowed Noyes to ponder the politics of war and the brotherhood it created in men from different states and backgrounds. By this time the novelty of war had been replaced by the worst kind of reality, Noyes said. With these thoughts in his head, the march to the Monocacy River ended as Noyes and his fellow soldiers halted to set up camp near the river on September 13. The same day, and only a few miles away, a soldier in the Twenty-seventh Indiana Infantry was walking through a field two miles south of Frederick where he found three cigars wrapped in papers. He picked up the cigars and removed the papers. The soldier discovered he had found Special Orders 191 written by General Robert E. Lee. The orders unveiled Lee's plan to invade the North. These plans gave the Union an advantage, but the ever cautious McClellan failed to move quickly. The next day, Sunday, September 14, would be spent marching through the City of Frederick and the long line of men in blue began to snake its way up the foothills of the South Mountain range to the west of the city where Doubleday admired the scene below.

The land became so steep, several officers and staff had to lead their horses, in an effort to save the animals' energy for the top of the mountain, said Noyes. Not long after they began their climb, the booming sound of cannon could be heard. Somewhere up ahead a fight had begun and the men heard duty calling their names. By noon, the men had reached Middletown and it became clear Union batteries were already responding to the call. The blasting of cannon reverberated off the hillsides and was heard through the dust made by thousands of feet long before the troops arrived to form a line of battle among the stones lying in the tall grasses. In some places, it was even too rocky for grass to push through.

As the men moved into position it became all too clear the battle would be fought literally on the side of a mountain; not just a nice steady rise, but nearly straight up with it cresting at nearly 1,200 feet. Union soldiers stumbled over rocks, trees, and uneven terrain as they tried to dodge enemy fire. The Army of Northern Virginia had already gotten into position using the mountains to obscure their northbound movements. The war that had so devastated Virginia was now taking its ugliness into lush Maryland. Ahead, the troops under General Jesse Reno were already engaged with the enemy. Bodies of soldiers were proof of earlier action and the wounded were quickly being carried toward the rear, noted Noyes. What had been a quiet mountain ridge was now bloodstained earth.

In mid-September the Maryland countryside is green with crops ready for harvest and the men in both armies enjoyed corn and apples, a bad combination for men on a march; more than a few suffered from diarrhea.

The South Mountain range has three passes: Crampton's Gap, Fox's Gap and Turner's Gap. At Turner's Gap Doubleday's men made their stand. The land is rocky with ledges and small depressions or ravines where a man could take cover, and take aim without being easily detected. The topography served as both advantageous and hazardous for each army. Just over the ridge, were Confederates of Colonel A. H. Colquitt; men who spoke with the soft drawls of Alabama and Georgia, a thousand strong waiting in the late afternoon sun in a cornfield behind trees, rocks and a fence.

General Burnside, who sported long, fuzzy whiskers from in front of his ears down to his jaw line (which became known as "sideburns," in a clever reversal of his name), ordered Gibbon and his troops to march up the National Road. Patrick's Twenty-first New York and Thirty-fifth New York forged ahead as skirmishers. The men moved up the mountain to meet the enemy, but due to the rocks, ridges and the low spots formed along the undulating land, they lost sight of each other and failed to connect their lines. Behind them were Hatch's Brigade under Colonel Walter A. Phelps and Doubleday's brigade. Fatigue from marching on a hot day had to be put aside and a mountain had to be climbed. It took an hour and a half before getting within range of the enemy's guns.[352] Patrick's men were soon in the sights of the Confederates who fired into the Union skirmish lines. Hatch's men, with Doubleday as second in command, were still struggling up the mountainside. Ricketts was ordered to reinforce Hatch's lines. William Henry Miller of the Fifty-sixth Pennsylvania, in Doubleday's brigade, wrote to his sister that the Confederates were waiting in a cornfield at the top of the mountain as the Union troops moved forward. Miller found the sounds of muskets firing all around him to be a terrible noise, "the worst."

The men of both sides fought furiously across the uneven ground in the woods. Bullets popped and zinged through the trees as leaves and branches were ripped from the trunks. The men from New York and Pennsylvania squared off with Virginians, Georgians, and Alabamians. The men under Phelps who was leading the First Brigade (mostly New Yorkers) pushed up the hill. Phelps gave the command for attack just as Hatch, riding on his horse, was shot through the calf of his right leg. The shot came from behind the fence separating the two armies.[353] Also suffering a leg wound in this push for the crest, was Second Lieutenant Charles S. Doubleday (possibly a relative of Doubleday) of the Twenty-second New York Infantry. Hatch was taken to the Sheffer farm nearby and Doubleday assumed command. The Seventy-sixth New York, Ninety-fifth New York and Fifty-sixth Pennsylvania were hurried forward (some having gone foraging during the short delay). The fighting was intense for an hour and a half; the Fifty-sixth Pennsylvania's Captain Williams reported his men ran out of ammunition.[354]

Hugh C. Perkins, Co. I, Seventh Wisconsin, wrote home a few days later. He said orders directed him and his fellow troops to support a battery. "We done so, and repulsed the Rebs four times. As they was approaching the fourth time, we got prety near out of cartridges. At that time Gen. Doubleday came up to our Brigadier General and told him in great excitement that his brigade was out of cartridges." Brigadier General John Gibbon told Doubleday, "Don't be alarmed about my brigade, they have got a few cartridges, I guess, and when them are gone they will hold if they have to do it by the point of the bayonet." Perkins said because there was little or no ammunition, bayonets were used.[355]

Charlie Stamp, color bearer for Company A of the Seventy-sixth New York who had saved the colors during the fight at Second Battle of Manassas, rushed ahead of his company and planted the colors in the ground, yelling at the Rebels, "There, come take that." Stamp became a clear target and took a bullet in his head.[356] His bravery is mentioned in many battle accounts. Confederates and Union men were so close the firing of weapons took an enormous toll on both sides. Colonel Wainwright of the Seventy-sixth New York, reported the Confederates tried to flank the regiment, but were discovered by Captain Goddard, thus possibly saving many lives as the men swung to meet the attack. The order to fire was followed closely by screams of "Stop, stop." The regiment was firing into its own men.[357] Colonel Wainwright of the Seventy-sixth New York was wounded in the arm. Even though he was down and his horse killed, Wainwright managed to fire his revolver at the Rebels.[358] Doubleday, as he had done at Fort Sumter, preferred to fool the enemy. Doubleday simply commanded a cease fire. In his memoirs, General Oliver Otis Howard gave Doubleday credit for this maneuver and noted the lack of fire caused the Confederates to believe they had "cleared their front." The Southerners moved forward, right into an ambush by the men of Doubleday's brigade.[359]

Noyes climbed the fence, ignoring the bullets and shells flying across the fence from both directions, and cheered his fellow soldiers. Halstead and Marten carried orders from Doubleday and dodged bullets. Later during the night, the two of them did an intelligence sweep to determine the enemy's position.[360]

Gibbon's men, on Doubleday's left, ran into two Confederate regiments at the top of the ridge. Fierce fighting took place, and the Confederates were soon reinforced with three more regiments. Gibbon moved his men forward and the firing took many a life, but the black-hatted fellows continued to press the enemy. Gibbon ordered, "Fix bayonets!" The men pushed forward again and the struggle was intense.

It was getting dark and the shooting was slowing down. Burnham said the man could "only see shadows and flashes of rifle." Ricketts' men rushed to reinforce the division but essentially the battle was ending. Firing could be heard to the left, and then it was quiet except for the sounds of the wounded. Night enveloped the dead, the dying and the survivors. The Union troops had proved their mettle, but Lee still had the mountain and would slowly creep away during the darkness. Gibbon's men had earned a new nickname for their fierce fighting at the fence. The black-hatted fellows were now the men of iron, the Iron Brigade. On September 16, Colonel Wainwright of the Seventy-sixth New York sat down at the Sheffer house, the same place Hatch had been taken when wounded. There Wainwright wrote his battle report. He stated the Seventy-sixth New York entered the battle with forty lines of men. "I doubt, 'whether they can now furnish more than thirty files (lines),'"[361] he said. Two days later, they would face even more deadly fire across the fields of Sharpsburg a few miles away.

Endnotes

[348] Noyes, 172

[349] Gen. Alpheus Williams and Milo M. Quaife, ed., *From the Cannon's Mouth*, (Detroit: Wayne State University Press and Detroit Historical Society, 1959), 40

[350] Noyes, 161

[351] *The National Tribune*, May 24, 1928

[352] Smith, 152

[353] Welch, 159; and Oliver Otis Howard, *Autobiography of Oliver Otis Howard, Major General, United States Army*, (New York: Baker & Taylor Co, 1907), Vol. I, 283

[354] OR, Vol. 19, (1): 240

[355] Hugh C. Perkins letter, Sept. 26, 1862, Thomas R. Stone Collection, USAMHI

[356] Smith, 153

[357] Smith, 154

[358] Ibid

[359] Howard, Vol. 1, 283

[360] OR, Vol. 19, (1): 223

[361] OR, Vol. 19, (1): 237

CHAPTER 17

"Poured in a deadly volley"

"Tell the men they can start small fires for coffee," Doubleday said. He and his staff were soon joined by Ricketts and his staff. Biscuits and hot coffee provided the only comfort in the early morning light as they began to discuss the battle and their available troops.[362]

Sunday's battle at South Mountain had taken its toll. The Iron Brigade had suffered greatly. All the soldiers only a few remaining rations and had used much of their ammunition on the crest of South Mountain. The morning after the battle, as burial crews made their way across the battlefield, Doubleday and his troops prepared for a new day. Surrounded by death, the men made a fire for coffee. Doubleday's new orderly, Benjamin Van Valkenburg, Company I of the Seventy-sixth New York, went foraging for the ingredients of a chicken dinner for his general. Van Valkenburg found a farm, but sitting on the porch were seven armed Confederates. Mustering up his courage, he ordered them to surrender. The battle only hours before had understandably made the Confederates more than ready to comply. They threw down their rifles and Van Valkenburg marched his prisoners back to camp, picking up two more on the way. Doubleday was delighted with his new orderly's accomplishment.[363] Unfortunately, history doesn't record if or how many chickens were also captured.

Doubleday reported to Hooker who was with Edwin V. Sumner on the porch of a tavern at Turner's Gap. During their conversation, Sumner told Hooker the army needed to catch the enemy.[364] Hooker, a Massachusetts native, was the grandson of a Revolutionary War soldier. Hooker said he was satisfied with the fighting by Doubleday's men the previous day on the mountainside. Sumner, also a Massachusetts man, was the oldest field commander on either side. Doubleday's men were ordered to guard a waterway near Pry's Mill opposite a fording area not far from the Hitt Bridge, or what would come to be called the Upper Bridge on the Antietam Creek.

Skirmishing took place as the two armies sought better ground and each other. A mountain crest was less than ideal for fighting. Twenty-some miles south of Sharpsburg, Jackson captured Harpers Ferry. Lee could now concentrate his men near the tiny village of Sharpsburg situated a short distance west of Antietam Creek. The creek had four stone bridges crossing it. The first bridge, Hitt Bridge, was on the Keedysville and Williamsport road; two and a half miles below was the second bridge, Pry's Mill Bridge, on the Keedysville and Sharpsburg turnpike, a mile further down, was the third bridge, "Felfoot" Bridge, on the Rohrersville and Sharpsburg road. Three miles from there at the mouth of Antietam Creek was the fourth bridge, the Rorbach Bridge, (soon to be known as Burnside's Bridge) on the road between Sharpsburg and Harpers Ferry. Another clash of the armies was inevitable. Hooker would have his chance to catch the enemy.

The storm clouds of an impending battle were gathering and yet the Federals did not aggressively pursue what could have become an advantage. Reports of Confederates positioning themselves at the third bridge were received. The ground gave them an advantage they weren't ignoring. The Union began to concentrate its forces by this third bridge. In mid-afternoon,

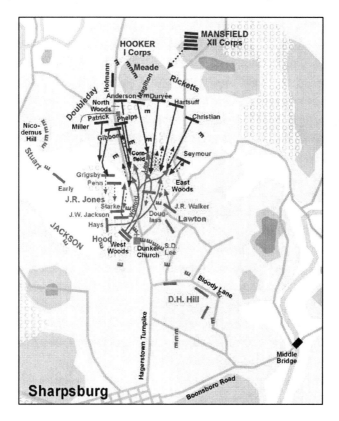

This map of Antietam shows the area where Doubleday's men were located near North Woods. *(Map courtesy of Hal Jespersen)*

the divisions of Doubleday, Meade and Ricketts were sent to cross the bridge near Keedysville with orders to turn the enemy's left. Some shooting broke out and the Confederates were driven back into the woods. By nightfall of Tuesday, September 16, men of both armies were within striking distance of each other. Doubleday and his men threw down their arms and uneasily slept about a mile from Joseph Poffenburger's peaceful farm. With thinner ranks and fewer cartridges than they started this march with, would they be able to survive another battle? Would they be able to claim a victory?

Just as daylight found its way over the eastern horizon on September 17, the Confederates announced their presence via artillery. The message was quickly understood, generals issued orders, and soon the Union guns roared in response. Gibbon's Iron Brigade led the way and went forward and to the right of the Hagerstown Turnpike. Doubleday ordered Phelps' men to support Gibbon by moving about fifty steps behind them. Twenty minutes behind Phelps was Patrick and his men. Hofmann sent men to protect a section of Capt. Joseph B. Campbell's batteries under the command of Lieutenant Stewart as it fired above the Union infantrymen's heads at the enemy in the cornfield.

Early in the day's action, a shell burst under the nose of Doubleday's horse. The horse took off running over rocks and fell, taking Doubleday with him. Now bruised, his hands smarting from trying to rein in his horse, Doubleday had to give up using the reins which put him at a disadvantage for the remainder of the day. [365]

It wasn't long before Gibbon's men reached the cornfield. Confederate troops moved forward and tried to flank the lines of the Federals who saw the move and tried to counter it. The noise of the bullets, shot and shell joined the screams of the men and horses, and men booming out orders. Stalks of corn were cut down by the deadly missiles, and so were the men in the cornfield. The battle ebbed and flowed as ocean waves against a rocky beach, with neither side giving way. Heroes in blue and gray pushed forward determined to take and keep the ground. Battle flags were captured, bugles sounded, and it must have seemed like hell on earth to the combatants. Colonel Post, of the Ninety-fifth New York, captured two of the enemy's battle flags. He was also wounded during the battle.

By mid-morning Doubleday's Commissary of Subsistence, George F. Noyes, returned from an effort to locate food. He rode through Sharpsburg looking for his brigade. After several attempts he was directed to McClellan's headquarters. As Noyes looked across the fields from that vantage point, he learned his brigade was supposed to be beneath the smoke from gunpowder that formed clouds above the battle. The only way he could rejoin them was to return to Keedysville and cross the Antietam Creek north of Sharpsburg and the fighting. Noyes noted ambulances were already taking Union wounded to the rear and bloody amputated limbs could be seen outside a barn as he rode his horse back to the Hagerstown Pike. There he found his brigade holding its position. It had taken Noyes nearly an hour to make his way around the battle to reach his brigade.[366]

Noyes infers Doubleday and his staff gathered west of the Hagerstown Pike for a short rest when an orderly from Meade (who now commanded the First Corps due to the wounding of Hooker) brought orders to move to the east side of the pike and form a line of battle at the rear of an artillery battery. The Confederate cavalry was threatening their flank. Then there was a lull in the fighting, said Noyes. It was then his fellow staff officers told Noyes of the terrible fight thus far. Among the stories told, two staff officers who were hungry relieved a dead Confederate of a "hoe-cake" he no longer needed. They learned of a shell killing the horses of three orderlies who were riding behind Doubleday. The battle would continue into the afternoon, but for Doubleday and his men, the battle had ended by mid-day. They had lost too many men to be effective and they were out of ammunition. The battle moved from the cornfield and Dunker church toward the Sunken Road and the Rorbach Bridge, the lower bridge crossing Antietam Creek where Burnside's troops would fight for hours against Confederate troops. As Doubleday's men remained in their position they could hear the din of battle, sometimes close, other times far. The afternoon wore on, and it was late afternoon when McClellan and his staff showed up to check the lines. They learned the Union had been successful in the center and on the left.

An hour later, enemy shot and shell rained down upon the men again, and it took only a moment to answer with the thirty guns that were posted nearby, said Noyes.[367] It would be the last time the guns of the Union right would be used that day. As daylight gave way to the darkness of night, the exhausted living would lie near those who would never wake.

For the next two days, the Union army tried to rest and waited for orders to chase the enemy. The orders never materialized. As Noyes and a friend rode the battlefield, near the haystacks where Doubleday and the staff had taken a short rest during the morning's fight, they found the body of a dead horse that died as he was attempting to rise. It looked so lifelike; Noyes ventured closer to confirm his observations.[368] The dead horse was one of many; nothing near the battle seemed untouched by bullet or shell. As the two men continued their exploration of the battlefield, they rode next to the bloody lane filled five and six deep with the dead. The burial parties had much to do. The following day, civilians began to arrive to claim the wounded and the dead.[369]

The battle had not been the resounding victory for the Union that Lincoln wanted, but it was close enough. The president announced his Emancipation Proclamation on September 22. A week later, General John F. Reynolds, who had been commanding militia troops from Pennsylvania, took command of the First Corps.

Doubleday prepared his battle report. He had kind words for Phelps, Wainwright and Hoffman. He praised staff members Halstead, Marten and Noyes. Doubleday even had praise for the man who had found Doubleday's behavior embarrassing the previous spring, General Marsena Patrick.[370]

The army, in spite of good marching weather set up camp and waited for orders to move. Noyes said he seldom saw any "of our troops playing base ball," instead they played cards, read and wrote letters home.[371] In early October, Lincoln visited Harpers Ferry and the battlefields of South Mountain and Antietam. Lincoln left Harpers Ferry at noon, October 2. He arrived late at McClellan's headquarters near the Antietam battlefield where the president slept in a tent near the general's. Early the next morning Lincoln and a friend, walked about the battlefield. Stopping on a nearby hilltop overlooking the Army of the Potomac's campsite and viewing the scene below, Lincoln said to Ozias M. Hatch, secretary of state in Illinois, "This is McClellan's bodyguard." Lincoln was obviously unhappy that the Union army was not pursuing the enemy.[372] Lincoln and "Little Mac" journeyed to Frederick the next day and visited the wounded before Lincoln headed back to Washington late that night.

Doubleday's headquarters were located across the way from those of Meade, and many officers and men who had cause to visit Meade, also stopped by the tents of Doubleday and his staff. There they would pass the time by talking about other times and other battles. Doubleday always had a tale to tell of Mexico, West Point and even those who had left the Union army for the Confederacy. Noyes and others found Doubleday's tales "constantly fresh and new."[373] By mid-October, Doubleday rented rooms in a Sharpsburg home, where he was joined by Mary and they would be more comfortable than living in a tent. He was sick for a few days, but soon returned to duty. His staff was camped nearby.[374] The waiting for orders to move continued. In mid-October Reynolds stated there was a great need for "shoes, tents, blankets and knapsacks. None to be found at Hagerstown."[375] More horses were needed and by the end of October, Harpers Ferry became a point for clothing being shipped for the use of the troops. All that had to be done was to pick up the clothing and distribute it to the men.

Then in late October, Doubleday received orders to move to Bakersville, Maryland, a few miles from Sharpsburg and the battlefield. He again took rooms for himself and Mary.[376] As the days passed, Doubleday took time to become acquainted with the area, but an army has to move and they soon were on their way back to Virginia.[377]

Endnotes

[362] Noyes, 183; Sometimes hardtack was also called biscuits, and it is difficult to tell which food was eaten.

[363] Smith, 163-164

[364] Abner Doubleday, diary, Harpers Ferry, 104

[365] OR, Vol. 19, (1): 226

[366] Noyes, 195-199

[367] Noyes, 200-204

[368] Ibid, 216

[369] Ibid, 220

[370] OR, Vol. 19, (1): 223

[371] Noyes, 224

[372] United States. 1960. *Lincoln day by day; a chronology, 1809-1865*, (Washington: Lincoln Sesquicentennial Commission, 1960), Vol. 3, 143

[373] Noyes, 226; Patrick's notes, 155, Abner could not see Patrick due to being "unwell" Oct. 2, 1862

[374] Noyes, 256

[375] OR, Vol. 19, (1): 75

[376] Noyes, 261; Post letters, Oct. 16, 1862

[377] Noyes, 262

CHAPTER 18

"A furious cannonade"

Carrie Post held a letter from her husband in her hands. "It is rumored that through some monkery or other General Doubleday is to be removed to another command somewhere, to make room for General Gibbon who is one of McClellan's protégées," wrote her husband who was still commanding the Ninety-fifth New York in the absence of Colonel Biddle. [378] A few days later, Post wrote again. "How many cripples there will be after this accursed strife is done and to think the infernal abolitionists are trying to make it a war to serve a people who for 6,000 years have never risen from the dust." He added, "General Doubleday was quite indisposed from neuralgia for some days but now is quite himself again his wife is now with him which don't look as like if we are intending to move very soon."[379] And in still another letter home in late October, Post said the anticipated changes in command had not happened yet. He told his wife he hoped the changes would not take place "as all the officers in the brigade are very much attached to General Doubleday and he is a cool, brave and able general."[380]

As Doubleday and his men were marching back into Virginia, events were taking place in Washington—McClellan was relieved again and Major General Ambrose Burnside was the new commander of the army. For those who loved "Little Mac," the change of command was hard to bear.

Burnside reorganized the army. Doubleday and his troops became part of the Third Division of the First Army Corps under Lancaster, Pennsylvania native John F. Reynolds who was glad to return to duty with the Army of the Potomac in late September. Reynolds had been on detached duty commanding the Pennsylvania Militia at that time and wrote to his sisters, "My own private opinion is, however, that if the militia of Pennsylvania is to be depended upon to defend the state from invasion, they had all better stay home, they can be of no use in any military point of view is they are to act as they did here [Sharpsburg, Maryland]"[381]

The Union army retraced its steps through the small, familiar towns seen only weeks before. They were returning to Falmouth, Virginia, where they learned the Confederates were occupying the heights of Fredericksburg.

The First Corps set up camp near White Oak Church, a short distance from Fredericksburg. About midnight December 10, Doubleday returned to camp; he had taken a rare trip to Washington.[382] That same day, a soldier of the Seventy-sixth New York wrote home that about "50 men in the Regiment" had no guns.[383] The Ninety-fifth New York boasted 909 Austrian rifles with a .54 caliber, of those only 251 were serviceable and twenty-three needed repair.[384]

The Union army prepared to take the heights. All they had to do was cross the Rappahannock River in front of the heights, with the Confederates watching their every move. In hindsight, such a battle could only result in losing a great many men for the North and would give the South a victory, but in December 1862, the leaders of the Union army

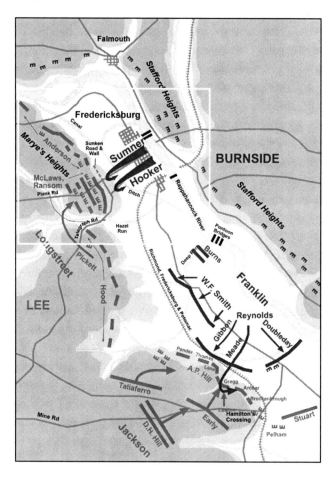

This map shows Doubleday's position at the Battle of Fredericksburg.
(Map courtesy of Hal Jespersen)

wanted and needed to get the Confederates off that hill.

Doubleday and his troops, as part of the Left Grand Division, were assigned to a position at the lower end of town, not far from where George Washington's boyhood home had been sited. Again, they would face the lemon-sucking, pepper hating general, Jackson and his hardy soldiers.

To cross the river, pontoon bridges were needed, and pontoon bridges were obtained, but having a pontoon bridge is one thing, being able to position it across a river under the nose of the enemy is quite another. That task fell to the army engineers. The plan called for two bridges to be placed in the Rappahannock River nearly in front of the town and one bridge to be placed south of town, but as with many plans there were changes as the plan went forward.[385] The infantry would go across the bridges and then cross an open area below the heights of Fredericksburg. These heights, known also as Marye's (pronounced by Fredericksburg citizens as Marie's) Heights.

On December 11, the work began. Getting the pontoon bridge placed at the lower end of town fell upon the shoulders of Captain McDonald and two companies of the Fiftieth New York Engineers. About 3 a.m. the engineers arrived at the site. It was dark and cold. Should a man take an unexpected swim, it would not be pleasant for there was ice on the river. Placing the pontoons would require stealth and total quietness.[386] Silence was golden, and nearly impossible.

Fourteen miles away, men of the Fourth Maine Infantry had completed their part in the crossing. At sunset, they had begun the construction of a corduroy road in hopes the Confederates would believe the Federal troops soon would use the new road soon. Perhaps the enemy would split its forces, or at the very least draw attention away from the laying of the pontoon bridges.[387]

At the river, the engineers continued their work. Federal artillery batteries took their positions on the banks above the water, ready to silence any enemy fire and to protect the construction crews who were unarmed. Similar actions were taken at the other planned bridge sites further north. At one of those sites, First Lieutenant Charles E. Cross of the engineers, and his men, used thirty boats to hold the unassembled bridge. Cross was uncertain how to proceed; he wouldn't be able to get the boats close enough to the site to unload them; the parts would have to be carried by hand to the river's edge. Commanders estimated it would take Cross and his men more than two hours to unload the boats, but it actually took four hours and they finished at daylight.[388]

In the stillness of the dark night, McDonald and his men began to unload and assemble the various pieces that would become the bridge at the lower site. They didn't run into any problems until about eighty feet from the dock on the opposite shore. Hidden Confederates along the shore line opened fire. Two soldiers of the construction crew were wounded. It didn't take long for Union artillery to roar. The firing went on for half an hour before the guns on the Fredericksburg side fell quiet. The work commenced again, and so did the enemy's guns, even hotter than before. McDonald was wounded along with a sergeant and three privates. With the heavy fire, the men dove for cover as the Federal guns opened up. Again it lasted about thirty minutes. With McDonald wounded, Lieutenant Michael H. McGrath took command and the construction began again. Again the artillery duel opened with even more determination exhibited on each side of the river. The cannon fire was deadly and resulted in the death of two men and with several others being wounded. With too few men, McGrath withdrew and turned the work over to the rest of his regiment; it took four attempts total to find success. [389]

At the upper bridge sites, laying the pontoon bridges wasn't any easier. At one point, infantry was called on to give assistance, but the soldiers would not get into the boats or on the bridge.[390] Time was passing, and the work was slow. How do you convince an unarmed man to erect a bridge while he's being shot at? Although many did their duty, others did not. They were panic-stricken.[391] To add to the difficulties, pontoons for one of the bridges had been left in the wrong place, so a second bridge was built on the lower site, instead of at the upper location.[392]

As the work at the upper site took place, shooting was taking place in both sides of the river. From near the Lacy House, on a bank more than a hundred feet above the Rappahannock River, the Federal guns shelled the town and directed their heaviest firing at houses closest to the river where Confederate soldiers were hiding.[393]

Once the pontoon bridges were in place, the infantry began its march across the river onto the open plains beneath the heights in the town. It too was attacked and fighting took place in the streets of Fredericksburg as the Federals refused to retreat. Unfortunately, some of the Union men then took to looting and ransacking homes in the city.

The day ended and wounded soldiers on both sides were sent to the rear. Doubleday and his men were positioned about a mile and a half away from the lower bridge. Before long, the men settled down for whatever sleep they could get. Just after daylight December 12, Doubleday and most of his staff, rode at the head of the division as they prepared for battle. The surrounding fields where thousands had spent the night looked vacant.[394]

A heavy fog hung over the area obscuring enemy lines, so it would be one more day before the anticipated battle began. The Union army used the time to get into position. While waiting, sporadic cannon fire was heard. Doubleday's Third Division crossed the river via the pontoon bridges and followed Meade and Gibbon to a point south of Fredericksburg. They took up their position near the building known as Bernard's house. As they got into position, Union artillery blasted away at Fredericksburg.

Meade and Gibbon settled into their positions. Men of the Seventy-sixth New York guarded the bridge before forming reserve lines. Meade would lead the fight, with Gibbon's support, and Doubleday's men became the left flank of the Union army.

Paralleling the river, the ground in front of them rose about ninety-feet giving the Confederates a huge advantage where Jackson and his men waited at the crest. On the Confederate right were the troops of Major General Ambrose Powell Hill, comprised of John A. Brockenbrough, James Jay Archer, James Henry Lane and William Dorsey Pender. Hill's lines were a mile and a half long.[395] At the foot of the heights were the rails of the Richmond, Fredericksburg and Potomac Railroad. A little further on was the Bowling Green Road. From the road to the river was an open area. Doubleday's Third Division was located in this area between the road and the river. On the right, was the New Hampshire battery under Captain George A. Gerrish; on the left, the Fourth United States Artillery's Battery B, under Lieutenant James Stewart.

The morning of December 13 came, and with it enough firing to tell the experienced soldier there would be a great deal more before the day would end. By mid-morning, the fog had lifted. In front of the well-entrenched Confederates were the Union soldiers positioned in three lines. With the Confederate artillery on one side and Union on the opposite, infantry found itself in the uncomfortable middle. Hill said he could see at least "ten full batteries." As the Union lines advanced, they were met with the cannon fire from the artillery assigned to Stuart's cavalry.[396] Pelham kept the Union troops busy, but they began an hour-long barrage as the infantry advanced. As Archer's men fired, Federal troops found shelter at the railroad bed a few hundred yards to the front. The Confederates pressed hard.

Under the watchful eyes of the Confederates, Meade's men advanced on the enemy's stronghold. Meade ordered the First Brigade to face the direction of the railroad. The Third Brigade then faced left and the two formed "two sides of a square."[397] Doubleday and his men were to keep the left flank of the army safe—no small job.

Doubleday's men moved forward "driving in the enemy's skirmishers."[398] As they pushed ahead, Doubleday ordered Meredith's men to take the woods in front of them, where the enemy laid waiting. The men of the Seventh Wisconsin, Twenty-fourth Michigan and the Second United States Sharpshooters took the woods, prisoners and horses. It was the first action for the Twenty-fourth Michigan and Doubleday was favorably impressed with the men.[399]

Doubleday ordered Phelps' mostly New York troops to move parallel with Bowling Green Road on the right of Colonel Rogers' men. The soldiers under Colonel James Gavin moved to the right of Phelps. Bullets and shells flying, Doubleday then moved Meredith left in response to enemy fire. Stewart's battery was moved to assist Gerrish's.

Meade's men made several attempts to send the Confederates reeling. Although the enemy broke through, they were unable to hold. On the left, Doubleday's men were fighting with such intensity they couldn't send aid to Meade whose men were forced to retreat with the aid of troops from General David B. Birney's division.

Doubleday's men held off the enemy; he ordered Meredith and Rogers to send out pickets as night fell. The troops were ordered back to safer ground. Doubleday worried that the Confederates might attempt a night attack. As he thought the battle was ending with winter's short day, about 4:30 p.m., cannons opened up and bellowed. The troops were pelted with shell fragments until "long after dark," said Doubleday.[400] Stewart's battery returned fire. As the battle progressed, Stewart's artillerists blew up one of the Confederate's caissons, killing the men with it. More batteries were added to meet those across the way. Captain Reynolds's battery went to the aid of Meredith on the far left.

After checking on Meredith's pickets, Doubleday discovered that although he had given an order two hours earlier to move the pickets, the order had not been carried out. Doubleday removed Meredith and replaced him with Cutler. Curiously in their battle reports, neither Meredith nor Cutler mentioned a change in command. Cutler simply refers to "When I took command." [401] Meredith and Cutler may not have mentioned Doubleday's decision from embarrassment or respect for military decision and decorum. Neither man was wet behind the ears. Meredith was fifty-two years old and would live another thirteen years. Cutler was fifty-five and had but four more years.[402] Even with a change in commanders, the men in the

Iron Brigade stood as firm as their name. Doubleday noted that even under the heavy fire of the enemy, the men "stood as if rooted to the spot."[403] The losses were heavy, but the men did not give way. It was totally dark when the gunfire slowly faded away in the night. The troops were moved in the darkness; they had to be ready should the battle begin again at sunrise.

Morning came and it was nearly noon before the screaming sound of a shell leaving a British Whitworth was heard. Whitworth breech-loading cannon were rifled creating an artillery piece that had a very long range. When a shell left the rifled cannon tube, it emitted a shriek that was unnerving to troops on both sides. Doubleday said the shell did no harm and even though many Confederates could be seen, no attack was launched due to the many Federal batteries now on the opposite side of the Rappahannock River.

On December 15, Reynolds directed the First Corps back across the Rappahannock River. Losses were tallied, the wounded sent to hospitals, and the dead buried. It would be a cold winter for both armies as they hunkered down and tried to keep warm.

Endnotes

[378] Post letters, Oct. 29, 1862

[379] Post letters, Oct. 16, 1862

[380] Post letters, Oct. 31, 1862

[381] John Fulton Reynolds papers, Franklin and Marshall College, Lancaster, Pa.

[382] Noyes, 290

[383] James Coye, letter, Pitcher, N.Y., Dec. 10, 1862, Vol. 1, 147, FNMP

[384] Orders Book, Ninety-Fifth New York Volunteer Infantry Regiment, NARA

[385] OR, Vol. 21, 175

[386] OR, Vol. 21, 169

[387] OR, Vol. 21, 169

[388] Ibid

[389] OR, Vol. 21, 179

[390] OR, Vol. 21, 175

[391] Ibid

[392] Ibid

[393] Noyes, 293

[394] Noyes, pg 299

[395] OR, Vol. 21, 645

[396] Ibid

[397] OR, Vol. 21, 509

[398] OR, Vol. 21, 461

[399] OR, Vol. 21, 462

[400] OR, Vol. 21, 463

[401] OR, Vol. 21, 478

[402] Stewart Sifakis, *Who Was Who in the Civil War*, (New York: Facts on File, Inc., 1988), 163, 444

[403] OR, Vol. 21, 464

CHAPTER 19

"Stays with his command"

Doubleday looked again at the orders he held in his hands. The wording caught his eye as he read his instructions:

"The Gallant Soldier and Accomplished Gentleman, Brigadier General Doubleday (the Hero of Fort Sumter) is assigned to the Third Division of the First Army Corps.

He is a graduate of West Point, etc.

"In passing the command into his hands, I feel assured that we have a general finally equal to the Exigencies of Campaign and to whom we can look, with perfect confidence in the changing and exciting scenes of the battlefield."[404]

Doubleday read it again, probably with a little smile. It offered official recognition for his actions; his career.

While the troops were recovering from the hard-fought Battle of Fredericksburg, the commanding officers were engaged in a less violent battle, but one that was no less intense. The "monkery" that Post had written about in October would soon rear its ugly head again. The day after Christmas 1862, Post wrote home again: Doubleday had been relieved by Wadsworth and sent back to his old brigade that had only 900 men remaining of the original 2,700. "We all like him very much but feel sorry for him, for it must be unpleasant to be changed from commanding 5 or 6000 men in a division to a single brigade. It is not however because of any misbehavior but simply because Wadsworth being senior and assigned to the division outranks him." Post said there was a letter-writing campaign to make Doubleday a major general and that General Reynolds sent Doubleday a very complimentary letter for action at Fredericksburg.[405]

The letter-writing campaign succeeded. While in camp with his new command near Belle Plain, Virginia, Doubleday received his major general appointment retroactive to November 29, 1862. The new rank had been recommended by several officers after the battle of Fredericksburg: Lysander Cutler, Walter Phelps, James Gavin, Gabriel R. Paul and his old artillery comrade, John F. Reynolds who now commanded the First Corps; all had put pens to paper on Doubleday's behalf.

Meanwhile in Washington, in the army and in many homes across the Union, people were asking why the army lost at Fredericksburg. Many questioned the commanders and the war itself. In Lincoln's cabinet men quarreled. In his army, generals quarreled. And the most serious quarrel was within the country itself. How would the Union survive? As 1862 came to a close, Lincoln was polishing his Emancipation Proclamation which would take effect on New Year's Day. On Christmas Day, the President and Mrs. Lincoln visited the wounded in hospitals. With the Lincolns, was Doubleday's wife, Mary. At the White House, the traditional New Year's reception was held, although the war and the events at Fredericksburg made it more subdued than normal. One young man on guard duty took up his pen and described the event: "The people came in, not by ones and twos, but by THOUSANDS."[406] The president shook so many hands, his own was swollen. Lincoln worried that his handwriting would not appear strong enough as he signed the Emancipation Proclamation. The proclamation would change the focus of the war and create a new nation in ways Lincoln could not have foreseen.

While many officers celebrated in Washington, a few stayed in the field. At Halls Landing, Virginia, the holiday was not ignored. Officers called on each other. Colonel Theodore B. Gates, Lieutenant-Colonel Jacob Hardenbergh and others, paid a visit to Doubleday and many of the brigade officers on New Year's Day.[407]

For Doubleday the winter of 1863 was beginning to look like the winter of 1862. What regiments would he command? So many men had been lost either by a bullet or by illness, the army's regiments were low in numbers and would soon go even lower as the enlistments of two-year men expired and they headed home. That was especially true of those who had served in the First Corps. Doubleday was initially given the Pennsylvania Reserves in mid-January. Demonstrating his animosity toward Doubleday, Meade wrote to his wife, "Doubleday has been assigned to the (Pennsylvania) Reserves which is a good thing for me, for now they will think a great deal more of me than before."[408]

Meade must have forgotten an incident that took place only a few months before. Colonel Horatio N. Warren of the 142 Pennsylvania wrote home and told this story: The men under Meade were on the march. The regiment halted along the way and dubbed the place "Starvation Hollow." They were hungry. As Meade rode past the division, the men began to yell for crackers and hardtack. Meade got so angry, he ordered "the whole division under arms and made them stand in the rain for about two hours."[409]

In a flurry of correspondence about the Pennsylvania Reserves, Doubleday and Hooker complained to Henry W. Halleck, the general-in-chief, that the men now assigned to Doubleday were short by approximately 250 men. Doubleday requested another regiment, even if it was not comprised of all Pennsylvania troops.[410] Even Reynolds requested more men for Doubleday's command. It was claimed that an agreement with Major General Heintzelman called for him to send men from his command (that was defending the nation's capital), called for only Pennsylvania men. Doubleday stated there had been no agreement, and that he had visited the offices of Heintzelman and Halleck daily trying to get the matter resolved until Reynolds ordered Doubleday to return to camp. It was finally decided to leave the Reserves in Washington and assign new regiments to Doubleday.

Summing up Doubleday's problems, Lieutenant William O. Blodgett of Co. F, 151 Pennsylvania Infantry, was in a sarcastic mood when he wrote home to his family, "He [Doubleday] is deficient considerably in the requisites of a commander. He does not drink whiskey, or at least I never saw him drink. Stays with his Command—and seems anxious to do his duty and fight Rebels. He came very near losing his confirmation as a Major General, and ought to have done so, for these reasons. He also allows his wife to stay with him when he ought to keep a mistress. Of course, the Army cannot succeed with such men, but it is a consolation to know there are but *few* *such* men in it and that those that are, are nearly powerless."[411]

New orders placed Doubleday in command of the Third Division of the First Corps. Doubleday had but two brigades. His new troops were the 121 Pennsylvania Infantry, the 135 Pennsylvania Infantry, the 142 Pennsylvania Infantry and the 151 Pennsylvania Infantry, all under the command of Thomas A. Rowley of the First Brigade. The Second Brigade commanded by Roy Stone was comprised of the 143 Pennsylvania Infantry, 149 Pennsylvania Infantry and the 150 Pennsylvania Infantry. Ezra W. Matthews commanded the artillery under Doubleday's new command: First Pennsylvania Light Artillery: James H. Cooper's Battery B, R. Bruce Ricketts' Battery F and Frank G. Amsden's Battery G.[412]

These were the men who would fight during the Battle of Chancellorsville. They were a mixed blessing for Doubleday. The men of the 121 Pennsylvania had fought at the Battle of Fredericksburg. All the others had been guarding the forts in the nation's capital. Real battle experience was lacking. Men of the 135 Pennsylvania would be mustered out after the battle at Chancellorsville.[413] A division usually had a third brigade, but this new division did not. Doubleday was challenged by circumstances he could not control. As the army prepared for another bloody summer, Hooker boasted, "My plans are perfect . . . may God have mercy on General Lee, for I will have none."[414]

During the time at Belle Plain, the men prepared for what would lie ahead. Private Charles D. W. Hoover of the 143 Pennsylvania Infantry noted in his diary, that drill and inspection took place before being reviewed by Doubleday.[415] On April 6 they participated in a review for the presidential couple who brought their son "Thady" along.[416]

By late April the weather and roads had improved. The army was on the move again. Doubleday and his men left Belle Plain and marched toward Port Conway. He and his men were to draw the Confederates under Jackson in that direction. Quaker guns (logs painted black to give the appearance of cannon) were placed, large fires were lighted to give the appearance of a large force, and pontoons were taken for a crossing of the Rappahannock River.[417] The troops then returned to Belle Plain and waited.

A similar demonstration was done at Port Royal by the Twenty-fourth Michigan and this time Jackson took the bait, but not much fighting occurred. By the end of April, the First Corps headed the seven miles from Belle Plain to Pollock's Mills. There seventy-five men from Wadsworth's Division were detailed to carry boats to the water's edge. It took two days to complete the task. When the Confederates discovered the Federals, they opened fire. Men from Wadsworth's Division dug rifle pits. Once the men were able to cross the river by boat, these same men began the work of bridge building. For two days the men endured the heavy shelling of cannon fire. Plans called for the Third and Sixth Corps to join the First Corps if the Confederates headed north. However, events don't always go as planned and soon Hooker ordered the First Corps to move toward the United States Ford near Chancellorsville.

Doubleday went on record saying the dividing of the army by Hooker, leaving Lee in the middle was not a good move. However, he also noted Hooker may have had information unknown by the rest of the army that could have affected the strategy.

After an exhausting march of more than twenty miles, the troops reached Chancellorsville. Doubleday described his men as "worn out."[418] Word came

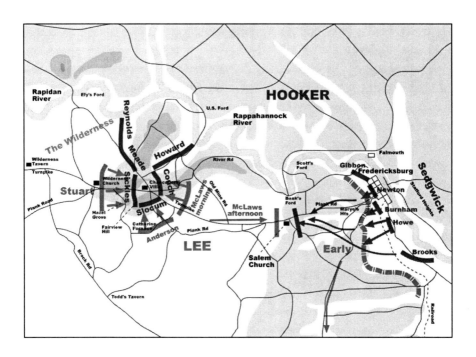

Map of the Chancellorsville battle action.
(Map courtesy of Hal Jespersen)

the Eleventh Corps had fled and defeat was imminent. The First Corps was ordered forward into the woods where they could use the cover of trees. The men under Doubleday were fortunate they were not attacked and the heaviest action was to their left.[419] Doubleday's men remained in that position for the remainder of the battle. During his testimony about the battle to the Joint Committee on the Conduct of War the following year, Doubleday said his troops took 132 prisoners.

During the Battle of Chancellorsville, the namesake of Doubleday's father, a twenty-six year old Lieutenant Ulysses F. Doubleday of Company H, 121 New York Infantry, commanded by Colonel Emory Upton in Sedgewick's Sixth Corps, was killed in his very first battle. This young man was brother to William A. Doubleday in Pierstown, New York, not far from Cooperstown. He had mustered in the regiment at Herkimer, New York the previous August, gone home on leave in March, and it was the first time his regiment had seen action. Upton reported Ulysses had fallen as he cheered on his fellow soldiers. As the regiment advanced into the woods, one soldier of the unit remembered the eerie quietness of the woods. No birds chirping, no sounds at all. They had no "premonition of any impending calamity," said Isaac O. Best.

The regiment was ordered to fix bayonets and move forward. Across the fields they crept, "when as if by magic, a line of men rose up" in front of them and delivered a terrible fire. It was Salem Church and the enemy seemed to be everywhere, even inside the house of worship, Best said. Once the battle had ended, "the full realization of our loss" hit the men of the regiment.[420] Like many other families during the war, the Doubledays of Central New York, would grieve their loss.

During the battle, Hooker was wounded. He was standing by the porch of a house he used for headquarters as he watched the battle. As Major Henry Tremain, a staff officer for Daniel Sickles, rode up, Hooker was hit by a piece of the porch column blown away by an enemy shell. According to one soldier, Hooker was no longer able to think clearly. In Doubleday's papers at the New York Historical Society, he states Hooker "was in great pain and was in a comatose condition for most of the time." Yet when giving testimony to the Joint Committee on the Conduct of War, Doubleday stated he had not seen Hooker on the day of the battle and knew nothing of the injury. However, Hooker's own staff officer, Captain William Candler said Hooker wasn't himself for the rest of the day.[421]

Could Doubleday have forgotten he saw Hooker that day? Did Doubleday embellish the story in his diary? The obvious answer is yes to both questions. Given Candler's statement but a short time after the battle, it seems likely Hooker was not in condition to continue command of the battle. What Doubleday said and wrote remains open to speculation and interpretation.

Once the final bullets had been fired, attention then turned to the wounded and the dead. Even as these tasks were performed, another problem had been brewing for the Army of the Potomac. Enlistments for nine-month men and two-year men were about to expire. Men would go home, new enlistees sought, and regiments reformed. As events unfolded, the Army of the Potomac would see major changes just as the fighting season began heating up.

Endnotes

[404] Abner Doubleday, GR

[405] Post letters, USAMHI; Reynolds' letter has not been located

[406] Andrew B. Hart, letter to mother, Civil War Misc. Collection, pension file, 150th Pennsylvania Infantry, USAHMI

[407] Seward R. Osborne, *The Civil War Diaries of Col. Theodore B. Gates, 20ᵗʰ New York State Militia*, (Highstown, NJ: Longstreet House, 1991), 57

[408] Meade, Vol. 1, 349

[409] Horatio N. Warren, letter, 142d Pennsylvania Infantry, USAMHI

[410] OR, Vol. 25, Part II, 63, 69, 87, 90, 91

[411] William O. Blodgett, letter, March 21, 1863, FNMP, (by permission of Rosemary McCorkel)

[412] Frank J. Welcher, Frank J., *The Union Army 1861-1865 Organization and Operations*, (Bloomington, IN: Indiana University Press, 1989), Vol. I, 304

[413] Frederick H. Dyer, *A Compendium of the War of the Rebellion,* (Des Moines, Ia: Dyer Pub. Co, 1908), 1613, 1615, 1617, 1618, 1619

[414] Charles Scribner's Sons, *Dictionary of American Biography*, (New York City, 1936) Vol. IX, 197

[415] Charles D. W. Hoover, Charles D.W., diary, FNMP

[416] *The Evening Star*, April 7, 1863

[417] CCW, Vol. 1

[418] CCW, Vol. 1

[419] CCW, Vol. 1

[420] *OR*, Vol. 25, 589, and Isaac O. Best, *History of the 121ˢᵗ New York Infantry*, (Chicago, Ill., 1921), 68, 75

[421] Stephen W. Sears, *Chancellorsville*, (Boston: Houghton-Mifflin Co, 1996), 338; and Abner Doubleday, March 1, 1864, CCW

CHAPTER 20

"General Reynolds sent for me"

Doubleday mounted his horse and headed down Bullfrog Road, a few miles south of Gettysburg, Pennsylvania. It was early morning on July 1, 1863. Doubleday did not know it was a day that would be remembered for years to come. Early daylight revealed a cloudy sky, and the troops he left behind were preparing for whatever the day would present. As he rode, he considered recent events. The man he knew when they were both stationed in New York City; the man he had bought a horse from, like so many men in this war, Jackson, had fallen. As Doubleday passed the fields around him, he noticed the flattened crops his own men had trampled, the fences that had been broken to allow men and supplies to cross fields more easily as they arrived and set up camp at the home of a local farmer. Most likely, Doubleday was aware of a Confederate presence in the region. There was much to consider as he rode along.

The Battle of Chancellorsville had ended badly for the Union, and its battered troops were on the move again. The Army of the Potomac licked its wounds, rested, skirmished and prepared for the next big fight that was sure to come. In the Confederate Army, Lee had lost his "right arm," Jackson, who had been accidently shot in night fire by his own men during the Battle of Chancellorsville. Jackson died a eight days later from complications. Although the Army of Northern Virginia was saddened by Jackson's death, it was also jubilant with the win at Chancellorsville. As the two armies struggled within, they looked outward for a battle to end all the bloodletting.

Lee and his troops needed food and supplies. The Virginia countryside was devastated. Supplies were low or nonexistent. Lee looked north—to the fine, productive farms of Pennsylvania. A strike there could threaten both Harrisburg and Washington, create fear in citizens and politicians and quite possibly demoralize all to the point of surrender. Lee surely thought that maybe one more battle would end it all. Maybe the Yankees would leave the South alone to determine its own future.

The one bright spot for the north in that spring of 1863 happened in the fields all around the tiny crossroads of Brandy Station, Virginia on June 9. The thunder of 20,000 horses' hooves shook the ground as the cavalry of both armies battled fiercely across the meadows and Fleetwood Hill. It would be the largest cavalry battle ever in North America. Stuart's staff officer, Henry B. McClellan, estimated the men under Stuart and Union cavalry commander, General Alfred Pleasanton at a combined total of more than 20,000 men on horseback.[422] This time, the Union cavalry held its own against the Southern swordsmen. Stuart's staff officer, McClellan noted, "One result of incalculable importance certainly did follow this battle,—it *made* the Federal cavalry."[423] Proud of their accomplishments, Pleasanton's men were more confident with the knowledge they were, at last, equal to the enemy's horsemen.

The two armies headed north with the Confederates leading the way and staying slightly ahead of Union forces by using the mountains to hide their movement. By June 25, Meade wrote to his wife telling her the Confederates were near Winchester and Martinsburg. In the same letter Meade acknowledged his wife's fears that he would be put in a higher command.[424]

With the defeat of the Union army at Chancellorsville and the wounding of "Fighting Joe" Hooker, the future looked bleak. Hooker was falling out of favor with the administration. He got into a tussle about leaving troops at the Harpers Ferry arsenal. Hooker offered his resignation and it was accepted. Lincoln was searching for a general, a man who would win and end the war. Mrs. Meade's worries came true. Her husband was ordered to take command of the Army of the Potomac, June 27, 1863, the day after Doubleday's forty-fourth birthday.

As the two armies headed northward, Union commanders in several locations had been getting reports the Confederates were moving through Winchester, Virginia, Hagerstown, Maryland and Chambersburg, Pennsylvania. Meade began to position the army at strategic points. On June 29, Meade notified Halleck that the First and Eleventh Corps were headed toward Emmitsburg, Maryland; the Third Corps and Twelfth Corps at Taneytown, Maryland, and the other corps spread out from Frizellburg to New Windsor. Meade tried to reassure Washington officials the city would be protected from a Confederate attack.[425] On June 30, Meade sent a report to Major General Darius Couch, stating he (Meade) was located between Emmitsburg and Westminster, "The enemy (A.P. Hill) holds Cashtown Pass, between Gettysburg and Chambersburg."[426] When Meade placed Reynolds (who had commanded the First Corps) in command of the Army of the Potomac's Right Wing as it headed north, Reynolds moved Doubleday to command of the First Corps.[427]

The same day Meade sent his report to Couch, the men of the First Corps pushed northward. They crossed the Mason-Dixon Line dividing Pennsylvania and Maryland; North and South; slavery and freedom. A hundred years earlier Charles Mason and Jeremiah Dixon created the boundary line, and settled a long-time argument continued by the descendants of Lord Baltimore and William Penn. In the middle of the nineteenth century, it became the invisible line of demarcation between free and slave states, with many slaves crossing the border to freedom in the north; ten miles north of that line is Gettysburg. In 1863, the population of Gettysburg was about 2,400. The major roads leading to Gettysburg surround the borough much like the strands of a spider web. The community boasted a college, a seminary, three tanneries, newspapers, several shoemakers (but no shoe factory), an assortment of stores and had a several carriage making businesses. A railroad had been built a few years before and Gettysburg also had several hotels.

Doubleday's long-time aide, Lee, said that as the First Corps had left the Rappahannock on its way north, Doubleday had studied the maps carefully and pronounced Gettysburg "would be the field of a second Antietam if Lee crossed into Maryland." In hindsight, Doubleday's aide could have been telling the truth, but one must wonder how Doubleday could have predicted a battle at Gettysburg. Perhaps Lee was continuing his faithful support, perhaps the number of roads in and around Gettysburg tipped Doubleday off as he mentioned during his testimony to the Committee on the Conduct of War, but it is one of those areas where no clear answer has been discovered.

By nightfall, the First Corps had crossed the Mason-Dixon Line and were headed toward Gettysburg when they stopped for the night. They were in the Bullfrog Road barnyard of Jacob Brown, not far from Marsh Creek. As it was the last day of the month, the men lined up to muster in for pay. Farmer Brown's home became Doubleday's headquarters; his barn and fields became an army camp.[428] The ground was damp from the recent rain and Farmer Brown wasn't happy about his unexpected guests. After the war, Brown claimed the First Corps used fifteen acres of grass for forage, trampled through his crops of corn, oats, hay and straw. Nine hundred and thirty-seven fence rails were damaged and two horses taken, he stated on his claim totaling $520.59. His claim was rejected by the United States government saying, "there is no evidence the claimant had taken an oath of allegiance to the government at the time of the alleged seizure." The findings of the government also stated "disinterested witnesses testify he was disloyal to the U. S. government." However, no details of the alleged disloyalty are provided.

The march northward had been anything but easy. The troops had marched fully equipped, haversacks with three days rations and sixty rounds of ammunition. The roads were bad from heavy rain and some men didn't even have shoes, said Colonel Orland Smith of the Seventy-third Ohio in the Eleventh Corps.[429] The day held the promise of warmth and humidity. A man could feel little rivulets of sweat trickle down his back as he trudged along attired in his woolen uniform, cotton drawers and shirt. If he was fortunate, he might have a good pair of home-knitted stockings inside his leather brogans. Many men didn't. The following day, the men would not be thinking about their feet.

Not far away from where Bullfrog Road intersected with the Emmitsburg Road, Reynolds set up his headquarters at Moritz Tavern about three-quarters of a mile from the Mason-Dixon Line and an even shorter distance from Brown's farm. As Doubleday would learn, during the night Meade sent orders to Reynolds. Major William Riddle, an aide de camp to Reynolds, had made his way from Meade's headquarters in Taneytown to the Moritz Tavern and arrived about four o'clock in the morning. Doubleday would learn later that Reynolds was wrapped in a blanket, sleeping on the floor when Riddle arrived. Riddle looked at the dispatches before deciding to wake his commander. Once Reynolds was awake, Riddle read the information sent by Meade, not once, but three times as Reynolds listened stretched out on the floor, his head in his hand.[430]

About the same time, Meade notified Halleck he was in Taneytown and told the general-in-chief, that Confederate General Ewell and his troops were somewhere near York or Harrisburg, Pennsylvania. "I fear that I shall break down the troops by pushing on much faster, and may have to rest a day." The Army of the Potomac's new commander informed Couch of Longstreet's presence near Chambersburg. Meade was headed for Hanover.[431] The exhausted troops would not get the rest so badly needed; unseen events would change that plan.

In camp the next morning, the soldiers rose under a cloudy sky. Breakfast was no more than a piece of hardtack, pork and coffee for those lucky enough to have rations. For many, it would be their last meal; others would not eat for another two days. The men of the Twenty-fourth Michigan gathered for morning prayer, but as they communicated with their God, they were handed cartridges.[432] Reynolds and his staff had fared better. They would have full stomachs when they met the enemy. Mrs. Christen (Alice) Shriver and her family had been asked to furnish breakfast for Reynolds, his staff, and any others who might be at the tavern. The Shrivers gathered up meat, eggs, and potatoes and loaded it all into their wagon and headed for what was known as The Commons.[433] The food was unloaded and cooked. The hungry soldiers made quick work of breakfast.[434] It could not have been a leisurely meal—the enemy was close and there was work to do. The men were in "wonderful spirits that bright sunny morning," wrote one man. They were happy to be in Pennsylvania and said, "We've come to stay." Before night fell, many would stay forever.[435]

It didn't take long for Doubleday to cover the short distance to Moritz Tavern where Reynolds established his headquarters. Doubleday arrived and strode inside to meet with Reynolds, who had "sent for me for the purpose of explaining the telegrams received by him," Doubleday said in his battle report later. There, Reynolds went over the information he had including the location of both Confederates and Union troops. Reynolds laid out his battle plans and told Doubleday a large number of Confederates were at Cashtown to the west and Mummasburg to the north. Buford's cavalry was already engaged along those roads, according to reports Reynolds had received. After reviewing the most recent correspondence and available maps, Doubleday returned to his own headquarters. By the time Doubleday left, Reynolds had handed the command of the First Corps over to him and the meeting ended.

Confident Doubleday had a good grasp of the situation; Reynolds rode on ahead as Doubleday prepared to bring up the rest of the corps.[436] Obviously, Reynolds trusted Doubleday's judgment and ability to lead men as the possibility of a pitched battle loomed.

Back at his headquarters on Farmer Brown's land, Doubleday ordered the pickets in and the lines to be formed for the march. He said it took "an hour and a half to two hours" before the corps was ready to move out. This meant politician-turned-general Wadsworth would be on his own for the early part of what would become an all out battle. Once the men under General John Cleveland Robinson and General Thomas A. Rowley were on the road, like Reynolds, Doubleday rode on ahead.[437]

Wadsworth left Marsh Creek about 8 a.m. His First Division of the First Corps included the Iron Brigade under the command of General

Solomon Meredith, who was claimed to be a Quaker general,[438] and the Second Brigade under General Lysander Cutler. As the troops marched at the double-quick toward Gettysburg, what had begun as a skirmish between the men of Confederate General A.P. Hill's corps and Union cavalry General John Buford intensified into an all out battle. Earlier in the day, Lieutenant Marcellus Ephraim Jones of Company E, Eighth Illinois Cavalry fired the first shot that began the three-day Battle of Gettysburg. Buford and his men engaged in a desperate, sharp battle with the Confederates before Reynolds and Wadsworth's men came to their aid.

As Reynolds and Wadsworth's troops approached Gettysburg, the distinct boom of cannon could be heard. The column changed its direction of march toward the unmistakable sounds of battle. They arrived at the Cashtown Road about 10 a.m. and Cutler and his men were ordered to move toward the Lutheran Theological Seminary that stood on the western outskirts of town along a low ridge.

Endnotes

[422] H. B. McClellan, *I Rode with JEB Stuart*, (Bloomington, IN: Centennial Series, Indiana University Press, 1958), 293

[423] H. B. McClellan, 294

[424] Meade, Vol. 1, 387-388

[425] OR, Vol. 27, (1): 66-67

[426] OR, Vol. 27, (1): 67-68

[427] Abner Doubleday, *Chancellorsville and Gettysburg*, (NY: DeCapo Press (reprint),1994) p.124

[428] Jacob Brown, Office of the Quartermaster General, Claims Branch, Box 609, RG 92, NARA

[429] OR, Vol. 27, (1): 723

[430] William Riddle, letter to Lebouvier, Aug. 4, 1863, Reynolds Folder, vertical file, GNMP; (original in Reynolds papers, Franklin & Marshall College, Lancaster, PA)

[431] OR, Vol. 27, (1): 69

[432] Alan T. Nolan, 1961. *The Iron Brigade; a military history*. (New York: Macmillan, 1961), (reprint 1983), Hardscrabble Books), 233

[433] Thought to be located near the Greenmount Fire Station.

[434] Shriver Family, "*Shriver Family Fed Reynolds' Last Meal*," Vertical files, folder 1000, Adams County Historical Society, Gettysburg, PA

[435] Thomas W. Hyde, "Recollections of the Battle of Gettysburg", Ken Bandy and Florence Freeland, *The Gettysburg Papers*, (Dayton, OH: Morningside Bookshop, 1978), Vol. II, 742

[436] OR, Vol. 27, (1): 243-257

[437] OR, Vol. 27, (1): 244

[438] Sears, 115

CHAPTER 21

"For God's Sake Come Up with All Speed"

Traveling ahead of the First Corps, Reynolds stopped his horse when he arrived at the seminary. He yelled up to Buford who was standing high above the ground in the cupola, "What the matter, John?"

Buford hollered back, "The devil's to pay!"

The cupola gave a fine view for military eyes. When Buford arrived there, he had rushed up the ladder, pulled out his binoculars and focused on the road toward Cashtown. Buford didn't like what he saw. There was an intense battle with each side trying to keep the other from advancing while attempting to push the other back. The winner would take the ground; ground that had several ridges that could prove advantageous in battle.

The seminary would soon be at the center of the early action between the two armies. In examining the many battle reports and accounts of soldiers, the seminary became the landmark used to explain their troop movements. The Chambersburg Pike runs west to east from Cashtown to Gettysburg and beyond to York and Lancaster.

Beyond Gettysburg that Wednesday morning on the first day of July, troops under red-shirted Confederate General Ambrose Powell Hill were moving east from Cashtown toward Gettysburg. Men from North Carolina, Tennessee, Virginia and Alabama had gone but three miles when they ran into Buford's pickets between eight and nine in the morning, the same time Wadsworth's men broke camp and marched north.[439] Bullets began whizzing through the air.[440] Buford's men answered and the results could be heard a few miles away south along the Emmitsburg Road as it enters Gettysburg. Buford's horsemen had been holding off the enemy in hopes the First Corps would soon arrive. Only the night before, Buford had written a note to headquarters stating the location of Hill, Ewell and Longstreet. On Gettysburg's southeastern side, there was a cemetery on a slight ridge; and about a mile further were two hills, one larger than the other, known as Little Round Top and Big Round Top.

After Buford and Reynolds rode toward the battle and assessed the situation, Reynolds quickly sent a messenger with orders for Doubleday and the First Corps to press forward with "all possible speed." Reynolds was pinning his plans on the roughly 8,000 men of the First Corps. Could Buford's men hold off the enemy until the First Corps arrived?

Doubleday was riding along the Emmitsburg Road and heard the unmistakable sounds of cannon fire. Gettysburg citizens were hurrying away from the booming cannon; others hid in their cellars. Doubleday urged his steed forward at a gallop and soon caught up with Wadsworth's troops; it was now about 10 a.m. As the troops hurried forward, there was a momentary pause as the commanders discussed the situation at hand. As the officers talked, the men of the Seventy-sixth New York, if its historian is to be believed, went into a grove of cherry trees and liberated the ripening orbs.[441]

Cutler's lead regiment was the Seventy-sixth New York followed by the Fourteenth Brooklyn (Eighty-fourth New York), Ninety-fifth New York, 147th New York and the Fifty-sixth Pennsylvania. Cutler ordered the Seventy-sixth New York, 147th New York and the Fifty-sixth Pennsylvania men across an unfinished railroad cut. Reynolds sent the men of the

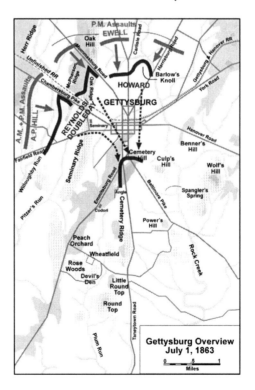

The morning of July 1, 1863 the fields to the west of Gettysburg were filled with soldiers.

(Map courtesy of Hal Jespersen)

Ninety-fifth New York and the Fourteenth Brooklyn to the left in support of the Second Maine Artillery (Hall's Battery).

When the remainder of the First Corps arrived, the Iron Brigade under Meredith, moved across the fields and into Gettysburg. Rufus R. Dawes, commander of the Sixth Wisconsin, said he wanted his regiment "to make a show in the streets of Gettysburg." Dawes ordered the drum corps to the front as the colors were unfurled. The sounds of cannon were joined by the drum-major's version of "The Campbells Are Coming."[442]

First Lieutenant Jacob Slagle, of Company D, 149th Pennsylvania Infantry and assigned as advocate general of the Third Division, was a very busy man that morning. Doubleday used Slagle as a messenger carrying orders to commanders who were moving toward Gettysburg. Slagle wrote home two months later with his story of events. Doubleday sent him with orders to hurry the artillery and the Second Division. When Slagle returned, he found Doubleday in his usual position at the rear of the First Division. Once closer to Gettysburg, Slagle was dispatched again to hurry the Third Division (formerly Doubleday's division) under General Thomas A. Rowley forward. Slagle found it about two miles to the rear. Slagle was also ordered to inform Brigadier General John Cleveland Robinson's Second Division to wait near the Seminary in reserve.

The men of the Seventy-sixth New York Infantry advanced; they were the far right of the Union lines. They were still marching by flank when the Confederates, more than a hundred yards away and lying unseen in a field of wheat, unleashed a hail of bullets on the New Yorkers. It took several minutes before the regiment was able to return a heated response. They managed to hit the enemy's colors twice before falling back and reformed on the railroad cut before advancing again to its former position where it held firm for some time before having to retreat again. It wasn't long before the regiment's Major Andrew J. Grover was killed as he was ordering the realignment of his troops. The Seventy-sixth New York fired until it had no more ammunition to fire. The men who only moments before had been joyfully plucking cherries and popping them into their mouths while officers discussed strategy, were now falling to the ground, blood rushing from their gaping wounds as Confederate guns popped off rounds and shells.

The men of the Iron Brigade, wearing their famous black hats, were positioned on the McPherson's farm where they faced west toward Willoughby Run, a small stream at the bottom of a ravine. The rippling water would hardly be noticed as bullets whizzed across it. Along the higher banks of Willoughby Run, they soon became hotly engaged. Doubleday dispatched Lieutenant Benjamin F. Marten with orders for Colonel Rufus Dawes of the Sixth Wisconsin. Dawes was to halt as men of the guard detail joined the front lines.[443] The boom of cannon was now so deafening, the sounds of music could no longer be heard and the musicians were more concerned with safety than Scottish tunes.

When Slagle returned to Doubleday, he saw the Iron Brigade was hotly engaged in the woods not far from the Seminary. Doubleday sent Slagle back to General Rowley with orders to double-quick to the front where Slagle put them in position.[444]

It was shortly after 10 a.m. and Reynolds was riding in the trees as he shouted words of encouragement to the men who were rushing through the woods, "Forward, men, forward! For God's sake, forward!" A Confederate bullet zinged through the air and a heartbeat later as it found its target, Reynolds dropped off his horse. The bullet had penetrated Reynolds' skull and killed him instantly. The man who had slept on the floor of the Moritz Tavern and who had eaten Mrs. Shriver's home cooking was gone, and with his death much of the needed information about the current situation that he carried in his head was gone too. Doubleday's aide, Henry T. Lee, later wrote from his law office about Reynolds: "His unusual exposure of himself . . . was owing to his eagerness to occupy and hold the ridge beyond the one on which he fell."[445] In the same letter, Lee said, "We all knew we were fighting against time with no earthly hope of ultimately holding our position against Lee's advance."

Captain John P. Corson of the First Maine Cavalry later claimed he broke the news of Reynolds' death to Doubleday. The confirmed loss of Reynolds put Doubleday in total command of the field.[446]

With a fierce battle underway, mourning Reynolds would have to wait. Doubleday immediately took command and his orders would affect the outcome of the battle two days later. Doubleday had a job to do and little time to consider his options. This first day of July, Doubleday would demonstrate, to those who ridiculed him, that he was a very capable commander. Slagle said Doubleday did not have the entire battle plans developed by Reynolds and "very much" felt the weight of the new responsibility. Doubleday could have called for an immediate retreat. He didn't, proving that his nickname through time has been misunderstood. "Forty-eight Hours Doubleday" has always been used as a reference to slowness in making decisions. The nickname is easily explained by understanding nineteenth century humor—Forty-eight hours equals two days or Double-day. It has nothing to do with Doubleday's abilities to make a decision, as he proved when Hatch was wounded and could no longer command at the Battle of South Mountain, and again at Gettysburg, as Doubleday suddenly found himself in command again. With the loss of Reynolds, Doubleday had to make several decisions and make them quickly. Yes, a retreat was one option, but as the historian of the Seventy-sixth New York said, Doubleday was "always averse to a retreat."[447] The First Corps pressed forward to meet the challenge. The fight continued, "without a break in carrying out his [Reynolds] designs under his able successor, General Doubleday," General Martin D. Hardin of the Forty-first Pennsylvania Infantry (Twelfth Pennsylvania Reserve) said.[448]

Bullets flew like swarms of angry bees and sought soft flesh. Green and golden fields were swallowed up by white and gray clouds of smoke as the cannons made the ground shake. The acrid smell of gunpowder announced the devil was, indeed, collecting his pay.

Looking at the various markers on the Gettysburg battlefield, you can see Doubleday personally took position in at least two different places that were close to the action. One was not far from where Reynolds fell and is marked with an upright cannon tube. The second place is near a house at the southeast corner of the Fairfield Road and Confederate Road.

Although we can be sure adrenalin was running high, Doubleday wisely held the men of the Sixth Wisconsin as reserve troops. "Lt. Marten came galloping up and said, "General Doubleday is now in command and directs you halt your regiment,'" Rufus Dawes (lieutenant colonel of the Sixth Wisconsin) later recalled that Marten didn't mention the death of Reynolds.[449] The remainder of the Iron Brigade dashed forward. On the opposite bank of Willoughby Run were the determined men of North Carolina, Alabama and Tennessee. Ferocious fighting took place as the equally determined Iron Brigade rushed down into the ravine and then up the other side to meet the men of the Twenty-sixth North Carolina, the Fifth and Thirteenth Alabama and the First, Seventh and Fourteenth Tennessee of General James Jay Archer and General James Johnston Pettigrew's brigades. To the northwest, Confederate Major General Henry Heth's Second Brigade of Virginians under Colonel John M. Brockenbrough and Mississippians and North Carolinians under the command of Brigadier General Joseph R. Davis, a nephew of Confederacy President Jefferson Davis, also pressed forward.

Across McPherson's green fields and down in the ravine men were shooting and dying. Men dressed in blue and gray bled red. Cannon on both sides spewed forth their deadly missiles and their projectiles knocked out all in their path. The troops surged forward. Life's scarlet liquid entered

Willoughby Run making July 1, 1863 a date to be carved on tombstones in faraway places.

Men of the South surged through the woods by the stream. Many were captured by men of the Second Wisconsin. Private Patrick Maloney, Company G of the Second Wisconsin, took matters into his own two fists and with a few more Wisconsin men, convinced Archer to join the other prisoners.[450]

Known as "Sally" while attending Princeton University, Archer, a native of Bel Air, Maryland, just north of Baltimore, had served in the Mexican War and received honors for his action at Chapultepec. An attorney, Archer returned to his legal practice after the Mexican War, but enlisted as a captain in the regular army's Ninth Infantry in 1855. When the Civil War began, Archer put his faith in the South and was promoted to brigadier general in 1862.[451] Along the waters of Willoughby Run, Archer refused to give his sword to a mere private, so it was turned over to Lieutenant Dennis Burke Dailey of the Second Wisconsin.

Not far away on Seminary Ridge and the ongoing battle, the Men of Iron loaded, fired and re-loaded again and again as they fought to hold their position, action was also taking place to the northwest across Chambersburg Pike. The men who had led Wadsworth's division, the Seventy-Sixth New York Infantry, were fighting to hold their position against more North Carolinians. The men had moved across the pike and the soon-to-be famous railroad cut. The wide, deep gash in the earth was the result of plans by abolitionist congressman and one-time Gettysburg resident and lawyer, Thaddeus Stevens who wanted rail transportation to his iron furnace a few miles to the west. Dubbed the "Tape Worm" Railroad because of its many twists and turns, it was not finished when scandal arose over its financing thirty years before it won its ever-lasting fame in the first day's battle.

With Meredith's Brigade on the south side of the Chambersburg Pike and Cutler's men on the right (north of the road), battle decisions continued to be made by Doubleday. Knowing the Eleventh and Third Corps were hurrying forward, Doubleday dismissed any thought of retreat. History has proven it was a gamble worth taking, but on July 1, it was a bet filled with hopes, uncertainty and luck. It wasn't long before Doubleday sent orders with staff officer Lieutenant Meredith Jones to Dawes again: "Move your regiment to the right."[452]

The Confederates poured fire on Hall's battery and Cutler's men. Major Harney of the 147th New York Infantry was trying to hold its position. As Harney tried to retreat, the enemy got behind him at the railroad cut. Within thirty minutes the regiment lost 207 of the 380 men who began the battle.[453] The air was filled with shouts, screams, shrieking cannon fire, whizzing bullets and the shrill whinnying sound of wounded horses. Doubleday and the men of the First Corps hung on. Doubleday sent his aide-de-camp with a message to General Daniel Sickles of the Third Corps near Emmitsburg, Maryland: "For God's sake come up with all speed."[454]

The Union army was not the only one moving forward. Lee's army was advancing too. Ewell was coming toward Gettysburg from the north and would eventually run into the right of the First Corps. All Doubleday could do was hope the rest of the army would hurry to the front. He quickly ordered the Sixth Wisconsin Infantry to advance. They and the men of the Ninety-fifth New York and the Fourteenth Brooklyn rushed to the railroad cut where they captured many Confederate troops.

General Oliver Otis Howard reached the field ahead of his Eleventh Corps prior to 11:30 a.m., according to his official report. Howard, a native of Maine, was known as a Bible-thumper. He sent his brother, General Charles H. Howard, to find Reynolds, not knowing what had happened. Charles found Doubleday near the seminary, in command of the First Corps and directing the troops. Doubleday gave Charles the sad news that Reynolds was dead. Doubleday told Charles to pass the news on to his brother that he (Otis) was now the commanding officer on the field.[455] According to Charles, his brother learned of Reynolds' death as he made his way down from his post of observation, the roof of the Fahenstock building. Howard was also seen on Cemetery Hill, located on the southeastern outskirts of Gettysburg, where he observed the action.[456]

When the Eleventh Corps arrived on the field, it took its position on the far right of the Federal line leaving a half-mile hole between its left and the Union right of bearded New Yorker John Cleveland Robinson. Robinson would wear the title of the hairiest man in the army and would eventually become lieutenant governor of his home state. That half-mile gap would soon be filled with Confederates leading to the right flank caving under Confederate pressure on Barlow's Knoll and contribute to losing the day. The Bible-thumper would issue damaging words regarding Doubleday and his troops. Whether or not it was deliberate is lost in the dust of history.

Several hours later, Howard sent a message to Meade stating he had assumed command of the First and Eleventh Corps and had sent messages to Slocum and Sickles to advance. He then made a statement that would haunt many good fighting men that day. "The First Corps fell back, when outflanked on its left, to a stronger position." In the same message Howard said Winfield Scott Hancock arrived at 4 p.m. His message was marked 5 p.m. on the first day.[457] Even more disturbing given the number of casualties in the First Corps that day was Hancock's message sent to Meade about half an hour after Howard sent his message. Hancock said he arrived about 4:30 p.m. and "found that our troops had given up the front of Gettysburg and the town." Hancock provides a brief description of the situation and closes with, "Howard says that Doubleday's command gave way," and states General Warren has arrived on the field.[458]

It was around noon as the men of the Iron Brigade were fighting to hold their lines; several of them saw what must have seemed a strange sight: An old man in a swallowtail coat carrying a rifle was headed toward them. At first the men laughed at the old man, but then after asking why he was in the midst of the fighting, the soldiers learned that John Burns had a bone with pick with the Confederates—they were responsible for possibly milking his cows and maybe even driven the cows into their own lines. Burns wanted revenge, according to one account.

Bullets were flying in all directions and the soldiers hunkered close to the ground. Burns stood behind a tree and began firing at the Confederates. In all the confusion and smoke of battle the men lost sight of Burns. Doubleday would later write:

> My thanks are specially due to a citizen of Gettysburg named John Burns, who, although over seventy years of age, shouldered his musket and offered his services to Colonel Wister, 150th Pennsylvania Volunteers. Colonel Wister advised him to fight in the woods, as there was more shelter there; but he preferred to join our line of skirmishers in the open fields. When the troops retired, he fought with the Iron Brigade (Meredith's). He was wounded in three places.[459]

As the Confederate army pushed the Federal lines back, the men moved through the streets and alleys of Gettysburg itself. Residents of the town had taken refuge by either fleeing or by hiding in their cellars. As the two armies flowed through the streets, confusion reigned. Doubleday was seen in the midst of the wounded and stragglers as he tried to learn more details of the action. He "rode rapidly back to the front. His horse was covered with foam and the flushed face of the General bespoke the tremendous strain under which he was laboring," said First Lieutenant L. A. Smith of the 136th New York Infantry.[460]

Men of the First Corps were forced to retreat. They scrambled through the narrow Gettysburg streets and alleyways trying to avoid Confederate fire. Several Union soldiers, including Dailey, had run inside the home of Mary McAllister on Chambersburg Street. McAllister would later write that the Irish lieutenant was furious at being in a situation where he could be easily captured. The bayonets of Confederates could be seen in the garden behind McAllister's home. Dailey was faced with few options—be killed or be captured. Finding a place to hide was near impossible without bringing more Confederates to the McAllister home in search of Union soldiers. What to do with Archer's sword? Dailey handed Archer's sword to McAllister for safe keeping and she hid it in the parlor wood box.[461] When the Confederates entered the house, Dailey was taken prisoner. Eventually his sword would be in the possession of George New, surgeon for the Second Wisconsin.[462]

Back on Seminary Ridge, the Confederates took over the grounds and buildings of the Lutheran Theological Seminary. Samuel Schmucker, seminary president, would later claim $1,753.90 in damages. Schmucker said more than 100 books, silver, clothing and other items were plundered by the Confederates. The federal government dismissed his claim for lack of proof.[463]

The men of the First and Eleventh Corps headed for Ever Green Cemetery on the rise on the southeastern side of town.[464] Howard had already set up his guns there. At the cemetery gatehouse, a pregnant Elizabeth Thorn watched helplessly as the soldiers took over the land where the dead were peacefully unaware of what was happening. Thorn's husband, the cemetery gatehouse keeper, was in the Union army in Maryland. It would soon be her job to bury the dead from the battle that would rage around her for the next two days.

Doubleday would later claim that Howard "did a good deal of damage to us (First Corps) at Gettysburg, but that is not generally known.' According to Doubleday, Howard had placed batteries of artillery on Cemetery Hill and was firing toward the retreating members of the First Corps as they tried to reach the very hill where Howard's batteries were.[465] Howard was most likely trying to fend off the Confederate advance, but some shells may have hit areas where retreating Union troops were passing through.

The armed men of the First and Eleventh Corps spent the night on what would forever be known as Cemetery Hill sleeping among the headstones. In an ironic twist, a sign on the cemetery's gatehouse specifically forbade guns.

By late afternoon, General Winfield Scott Hancock, a veteran of the Mexican War and an excellent soldier, arrived on the field. With him were orders from Meade placing him in command. The issue of rank was immediately brought up, for Howard outranked Hancock. Howard did not go quietly; he did not believe that Hancock was now in command. It took several hours to convince Howard that Hancock was following Meade's orders. Hancock began to assess the position of the Union army, the terrain, the number of men available, the number of men that would soon arrive and what options were developing if they were attacked again.

Meade's battle plans were in shambles. Before the armies clashed on the outskirts of Gettysburg, before the Union troops even reached Gettysburg, Meade issued a circular, commonly called the Pipe Creek Circular. The directive said that the Union army would "form a line of battle with the left resting" near Middleburg, and the right at Manchester, "the general direction being that of Pipe Creek." The communities were in Maryland, not Pennsylvania. The document described placement of the various corps and put the Second Corps "in the vicinity of Uniontown and Frizellburg, to be thrown to the point of the strongest attack." The corps at Emmitsburg (First and Eleventh, with the Third coming up behind them) were to be withdrawn and moved toward Middleburg. Events of the day had changed the plans. [466]

Even though he was only thirteen miles from the battlefield, Meade did not arrive at Gettysburg until the early hours of July 2. He looked like a man who had been handed the immense responsibility for the Army of the Potomac only three days earlier; a man whose plans to establish a battle line to the south had not taken place; a man who now found himself riding in the dark to a battlefield he had not chosen nor even viewed. In short, he was under a tremendous strain and it most likely showed on his face as he went up the steps and into the house of a widowed woman, Mrs. Lydia Leister, who had left in a hurry as shot and shell dropped too close. Seeing Meade at daylight, Colonel Thomas Rafferty of the Seventy-first New York Infantry said Meade "seemed utterly worn out and hollow-eyed. Anxiety and want of sleep were evidently telling upon him." [467] The next day would be one of waiting. Waiting for the troops to be moved into position. Waiting to see what Lee would do. Waiting to be shot at.

The remnants of the regiments, who had fought so hard to hold their ground the previous day before retreating through the town, were now separated. Men from one division of the First Corps, including the Seventy-sixth New York, found themselves on Culp's Hill east of Cemetery Hill and on the far right of the Union lines. To the far left, the line ended on Little Round Top, one of the two hills seen the first day of battle. Unknown to the Union soldiers, Lee had decided to hit the Union at both ends of its long line. Two more divisions of the First Corps were now placed at the base of Cemetery Hill under Doubleday's command. Continuing to the left were men of the Second, Third, and Fifth Corps. The Sixth Corps was positioned to the rear of Little Round Top. The first day had ended with the Confederates taking Gettysburg. As daylight was slipping over the mountains west of Gettysburg, men from the Green Mountains of Vermont reached the field to take their place. The Vermont men had also been under the command of Doubleday as the Third Brigade of his Third Division. The Vermont men had reached the battlefield the first day around 5 p.m. according to Colonel Francis V. Randall of the Thirteenth Vermont.[468] Corporal J. C. Williams of Company B, Fourteenth Vermont, proudly wrote that Doubleday "has denominated this the 'flying brigade' for its ability to make the forced march to the battlefield."[469] The Vermont men would be held in reserve, but not for long.

JULY 2

Early on the morning of July 2, General John Newton reported to Meade. When Newton left, the man who had been court-martialed as a sixteen-year old shortly after entering West Point with Doubleday, he was in command of the First Corps. Doubleday was returned to his former command, the Third Division of the First Corps. The day dragged on with each army aligning itself for what was certain to come. The waiting ended in the afternoon as the Confederates made their move. Dr. William W. Potter of the Fifty-seventh New York Infantry was near where many of the First Corps officers were getting ready to meet the enemy. Potter saw the Confederates begin to advance and heard Doubleday, who had been talking with Howard, to announce, "'There, general, go the enemy's batteries.'"[470] Shells and bullets flew across the fields of what had been quiet farmland. The Confederate plan was to force the collapse the Union line with attacks at the end of each flank; one at the Round Tops and the other at Culp's Hill.

Although the Union lines at each end proved strong, in the center, the Third Corps' Brigadier General Daniel Sickles changed his battle lines. Sickles was not a military man; he was a highly controversial politician from New York City. Before the war, Sickles had shot Phillip Barton Key (son of Francis Scott Key, the composer of the *Star Spangled Banner*) for having an affair with Mrs. Sickles. In the ensuing trial, Edwin M. Stanton defended Sickles using for the very first time an insanity plea. The defense was successful, and Sickles was saved from serving time in a jail cell. A few years later, Stanton became the secretary of war under Lincoln. Sickles had proved to be fearless on the field of battle at Antietam, Fredericksburg and Chancellorsville, eventually winning promotion to the command of the Third Corps. At Gettysburg he ordered his men to move forward into the Peach Orchard, thus creating a breach in the center line. Scholars have long debated Sickles' action. Did it hurt or help the Union? Meade had not ordered such a move, and by the time he was aware of the action, it was too late. The Confederates were attacking. No matter which argument you espouse, Sickles' action certainly slowed the Confederate advance.

The Union troops were firing, loading, firing again all along its line. Doubleday and the remainder of his men were not far from the Widow Leister's house where they assisted Hancock's Second Corps near the copse of trees that would see bloodier fighting the following day. It was late on July 1, the Vermont men, including William O. Doubleday, a private in Company H of the Fourteenth Vermont, arrived behind the Union lines. William was a distant cousin to Doubleday. It's possible, but not recorded, that Doubleday didn't know William was in the ranks. William would be wounded during the third day of the battle.

Doubleday's testimony to the Committee on the Conduct of War gave little detail of the second day's battle. He and his troops became "a part of Hancock's force sent to help him." Doubleday said he had received orders to "bring up this force with all haste to Hancock's assistance."[471] Doubleday said his men formed five lines and made a charge. The men fought hard and continued firing even after the charge had been halted, Doubleday stated in his testimony.

The cannons of Battery C, Fifth United States Regular Artillery had advanced toward the Rodgers House along the Emmitsburg Road. The guns, under the command of First Lieutenant Gulian Weir, had advanced to close to the Confederate lines. The fighting was sharp for Weir, one of sixteen children born to Doubleday's West Point professor of art Robert W. Weir. The artillerymen fired, loaded and fired again, but were unable to hold the ground. As the fighting became too hot, Weir began to retreat, but in doing so, left four guns behind. His horse had been killed as he was riding and Weir was wounded.

It wasn't long before a galloping horseman approached Col. Francis Randall of the Thirteenth Vermont. It was Doubleday who had just left Hancock's position. Could Randall and his men get the four cannons back? Randall wouldn't refuse the challenge, even when informed that the mission would be dangerous and the decision would be his alone. The men of Vermont advanced, even after Randall's horse had been shot from under him. The Vermont refused to give up. Using fences, the road and a ditch, they moved forward to take the guns. They also captured three Confederate officers with eighty men as they sought to move the guns back into Union lines. During his testimony to the Committee on the Conduct of War, Doubleday said this happened "about dusk" of the second day.

The mortification for was too much for the man who cut his teeth on West Point ideals and regulations. Weir committed suicide twenty-three years later. Losing the four cannon at Gettysburg may have played a part in Weir's final act. He is buried at his birthplace, West Point.

Other pieces of artillery were also brought back into Union lines following the ending of the second day's battle. "The One hundred and forty-ninth and One hundred and fiftieth [Pennsylvania] Regiments, under Captains Glenn and Jones, were here advanced some 600 yards, until they encountered the enemy's pickets, and in the morning rejoined the brigade, bringing with them two pieces of artillery and caissons recovered from the field."[472] These soldiers had waited at the front all night and the following morning, the Confederates shot at them as they brought the prized artillery weapons back to Union lines.

That night, Meade held a council of war at the Widow Leister's house. Nine generals went to the meeting. Doubleday was not one of them, but Newton and Howard were. There were three questions posed: Should the army stay or leave? If the army stayed, should it attack or wait to be attacked? And lastly, if the Union army should go on the attack, when? They took a poll and when the council closed, Meade's generals decided to stay on the battlefield, without making an attack the next day but rather to wait for an attack. There was no clear decision to attack if the Confederates did not. As it turned out, it was a decision that would not be needed.

Endnotes

439   OR, Vol. 27, (1): 926-930

440   OR, Vol. 27, (1): 646

441   Smith, 236-237

442   Rufus Dawes, Bandy and Freeland, Vol. 1, 214

443   Rufus Dawes, 1888, Sixth Wisconsin Folder, GNMP

444   Jacob Slagle, letter dated Sept. 13, 1863, GNMP

445   Abner Doubleday papers, Henry T. Lee to Samuel P. Bates letter, Feb. 6, 1871, Robert L. Brake Collection, USAMHI

446   *The National Tribune*, Apr.14, 1910

447   Smith, 131

448   Gen. Martin D. Hardin, "Gettysburg Not a Surprise to the Union Commander," War Papers Read to the Commandery of the State of Illinois, Military Order of the Loyal Legion of the Unites States (hereafter MOLLUS), Vol. 5, Chicago: Cozzens & Benton Co. 1907.

449   Rufus Dawes, Robert L. Brake Collection, USAMHI

450   For more information about Archer and Doubleday, see the appendix.

451   Faust, 21-22

452   Rufus S. Dawes, "Service with the Sixth Wisconsin," Robert L. Brake Collection, USAMHI

453   OR, Vol. 27, (1): 245

454   OR, Vol. 27, (1): 129

455   Charles H. Howard, *The First Day at Gettysburg*, War Papers Read to the Commandery of the State of Illinois, MOLLUS, Vol. IV, pg. 314

456   Gen. Charles H. Howard, "The First Day at Gettysburg," Bandy and Freeland, Vol. I, 314

457   OR, Vol. 27, (1): 696

458   OR, Vol. 27, (1): 366

459   *Battles and Leaders,* Vol. 3, p. 276

460   L. A. Smith, Bandy and Freeland, Vol. 1, 342

461   Mary McAllister, diary, Adams County Historical Society, Gettysburg, PA; letter of Dailey, Mar. 24, 1890, GNMP

462   George New letter, Mar. 24, 1891, Batchelder papers, GNMP

463   Samuel Schmucker, Office of the Quartermaster General, Claims Branch, Book 214, Claim 719, RG 92, NARA

464   It was later that the cemetery name was changed to Evergreen.

465   Abner Doubleday to George B. Lincoln, Nov. 30, 1886, Dickinson College library, Carlisle, PA

466 OR, Vol. 27, (3): 458-459

467 Bandy and Freeland, Vol. 2, 543

468 OR, Vol. 27, 351

469 J. C. Williams, *Life in Camp*, (Claremont, NH: Claremont Manufacturing Corp., 1864), 139

470 John M. Priest, *One Surgeon's Private War: Dr. William W. Potter of the 57th New York*, (Shippensburg, PA: White Mane Publishing Co.), 1996, 72-73

471 CCW, Vol. 1, 309

472 OR, Vol. 27, 336

CHAPTER 22

"At least 125 guns"

Doubleday shook out his saddle blanket from where he had slept on the ground overnight and rose for another day sure to be filled with fighting. The night faded into gray, then gold and finally the blue skies of dawn. The sun rose revealing in its soft morning light the horrors of the previous day. The black night had not been silent; neither was morning. Men on the battlefield were moaning, calling for water, for home, for family, for their God.

As the first light pushed the cloak of darkness aside, it left the battlefield naked exposing the flattened crops, bodies of bloating horses and men, and the soldiers who needed medical attention, yet there was little time for attending to the dead and dying. Lee had hit both Union flanks the day before. Would he try the middle? Troop positions were changed and Union troops were concentrated along Cemetery Ridge all the way to the Round Tops.

As the day dragged on, a short distance across and behind fields and woods, the Confederates moved into position, the mid-afternoon sun shining on their backs. After a relatively quiet morning, the opening gun of the Confederate army belched forth ball and smoke. It was *the* signal all had been waiting for. The signal cannon was quickly joined by "at least 125 guns," testified Doubleday.[473] Doubleday's men scrambled behind rocks, trees, and fences. Horses were killed including two of Doubleday's mounts, and caissons were blown up.[474] The ill-fated charge, attributed to Virginian, General George Pickett, was underway. Confederate troops three to five lines deep advanced across the fields toward a clump of trees and a rock wall used to keep livestock in place.

The constant thundering, booming of cannon was described: "[It was the] most terrific cannonading I have ever heard, General Doubleday, an old artillery officer says he never before heard anything like it."[475] The cannon firing continued for an hour and a half.

Doubleday later told congressional committee members that Confederate lines were formed with wings in an attempt to prevent flanking fire. "The wing apparently did not understand the movement, but kept straight on," said Doubleday. This created a gap between the wing and the main battle line. It was this error that allowed the Vermont men to inflict a deadly, flanking fire into the Confederate troops as they neared the small copse of trees near a stone fence.

The cannon fire from the guns of the two armies sliced through the air and into the bodies of men who, if they survived, would never forget the sounds and sights before their eyes.

The Union soldiers peered across the fields toward the woods to the west. They soon saw a long, long line of Confederate gray emerge, the light glinting off their rifles and sabers, as they began their across the open fields, down the low swales and then over the slight rises where the ground undulates. Doubleday's men could see the troops of Pickett, Pettigrew and Trimble were heading right for them. Halstead suggested that reinforcements were needed. "Every general on the ridge can see where we are and will send whatever troops can be spared," Doubleday answered.[476] It wasn't long before the prediction was fulfilled.

The Vermont men proved their mettle that day, as even the Confederates admitted.[477] The persistent men of Vermont were green as grass when they were assigned to Doubleday only the day before. As Lieutenant Colonel Charles Cummings put it, "Doubleday knew we were green 9 months men . . . said he would risk it."[478] They could march and do picket duty, but that was their only qualifications as they marched to Gettysburg. On July 3rd, they conducted themselves as well as any battle-hardened soldier on the field.

The Vermonters moved forward, changed direction, moved again and repeated the maneuver a third time. Each time they advanced closer to the stone wall that ran along Cemetery Ridge, separating the fields a short walk from Emmitsburg Road. The maneuvers placed the Vermonters where they could fire into the flanks of the Confederates. The men were like old veterans, said newspaper accounts, and the Vermont men were praised by Doubleday, "The Major-General commanding the division desires to return his thanks to the Vermont brigade," including the 151st Pennsylvania, and Twentieth New York Militia, "for their gallant conduct in resisting the front line the main attack of the enemy upon this position, after sustaining terrific fire," of the Confederate artillery.[479]

Twenty-five years later Doubleday was invited to a reunion of the Fourteenth Vermont Infantry, but declined saying that he had received so many similar invitations that he was concerned that by accepting one over the other, it would not be fair to any of the troops he led at Gettysburg.

A short article by Doubleday stated: "yet I acknowledge that none have higher claims on me than the Vermont Brigade."[480] However, that was in the future.

The attack ended, the Confederates returned across the fields they had just advanced through, stumbling over the wounded, dead and dying who had stood shoulder to shoulder just minutes before.

Doubleday, still on horseback, began to get reports from his batteries and regiments very quickly after the firing had ceased. He sent men out with stretchers to pick up the wounded. The enemy was still firing and Doubleday believed the stretcher-bearers were the target. Doubleday, still mounted in a group of officers including Newton, the corps and division staff members, was hit by a shell fragment that had passed through his hat. The shell wounded one of Doubleday's staff officers, Lieutenant Cowdry. Doubleday was not seriously injured.[481] The shell piece stopped in the velvet coat collar that had been folded over to double its usual thickness. The force of the blow knocked Doubleday over the neck of his horse and on the ground. He even thought he'd been killed. He put a hand up to his head, to make sure he still had one. Once he got up, he walked around and lay back down as he tried to cope with being hit. Doubleday said the jagged edge of the shell piece landed away from his neck, otherwise he would have been seriously wounded or killed. He did experience headaches, but no permanent damage. The fragment tore a hole in his hat; a hat that is among his artifacts at Gettysburg National Military Park. Later Mary had the shell fragment mounted as a paper weight. Even though he was certainly shaken, he did not leave the field or his troops.[482] In an example of confusing events creating inaccurate reporting, the New York Times reported three days later, that Doubleday was "dangerously wounded."[483]

No stranger to the violence of the battlefield or being in danger, Doubleday had been talking with General Rowley, when a shell hit and killed Rowley's horse while Rowley was holding the bridle.[484] Rowley would later describe Doubleday on the first day: "He handles his troops under fire with the same composure he would exhibit at a review or parade." In Rowley's opinion Doubleday was "a man of unquestioned bravery, cool and clear sighted on the battlefield." That was high praise from a subordinate officer.[485]

After the battle had ended, men wandered about looking for their regiments. Captain John D.S. Cook located his unit, the Eightieth New York Infantry. His fellow soldiers were hungry. Cook went to the colonel who said requests for food had been sent to Doubleday. The colonel sent Cook to check on the request. On the way, Cook stopped to talk with a man in civilian clothes riding on a horse. Cook's interest intensified when he saw what the man held—an oversized slice of bread slathered with butter. "Do you have any more?" asked Cook.

The man reached into his saddlebag and pulled out another slice and a huge onion. He handed the food to Cook. Bread in one hand, onion in the other, Cook took a bite of each as he continued his search for Doubleday. Cook was still eating when he found him.

Doubleday was making himself a bed where two lines of a fence formed a corner, probably near the Pry farm. Cook noticed a bandage around Doubleday's neck, making Doubleday appear as a man of the cloth. Cook attempted a salute even though his hand full of bread and butter. Cook was tempted to take a bite as the hand moved upward, resisted, but could not resist as his hand was lowered. "Sir, I've been sent to inquire about food for the men."

Doubleday chuckled, "Well captain, you seem to have a supply."

Following a short conversation about the events of the day, Doubleday sent Cook on his way with the message that rations would arrive by morning.[486]

Later the same day, Doubleday requested a corps command. The death of Reynolds left an opening and as Doubleday put it, "I think myself entitled by my rank."[487] His request would not be granted and although he did not know it at the time, the battle of Gettysburg would become his last action on a battlefield during the Civil War.

The sun vanished and the guns of Gettysburg were silent; men and officers waited, wondering if there would be a battle in the morning. When daylight came, the Confederate army had left, the sky loosened its rains and the battle guns were, for the most part, silent; but the unending battle of words would begin all too soon.

Thirty years later and long after the carnage had disappeared; Doubleday visited the Gettysburg battlefield again. It wasn't what he expected: "I had formed the idea that it was covered with monumental abortions, and was agreeably surprised to see so many beautiful and attractive memorial structures." And the ground had not lost its familiarity.[488] The visit gave Butterfield time to observe Doubleday on the field he had commanded: "Doubleday's strength was sorely tested, invalid as his is, in the severe ascent to the cupola of the seminary. His clear and lucid description of Buford's works and his own on the first day of the fight, before and after Reynolds' death, and his explanation of the splendid coup of Robinson, with

Wadsworth's and Fairchild's work, were interrupted and broken, but not impaired, by inability quickly to regain breath and strength after climbing such a height."[489] The memories of those three days must have flooded over Doubleday and his companions like a waterfall. However, that would be three decades later.

The day after the cannon thundered, the nation's Independence Day, more than an inch of rain fell from the skies[490] and the Army of Northern Virginia picked up its dead and wounded and left the field to the victorious Union Army. As the Confederates retreated over the South Mountain range, Doubleday fumed over the way he had been removed from command the first day by Meade. It would be a thorn in his side for years to come. He requested the date of Newton's rank only to discover that Newton was Doubleday's junior. The thorn went deeper. On the following day, Doubleday flat out refused to obey an order made by Newton. That refusal led Meade to send Doubleday to the adjutant general's office in the nation's capital. Doubleday had been relieved from command and his future remained unclear. "The pro-slavery clique at headquarters took advantage of the opportunity to injure me as much as possible," Doubleday said.[491]

Endnotes

[473] CCW, Vol. 1, 309

[474] Ibid

[475] Marshall, 167

[476] Abner Doubleday, Col. G. G. Benedict, "*A Short History of the 14th Vermont Regiment*," Bennington, VT: C. A. Pierce, 1887. 35, USAMHI

[477] CCW, Vol. 1, 310

[478] Marshall, 169

[479] *The New York Times*, July 9, 1863; *Boston Evening Transcript*, July 9, 1863

[480] Abner Doubleday, Col. G. G. Benedict, 79

[481] Abner Doubleday, *Reports of the Battles of Gettysburg, July 1st, 2nd, and 3d, 1863*, Walton's Steam Press, Montpelier, Vt., 1865, 19 This injury is not mentioned in Abner's Dec. 14, 1863 official report of the battle. However, in a rarely seen report dated Sept. 19, 1863, he mentions the injury.

[482] David & Audrey Ladd, ed., *The Batchelder Papers*, (Ohio: Morningside, 1994), Vol. II, 1149-1151

[483] *New York Tribune*, July 6, 1863

[484] Jesse Bowman Young, *The Battle of Gettysburg*, (New York: Harper & Brothers Publishers, 1913), 50-51

[485] Theodore B. Gates, *The Ulster Guard*, (New York: Benjamin H. Tyrrel printer, 1879), 429

[486] Captain John D. S. Cook, *Personal Reminiscences of Gettysburg*, Dec. 12, 1903, 932-933, *War Talks in Kansas,* MOLLUS

[487] Abner Doubleday to Gen. Seth Williams, July 3, 1863, Generals' Papers, folder 1, RG 94, NARA

[488] Abner Doubleday, "Gettysburg Thirty Years After," *North American Review*, Feb. 1891

[489] Daniel Sickles, D. Gregg, John Newton, Daniel Butterfield, "*Further Recollections of Gettysburg*, North American Review, Mar. 1891

[490] Rev. Dr. H. E. Jacobs, "Meterology of the Battle," *Gettysburg Star and Sentinel*, Gettysburg, Pennsylvania, July 30, 1885

[491] Abner Doubleday, GR

CHAPTER 23

"What was just and right then is proper now"

On July 5 Doubleday, still on the muddy, horrific Gettysburg battlefield, wrote to Meade protesting the elevation of Newton who was a junior officer to Doubleday by four months. The same day Meade issued orders, "[Doubleday] is relived from duty with the army and will report for orders to the Adjutant General [in Washington]."[492] Once Doubleday reached the nation's capital, he picked up a pen and wrote a letter of protest to Lorenzo Thomas, Adjutant General of the United States Army:

> So far as I am concerned no fault whatever has been found, to my knowledge, with my military maneuvers or conduct on that occasion either by General Howard or General Meade. They both in conversation seem to have been satisfied that everything was done that could have been done. Before the result of the battle was known to General Meade he directed General Newton, who is my junior, to supersede, for no alleged fault or neglect that I can learn.

Doubleday goes on to say he believes that if:

> . . . . the principle of directing senior officers to obey their juniors, except by the President, under the instruction of the act of Congress, can not be established in the Army of the Potomac without resulting in the most violent discontent, disorder and even bloodshed . . . . The Army would no longer be a National Army but the property of an individual. When General Meade was a candidate for the command of the 5th Corps, he urged the same views with much earnestness . . . . What was just and right then is proper now.[493]

On the back of this remarkable letter, is an order for Doubleday to report to Buffalo where he would oversee the unpopular draft of eligible men for duty.

The three-day battle of Gettysburg had ended, but the war of words for history had just begun. This struggle for the written history included a desire for accuracy (from the participant's point of view), for glory (for posterity with sometimes less than accurate accounts—either intentional or unintentional), for personal honor (honor being a very important value of the day and could include promotions too) or revenge (in the guise of accuracy) and for political purposes (to sway citizens).

Doubleday, the son of a veteran of the War of 1812, the grandson of an American Revolutionary War soldier and grand-nephew of five more Revolutionary War soldiers, was now an angry general. He had done his duty and he had done it well. He had watched the men he commanded, determinedly and heroically, face the enemy, only to become wounded or killed. Now he had to deal with several issues: Why was his rank overlooked in favor of a junior officer? Why were his battered troops ignored? What would be his future? Would there be justice and honest recognition for his role at Gettysburg? Several pieces of correspondence, including the one above, provide us with insight.

On some level, Doubleday had to be glad to leave Gettysburg. With the stench, the insects, body parts lying everywhere he glanced, every building acting as a hospital, bodies of humans and horses lying all over; Gettysburg was as pleasant as a slaughter house in full swing.

In a July 11th letter Doubleday wrote to a friend on Wall Street in New York City: "You are right in your supposition that I have been treated badly." Doubleday asserts that Newton was, "a personal friend" of Meade. Doubleday states Newton was elevated to replace Doubleday's command position prior to July 2 and before Doubleday's version of events had even been heard by Meade.

Doubleday wrote his friend that he (Doubleday) had contacted Newton to determine who the ranking officer was at that moment. Discovering that he outranked Newton, Doubleday unwisely challenged Meade's orders and requested Meade to relieve him. Meade, who had no love for Doubleday, saw an opportunity to rid himself of Doubleday and took it. Doubleday was charged with not obeying the commands of Newton and taken out of action for the remainder of the war.[494] By this time it was very evident that Meade and Doubleday were on opposite sides of the abolition question. Personal politics affected their military decisions. *The Daily Courier* of Buffalo took note of Meade's politics by stating Meade was "highly conservative in his political opinions—his sympathies we think, being with the Douglas democracy."[495]

Doubleday's first written version of the events at Gettysburg was dated September 19, 1863. The report was barely three pages long in the Official Records of the War of the Rebellion and much of it was quotes from his own subordinate officers, General Stannard and Colonel Gates. Doubleday's report completely ignored the first day's battle. According to a document said to be the work of Doubleday's staff officer, Halstead:

> So great was Gen'l Meade's animosity to Gen'l Doubleday, founded on past political difference (that) he declined he would not mention his name in his report of the battle but would give the credit of all the success of the day to Gen'l. Reynolds. His first report to the War Department ignored Gen'l Doubleday entirely. He even went so far as to direct Gen's Newton to make a report of Gen'l Doubleday's operations and it was only after Gen'l N declined to do this that Gen'l Doubleday was allowed to make his own report. As all the sub-reports had been sent to Gen'l Newton, it was sometime before Gen'l D. could obtain copies.[496]

Meade's official report, written October 1, 1863, states: "In the early part of the action, success was on our side, Wadsworth's division, of the First Corps, having driven the enemy back some distance, capturing numerous prisoners, among them General Archer, of the Confederate army."

Meade continues to describe the action and noted the First and Eleventh Corps were pressed "so severely" that Howard called for a retreat. Meade only acknowledges Doubleday assuming command of the First Corps when Reynolds fell, giving credence to Halstead's notation.

Doubleday's September battle report was not accepted and a revised report was submitted in mid-December. However, Newton's report of September 30 begins by stating Doubleday's report about the actions of July 1 "are fully set forth." What report did Newton see? Was there another report by Doubleday that provided a more detailed description of the first day's battle? As of this writing, a report by Doubleday detailing the July 1 battle dated before September 19 has not been located, if it even still exists. Doubleday's two known reports were printed in Vermont in 1865. At the end of the small booklet is a handwritten note by Doubleday. The note states the report was printed through the Office of the Adjutant General of that state, "I have never been allowed to print it myself. A.D."[497]

Doubleday, as did many other Civil War participants, continued to write about the battle of Gettysburg for many years. The National Archives has his longest report on microfilm. The report is slightly more than 300 pages long, but contrary to popular thought, the report is not solely about the fighting at Gettysburg. The report encompasses all the Civil War battles Doubleday participated in.

Doubleday was not the only general to be upset by Meade. Major General O. O. Howard himself, complained to the commanding general on July 1. Howard had already been criticized for the actions of his troops at Chancellorsville, so he was understandably sensitive. Howard had read the order for Hancock to assume command. By then Howard had turned the command over to General Henry Slocum. Howard's message to Meade reads:

> I believe I have handled these two corps (First and Eleventh) to-day from a little past 11 until 4, when General H. assisted me in carrying out orders which I had already issued, as well as any of your corps commanders could have done. Had we received re-enforcements a little sooner, the first position assumed by General Reynolds, and held by General Doubleday till my corps came up, might have been maintained . . . ." Howard continues by saying "The above has mortified and will disgrace me.[498]

Howard was not alone in his mortification. Robinson read Meade's October 1 battle report, and mulled it over for a month before he responded. Robinson wrote Meade: "I feel it is my duty to inform you of the intense mortification and disappointment felt by my division in reading your report of the battle of Gettysburg." Robinson stated his men had battled for four hours on July 1, and he lost about half his men in the hotly contested action. "We have been proud of our efforts on that day, and hoped that they would be recognized. It is but natural we should feel disappointed that we are not once referred to in the report of the commanding general."[499]

While the embattled generals expressed their dismay regarding Meade's summary report, the citizens of Gettysburg were left with the effects of the three days' battle that had resulted in the death and wounding of approximately 51,000 for both sides combined. The small community found itself as one gigantic hospital; every house, barn or outbuilding was being used to hold the wounded. Crops and vegetable gardens to provide food for the coming winter had been destroyed. Its citizens cared for the wounded as they cleaned up after the two armies and tried to get their own lives back to some semblance of normalcy.

At the White House, Lincoln anguished over the losses and the fact that Meade had let Lee escape. Lee and the Confederate Army of Northern Virginia had been within Meade's grasp, but slipped away. After three days of intensive fighting, Meade believed he did not have enough men to stop Lee. Lee's retreat was comprised of those still standing and a twenty-six mile long ambulance wagon train over the mountains to Virginia soil on the south side of the Potomac.

Life went on for Doubleday and Mary even though he was no longer on a battlefield. Draft riots broke out and it appeared as though Doubleday would be ordered to a possible riot site in Buffalo, New York.[500] Once Doubleday arrived there, and though he was not officially on duty, he sent a letter to Colonel J. B. Fray, of the Provost Marshall General's Office back in Washington. Buffalo citizens appealed to Doubleday to request a light battery to deter any riots that could break out. Rumors claimed a group of armed Canadians had arrived in the city on behalf of the secessionists, wrote Doubleday. About 7,000 members of trade groups also opposed the draft.[501] The rumors persisted, but soon ran out of steam as the days went by without the type of riots seen in New York City. By early August, Doubleday was in New York City where he was honored with a dinner at Delmonico's restaurant. The event featured speeches by William Cullen Bryant and Horace Greeley.[502]

Not long after, the *Boston Evening Transcript* featured a brief biography of Meade:

"He is a member of the Protestant Episcopal Church, and his family holds a pew, where it has long been held in regular attendance, in St. Mark's Church. General Meade's relations in life, as regards politics, have ever been Whig. His family were all Whigs, and though opposed to the anti-slavery agitation before the war broke out, the General has since become an earnest supporter of the whole war policy of the national Administration, like Burnside, Grant, Rosecrans and other conservatives."

Doubleday continued his stay in New York City, where Colonel Gates saw Doubleday at the Astor House. Gates he had been recommended for a promotion, Doubleday told him.[503] However, Doubleday's stay in the city ended by late August. The sounds of the city were replaced with the quiet of Vermont mountains as Doubleday and his wife, Mary, accompanied Mary Todd Lincoln to Manchester to escape the summer heat of the city.[504] They enjoyed the hospitality of the Equinox House, not far from the site where many years later Robert Lincoln would build his home, Hildene.

While in Vermont, Mary Lincoln received a telegram from her husband: "The Secretary of War tells me he had telegraphed Gen. Doubleday to await further orders. We are all well, and have nothing new." The telegram baffled historians for years as the presence of the Doubledays was unknown. Two weeks later Mrs. Lincoln and the Doubledays left Manchester, but not before Doubleday was serenaded by the musical citizens of Manchester. As he thanked them, he told them that he believed the Confederacy was on its knees. [505]

They returned to Washington where Doubleday continued in a military limbo. Unassigned and with time on his hands, Doubleday certainly must have chaffed without orders. He was used to being in action on a battlefield, not seated in a parlor. The days slid by as green leaves put on their autumn colors and still no orders arrived.

In chilly November, Doubleday returned to Gettysburg by train through Harrisburg. Four months had gone by since the three-day battle and a new national cemetery was to be dedicated. The dedication would take place November 19, although burials were still taking place daily with only about a third of the graves finalized. This time Doubleday was part of a Union Army contingent that was honoring the men who had fallen and would forever rest in the new cemetery. A parade was formed with military representatives at the front, so it is likely that Doubleday was in this group as it marched down Baltimore Street toward the new cemetery. There he would take his place among the dignitaries on a wooden platform. Noted orator Edward Everett spoke, in the fashion of the day, for several hours. As Everett sat down, another speaker walked to the front of the raised platform that had been constructed specifically for the day. President Abraham Lincoln pulled out one or two pieces of paper with less than 300 words total and gave his speech. Lincoln's speech was so short that it caught the audience off guard; they could not believe it had ended. However, those few words changed the focus of the war and echoed long after he settled back in his seat. The hallowed ground had been consecrated.

The following month, one of the heroes of the Gettysburg battle was laid to rest in another cemetery. Doubleday bade farewell to a fellow officer. John Buford had died at the home of fellow cavalryman General George Stoneman in Washington, D.C. Stoneman had allowed the ill Buford to stay at the Stoneman home on Pennsylvania Avenue. Clement H. Barclay notified Lincoln that Buford was dying. The life and death drama in the

Stoneman home only increased as Barclay whispered into the ear of the dying man that Lincoln made Buford a major general that very day as a tribute to the thirty-seven year old soldier and West Pointer. Doubleday along with generals Silas Casey, Samuel P. Heintzelman, Daniel E. Sickles, John M. Schofield, Winfield S. Hancock, Christopher C. Augur, and Gouverneur K. Warren were named as pallbearers. Buford's body remained in the Stoneman home before his church funeral and West Point burial that would later be marked by a tall monument with several three-dimensional eagles carved in stone.[506]

Eighteen hundred and sixty-three had been a tough year; another year of life-changing battles. Surely, Lincoln, Doubleday and the nation were thinking about what the war in 1864 would bring.

Endnotes

492   Meade to Doubleday, Headquarters of the Army of the Potomac, M619 Letters Received by the Office of the Adjutant General (Main Series) 1861-1870, Roll 169, RG 94, NARA

493   Abner Doubleday to Lorenzo Thomas, July 8, 1863, Letters Received by the Office of the Adjutant General of the U.S. Army, M619, Roll 169, 432-437, RG 393, NARA

494   Abner Doubleday to A. Z. Huggins, July 11, 1863, Columbia University, NYC

495   *The Daily Courier*, (Buffalo), July 20, 1863

496   James W. Wadsworth papers, Wadsworth Family Papers, Feb.-July 1863, GNMP. This statement is attributed to Abner's staff officer E.P. Halstead.

497   Abner Doubleday, *Reports of the Battles of Gettysburg*, Walton's Steam Press, Montpelier, 1865

498   OR, Vol. 27, (1): 696-697

499   OR, Vol. 27, (1): 291

500   *The Daily Courier*, Buffalo, NY, July 20, 1863

501   Abner Doubleday to J. B. Fry, July 24, 1863, O.R., Series III, Vol. 3, 566

502   *Boston Evening Transcript*, Aug. 5, 1863

503   Osborne, 101

504   *The Manchester Journal*, Sept. 1, 1863

505   Long, 205; *The Manchester Journal*, Sept. 8, 1863

506   *The Evening Star*, (Washington, D.C.), Dec. 17, 19, 1863

CHAPTER 24

"It is inexplicable to me"

Doubleday strode across the Congressional Committee room and took the witness stand. Ohio Senator Benjamin Wade, chairman of the Joint Committee on the Conduct of War began, "You were with the army of the Potomac when the battle of Gettysburg was fought?"

"Yes, sir," Doubleday said.

Wade continued, "Give the committee an account of that battle in your own way."

Doubleday spoke clearly as he told committee members about the arrival of his troops at Marsh Creek, just a few miles south of Gettysburg, on June 30, 1863. Doubleday recounted conversations with Reynolds and the march to the small town. Doubleday described the unfolding of the action, the orders he gave, the placement of troops and the messages sent and received. He continued to relate the events of July 2 and 3.

Wade probed for more information by asking questions regarding the actions of other officers, including Meade. When Doubleday took the stand to testify, he was a general who was still angry with his commander, with good reason. Doubleday had come to the conclusion he had been unfairly removed from his command by Meade.

Doubleday told the committee the evening before the first day's action Meade had issued the Pipe Creek Circular regarding the massing of the Confederates around Gettysburg. Meade said the army should stay where it was, until the Confederates showed their hand, according to Doubleday describing the correspondence. "This was very much like saying that he would give us orders after the battle was fought, for he had already stated the intention of the enemy to be to take Gettysburg." said Doubleday.

Then he presented some startling news:

> During this time General Meade was at Taneytown, some ten
> or twelve miles off, engaged in laying out a very long line of
> battle—I should judge ten miles long at least—from Taneytown
> to Manchester along Pipe Creek. He seemed to have determined

that the battle should take place there. It is inexplicable to me that he could hear the thunder of that battle all day without riding up to see something in relation to it, as he could have come up in an hour.

If Meade had ridden to the battlefield sooner, said Doubleday, Meade could have sent in two more corps to reinforce those already on the field. (Doubleday was referring to the Third Corps under General Daniel E. Sickles and the Twelfth Corps under General Henry W. Slocum.) According to Doubleday, Meade replaced him with Newton (a junior officer) without a single question asked regarding the events of the first day's action.

As Doubleday described events, Meade, not surprisingly, was placed in an unfavorable light. When asked why he and Howard had been removed from command by Meade, Doubleday said:

> I think General Meade thought a couple of scapegoats were necessary; in case the next day's battle turned out unfavorably, he wished to mark his disapprobation of the first day's fight. General Meade is in the habit of violating the organic law of the army to place his personal friends in power. There has always been a great deal of favoritism in the army of the Potomac. No man who is an anti-slavery man or an anti-McClellan man can expect decent treatment in that army as at present constituted.[507]

Doubleday's appearance before the committee came three months after Buford's death and was followed by the arrival of the long-awaited orders. Doubleday would sit as president in a series of special military commissions and charged with overseeing a variety of legal matters. He no longer had a full staff; only his two trustworthy aides, Marten and Lee, the men who had been with Doubleday since late winter of 1862.

We get a look at another court room; one presided over by Doubleday in 1864, as he served as a participant in the special commission court proceedings. The court room became the last stop of a daily parade of people committing infractions and being involved in illegal activities. The following are a sampling of crimes that were endlessly repeated, only the names of the accused changed.

The previous August, H. G. Coburn, a former sutler for the Twentieth Maine Infantry was charged with "unlawfully proceeding to the front without a pass." Coburn apparently tried to impersonate a man known only as Knox, of that illustrious regiment. A. K. Mathews, another sutler of that same regiment, somehow got his hands on the pass and gave it to Coburn. Both Coburn and Mathews were found guilty and fined $200 each. They would be confined to prison until the fines were paid.

In other cases, men and women were found guilty of obtaining civilian clothing for soldiers who planned to desert. Rebecca Smith of "No. 540 12th Street, Washington, D.C." was not content with buying one suit of civilian clothes, but purchased three! She was pronounced guilty and given a six-month prison sentence.

Then there was Addison F. Brown, a citizen of Georgetown in the District of Columbia. In July 1864, "while the enemy were invading the District of Columbia," (referring to the battle at the Monocacy River north of the capital city) Brown hollered to the passing Union soldiers that he hoped that none of them would survive. Brown was charged with violation of the oath of allegiance. Doubleday and his fellow commissioners sentenced Brown to five years of hard labor off the coast of Florida in the Dry Tortugas.

Among the many cases Doubleday heard, was the somewhat unusual case involving Gorvin James whom history only records as a colored man. Gorvin was accused of recruiting men in the nation's capital, hiding them in a baggage car and sending them to New Jersey. Once the new recruits reached New Jersey they were to serve as substitutes to fill the state's quota of soldiers. Gorvin was found not guilty and released.[508]

At that time Doubleday and his wife, were most likely staying at The Willard Hotel, in essence, the "headquarters" for many of the Northern officers who were on duty in and around the nation's capital. Colonel Theodore B. Gates, of the Twentieth New York State Militia, sometimes called the Eightieth New York Infantry, would note in his diary several sightings of Doubleday at the famous place of lodging.

Living in the city meant there were social events to enjoy. One such event took place at the White House on March 12, 1864. Lincoln invited several of his generals to dinner. Among the guests were Doubleday, George Gordon Meade, John E. Wool (retired), David Hunter, and Daniel Edgar Sickles. With the animosity between Doubleday and Meade, it must have been a somewhat strained gathering for the two men. While information about the dinner is scarce, we can only hope that Doubleday sat next to Hunter, who shared Doubleday's views on slavery.[509] It had only been eleven days since Doubleday had slammed his former commander, Meade, in testimony at the Joint Committee on the Conduct of War.[510] Considering Doubleday's testimony wasn't flattering to Meade, dinner conversation must have been interesting.

Doubleday served on the commission for nearly a year, when he was promoted as colonel of the Seventeenth United States Infantry. The Civil War dragged on with Doubleday sidelined. In July, Lincoln called for more troops. General William T. Sherman was marching on Atlanta. The tide was turning, but it was a long, slow, painful change. By the following spring, people sensed the war was coming to the end. A ship was headed to Fort Sumter and Doubleday was on board. He and many others were marking the anniversary of Sumter's fall with a ceremony to restore the Union flag to its former place of honor above the fort. William Lloyd Garrison was one of many guests for the occasion. Garrison's letter home mentioned many of those attending including Rev. Henry Ward Beecher. At one point, "three thousand colored people" greeted the famous.[511] It was a congenial group, according to Garrison.

While Doubleday was participating in the events at Fort Sumter, back in the nation's capital, knowing the war was winding down, the president decided to go to the theater. "Our American Cousin" was playing at Ford's Theater. Part way through the play, Southern sympathizer John Wilkes Booth crept up the back stairway, entered the president's box and shot Lincoln. Lincoln died the next morning. There was hardly a family in the country that did not experience some type of loss in the war. Now, the Union as a whole was in shock and grieving.

Doubleday's career took another turn. He was assigned to the Freedman's Bureau in Texas. The Freedman's Bureau was created by Congress in March 1865. Its purpose was to provide humanitarian aid to newly freed African Americans and refugees following the war. The bureau assisted with clothing, medicine, legal assistance, and education. It took control over lands that had been confiscated or owned by the Confederate states. It was headed up by none other than General Oliver Otis Howard, the former commander of the Eleventh Corps.

Doubleday was kept busy with the many claims that crossed his desk. Most cases were small; not even worth the cost of an attorney, Doubleday said.[512] In another bit of correspondence, we see the results of racial hatred. Doubleday wrote Lieutenant Manning at Waco, Texas and requested a copy of a newspaper containing a particularly disturbing notice about two doctors that were in prison for castrating a freed boy.[513]

Endnotes

[507] CCW, 305-311

[508] United States Army, General Court Martial Orders, War Department, Vol. 5, 1864, USAMHI

[509] Both the *Washington Chronicle* and other Washington newspapers printed the guest list on March 15 and March 14, respectively. David Hunter issued the infamous order to abolish slavery in the Department of the South in March 1862. Lincoln immediately repudiated the order. Hunter would order the burning of Virginia Military Institute in June 11, 1864 and presided at the court martial of General John Fitz Porter and later the trial of the Lincoln conspirators. Controversial would be an apt description of Hunter.

[510] William Lloyd Garrison, Walter McIntosh Merrill, and Louis Ruchames, *The letters of William Lloyd Garrison*, (Cambridge: Belknap Press of Harvard University Press., 1971), Vol. 5: 266,269

[511] Abner Doubleday letter, Mar. 1, 1864, and Feb. 11, 1867, letters sent, Bureau of Refugees, Freedman and Abandoned Lands, Galveston, Texas, NARA

CHAPTER 25

"Another Hero Gone"

One of life's basic truths is that if you live long enough, you will see family and friends die. In 1866, Doubleday's father, at age seventy-four, died in Belvidere, Illinois. The old printer had developed pneumonia. He was laid to rest next to Hester at the Old City Cemetery in Bloomington, Illinois.[514] Notice of his death even appeared in the *New York Times* a few weeks later. At that time, Doubleday was on recruiting duty at Hart Island, New York, but news accounts do not provide us with a listing of those who attended, so we can only speculate that Doubleday was there.

After serving with the Freedman's Bureau, new orders arrived for Doubleday—he was off to San Francisco for recruiting duty. While there, Doubleday added his name to a document that has been the subject of some confusion over the years. Doubleday signed his name to sponsor a cable car company. This does not automatically translate to Doubleday inventing the cable car, as has been suggested. Doubleday was friends with the other men who were starting a business.[515] The documents were signed and the Clay Street Hill Railroad was born. Unfortunately, records have not been located to tell us if Doubleday took an active role in the railroad, but with his military duties it is likely he did not.

Doubleday's next assignment was, for two years, as commander of Buffalo Soldiers in west Texas; his last post in a long career. There he faced Indian attacks, an unforgiving landscape, and those who were seeking a new life in a new region. When he and Mary finally built a home, it was in Mendham, New Jersey—not too close to New York City, but close enough for a visit. As he grew older, like most people, his health declined. In August 1891, *The Kansas City Star* took note with an announcement that Doubleday was "dangerously ill" but did not give any details.[516]

Always seeking new information, Doubleday became involved with Theosophy—"Divine Wisdom." It combined the spiritual with a new way of viewing the universe and the people in it. Theosophy was founded by Helena P. Blavatsky. At one point when Blavatsky was out of the country, the reins of the Theosophy Society were handed over to Doubleday for safe keeping. His interest in Theosophy prompted him to study Sanskrit.

Doubleday made time to write letters; many were about his role at Gettysburg. He not only answered letters, but wrote many public works about the Civil War. He began to write his memoirs, but they were not published for many years.

In the fall of 1887, Doubleday said another farewell to a former colleague. Colorful "Fightin' Joe" Hooker died. Members of the old First United States Artillery gathered in New York City for a brief trip to Garden City, Long Island. The news of Hooker's passing was something of a shock. Hooker had not been ill and only days before had written a letter that found its way into the *New York Times*. Those attending the funeral service included Daniel Butterfield, Samuel Wylie Crawford, John Newton and Winfield S. Hancock as well as John Jacob Astor and Charles L. Tiffany. Just a few days later, the country said goodbye to Senator Zachariah Chandler, the man who had been so influential on the Joint Committee on the Conduct of War. On September 22, 1887, Doubleday's old friend James Ricketts died and was buried on the grounds of Confederate General Robert E. Lee's old home, Arlington House, at Arlington Cemetery.

As the years went by, Doubleday's health declined. He visited Gettysburg at least once, but turned down many invitations because of his age and health. He had Bright's disease, a disease of the kidneys that kept the former very active army general house-bound. Though he had been retired for many years, at least one of his former colleagues reached out to Doubleday. In a letter from a captain of the Twenty-fourth United States Infantry, the writer acknowledged the degree of seriousness of Doubleday's illness and said, "I sincerely trust and hope you will soon be entirely restored to health and that your life may be spared for many years . . . ."[517]

In January 1893, a doctor made his way frequently to the Doubleday home. On January 26, Mary, a minister, nurse and doctor gathered around the bed of seventy-four year old Doubleday and watched him breathe his last. Although he was not the picture of good health, the doctor had visited the day before and saw no indications death was twenty-four hours away, according to his hometown newspaper. Doubleday had seemed fine until about 5 p.m. when Dr. Begrood was summoned.

The following days must have been a blur to Mary. A funeral took place in Mendham, and then Doubleday's body was taken to New York City. There, Doubleday's body rested in an oak coffin and was given honor in the Governor's Room of City Hall in New York City. Thousands shuffled quietly past to pay their respects to the hero of Fort Sumter. Doubleday wore his major general uniform. White roses and a flag claimed to be the very flag that flew above Fort Sumter when the fighting began, were around the low catafalque. His sword and a small bouquet of violets were placed on the flag. Generals Joshua Lawrence Chamberlain, Francis Barlow and Phillip Sheridan were joined by other military men including Doubleday's long-time war aide, Marten They were all together again to say goodbye to the man they had served with for so long.

It was all too much for Mary who remained in Mendham following the private funeral. However, she did make the trip to Arlington Cemetery for the burial of her husband. They had been married forty-one years. Several relatives attended the public services, including Doubleday's brother Ulysses, his nephews Seth Ward Doubleday, James Stewart Doubleday, W.A. Eddy, Ulysses D. Eddy, H. J. Eddy and others. When at last the trip to Arlington began, Mary did not go alone. Doubleday's brother Ulysses, James, and Ulysses D. Eddy and T. A. Eddy kept her company. Major William L. Haskin, who wrote much of the history of the First United States Artillery, Doubleday's old regiment, and several other military men, also went with the family to the nation's capital. Doubleday's burial site is not far from the home of his old adversary, Robert E. Lee and his old friend, James Ricketts.

Eighteen days later, Doubleday's brother, Ulysses, died at his home in Asheville, North Carolina. Ulysses was sixty-nine. He became sick after Doubleday's burial and never recovered. Earlier that same day, he had learned that his son-in-law had died. One can only imagine how a family would deal with the loss of three family members in less than a month.

Doubleday's widow, Mary, later returned to the city of her youth, Washington, D.C. The woman who had followed Doubleday everywhere possible was acknowledged by the House of Representatives for her own contributions. She was awarded a pension; not only as Doubleday's widow, but for service she too, gave her country.

The wording of the 1896 document offers a rare view of Doubleday's wife:

> We find that after General Doubleday's retirement from the Army he lived very economically in the little village of Mendham, N.J., and devoted all his income above the amount necessary for his support to the providing of a policy of insurance in behalf of his widow; that shortly before his death the insurance company failed, and that his last hours were clouded with the fear that his widow would come to want.

We find that, independent of the notable services of her husband in behalf of the Union, she herself, during a long life as his companion upon the frontier and in campaign, rendered valuable service to the country. Particularly was the case in Florida wars, when she remained with her husband in the wilderness, and by her presence and influence over the soldiers associated in maintaining discipline and good order; also at Fort Sumter, when it was besieged and the garrison very small, she took her regular turn in relieving the guards and in keeping watch of the approach of the enemy, and also securing medical supplies from Charleston.

There in black and white it confirmed that Mary stood guard at Fort Sumter. She faced danger as much as any man in uniform at Sumter. The bill passed, and Mary would receive $100 a month.

The years slid by and Mary and Mrs. Ward Doubleday were among the 3,000 invited to a White House reception by Mrs. Theodore Roosevelt in February 1905. Two years later, Mary died suddenly of cardiac arrest at the Hotel Richmond in Washington, March 12, 1907. Her funeral was held at St. John's Church on Lafayette Square, just a few steps from the White House. Mary was laid to rest, next to her husband, in Arlington Cemetery. [518]

The Doubledays, Abner, Mary, Thomas, Ulysses, and their relatives including the six ancestors who stood firm during the American Revolution, contributed to the building of America. They had their weaknesses, but they used their strengths to the benefit of a growing nation.

Endnotes

[512] *Pantagraph,* Bloomington, Ill., March 13, 1866

[513] Benjamin Hassen Brooks, *Reminiscences of Hi Early Life; his father, Benjamin S. Brooks; life in California,* (Bancroft Library, University of California at Berkley,1925), 112

[514] *The Kansas City Star,* Kansas City, Kansas, August 5, 1891

[515] Writer's name is unreadable to Abner Doubleday, August 22, 1891, Abner Doubleday papers, Folder IV, National Baseball Hall of Fame, Cooperstown, NY

[516] "Reception at White House," *Washington Post,* February 16, 1905; Mary Doubleday death notice, *Washington Post,* March 14, 1907; also St. John's church records

[517] *Battles and Leaders of the Civil War;* Castle Publishing, Vol. III, p.285

APPENDIX

DOUBLEDAY AND THE MYTHS

For many years, the general public believed Doubleday invented baseball. In 1905 a commission was assembled with the intent of establishing the invention of American baseball, not as an evolution of the British game, Rounders. The commission was presided over by Abraham G. Mills, the fourth president of the National Baseball League.

As part of the search, the public, through a series of newspaper articles, was asked to submit their stories about the beginning of baseball. One response came from Abner Graves who claimed he and Abner Doubleday laid out the bases in the summer of 1839 in Cooperstown, New York. The unverified story was printed immediately.

Had the commission carefully reviewed the "facts" presented by Graves, they may have come to a different conclusion. We do know the following:

1) There were many Doubledays who lived in and around the Cooperstown area.

2) There was more than one Abner Doubleday. One, the subject of this biography, was a West Point cadet the summer of 1839 as the demerits in his records indicate. A cousin with the same name lived near Cooperstown, although this Abner Doubleday was only five years old in 1839.

3) Neither of the two Abners attended school in Cooperstown. In 1839, the man who became a general was already a cadet at West Point; the five year old lived in Richfield Springs, New York, about fifteen miles distant from Cooperstown and most likely attended school much closer to home.

Once the commission dissolved in 1907, Abner Doubleday's name was forever linked with the sport that became known as the National Past Time in America. Baseball was and remains a very popular sport although its origins are cloudy.

Another story that has been passed off for years as true, deals with Doubleday and Confederate General James Jay Archer when they "met" on the battlefield at Gettysburg.

Doubleday's staff officer, Eminel P. Halstead told the story of July 1, 1863 this way:

"General Archer and most of his brigade were captured early in the day by Meredith's 'Iron Brigade.' He evidently had expected an easy 'walk over,' judging from his disappointed manner after he was captured. A guard brought him back to General Doubleday, who, in a very cordial manner,—they having been cadets at West Point together,—said; 'Good morning, Archer! How are you? I'm glad to see you!'

"General Archer replied; 'Well, I am not glad to see you by a—sight!'"[519]

Like the baseball story, this incident has been written about so many times, it is taken for gospel.

However, a closer look at the records, reveal that Archer did not attend West Point with Doubleday. He went to Princeton University where he was known as "Sally." Halstead was not correct in his telling of the story. Perhaps, he was confused, or maybe he wanted to illustrate a friendship between the two men (real or imagined in a spirit of both sides coming together). Whatever the reason, it is a story that continues in the annals of Civil War history.

General Abner Doubleday's
Family Who Served in the Civil War

Author's Note: The following information was found in New York State Archives, The National Archives, regimental histories and other similar resources. Several men on Doubleday's staff came from the legal field. I have included their relationship, if known, to the subject of this book.

Abner D. (Demas) Doubleday (cousin, Civil War)

This Abner Doubleday had dark hair and eyes, stood 5' 10" and had a light complexion. In his private life, he was an accountant. He enlisted in Richfield, New York (not far from Cooperstown, New York) on December 16, 1863 and was mustered in January 11, 1864 with the Second New York Heavy Artillery. He served in companies D and L. He was discharged for disability with asthma/sunstroke January 20, 1865. He also suffered a disease of left lung according to his military records. His father was Demas Abner Doubleday.

Stephen Ward Doubleday (nephew, son of Thomas, Civil War)

A physical description has not been located at this time. Stephen Ward Doubleday was the son of Thomas, and nephew of General Abner Doubleday. He was eighteen when he enlisted on September 21, 1862 in Washington for three years with the Fourth New York Heavy Artillery. He received his commission as a second lieutenant of Company B October 30, 1862. He eventually transferred to Company D for promotion as First Lieutenant January 21, 1864. Stephen was discharged October 14, 1864 on tender of resignation per Special Order 35, War Department, October 20 1864. (Photo courtesy USAMHI)

Thomas Donnelly Doubleday (brother, Civil War)

General Abner Doubleday's older brother, Thomas Doubleday had blue eyes, dark hair and dark complexion. He was 5' 9" tall. Born in Ballston Spa, New York, in 1816, Thomas became an importer. He enlisted in New York at age forty-five, November 1, 1861 for three years. He mustered in

January 23, 1862 and was commissioned as colonel of the Fourth New York Heavy Artillery on March 4, 1862. Thomas was discharged March 7, 1863 for mental and physical incapacity. (Photo courtesy of USAMHI)

Ulysses Doubleday (brother, Civil War)

Born in Auburn, New York in 1824, General Abner Doubleday's younger brother Ulysses had blue eyes, brown hair, and a fair complexion. He was 5' 9 ½" tall. Ulysses was thirty-seven years old when he left his job as a clerk enlisted January 6, 1862 in New York for three years with the Fourth New York Heavy Artillery. He mustered in January 23, 1862 as a major. He was later discharged September 14, 1863 as a major to accept commission as lieutenant colonel of the Third Unites States Colored Troops Regiment. (Photo courtesy of USAMHI)

Ulysses F. Doubleday (probably a cousin, Civil War)

Son of Demas Doubleday and Sally Calkins Doubleday of Pierstown, New York, (also near Cooperstown, New York), Ulysses, at the age of twenty-five, enlisted with the 121st New York Infantry. He joined for duty August 18, 1862 at Mohawk, New York, and was mustered in at Herkimer, New York on August 23, 1862 for three years. He was assigned to Co. H as a first lieutenant. Records for 1863 show he went home for ten days, beginning April 10, "to visit my family and to attend to special business." Permission was granted, "Doubleday is a faithful officer and worthy of the favor he asks, no other officer on leave," said Colonel Comely. The regiment was at that time, camped near White Oak Church, Virginia, not far from Fredericksburg. Less than a month after his trip home, Ulysses was killed in action at Salem Church, May 3, 1863.

William Orlando Doubleday
(probably a distant cousin, Civil War)

William O. Doubleday, born in 1821 in Sharon, Vermont, was probably a distant cousin of General Abner Doubleday. William was a farmer/teamster when he enlisted as a private in Company H of the Fourteenth Vermont

Volunteer Infantry at Brattleboro in October 1862. He was about forty-four years old and 5'8" with light complexion, with dark eyes and hair, according to his military records. On July 3, 1863 he was severely wounded in the left leg during the battle of Gettysburg. His leg was amputated and William was in a field hospital, otherwise known as St. Francis Xavier Catholic Church on High Street, Gettysburg. According to an eyewitness account, William was lying near the altar when he looked up and asked the passerby to stop and talk. William talked about his wife and children. The passerby was president of the U.S. Christian Commission and wore an identifying badge. When William saw the badge, "tears came to his eyes." What comfort could be provided was given, but William died August 12 and was buried at the new national cemetery in Gettysburg. He left a wife and five children. (The description of William in the church comes from "*Killed in Action: Eyewitness Accounts of the Last Moments of 100 Union Soldiers Who Died at Gettysburg*" by Gregory A. Coco, Thomas Publications, Gettysburg, 1992, 111-112)

Adelbert S. Eddy (nephew, Civil War)

Adelbert S. Eddy was born at Scipio, New York, September 12, 1837 and educated in public schools of New York City. He was six feet tall with light hair and complexion, and left his job as recorder to enlist in Illinois, April 1861, for three months. As it became more evident the war would not end in three months, he enlisted again, this time in the Fourth New York Heavy Artillery at the age of twenty-four. The blue-eyed Eddy mustered in January 2, 1862 at Camp Ward for three years. He was a first lieutenant in Company C. He served on the staff of Brigadier General Whipple for several months in 1862. Later, he was promoted as the captain of Co. B at Cold Harbor. Adelbert S. Eddy was discharged June 30, 1864 at Petersburg. After the war, he worked in banking and resided in Bloomington, Illinois.

Herman J. Eddy (brother-in-law, Civil War)

He enlisted July 1, 1864 as a sergeant of Company H of the Fourth New York Heavy Artillery. When he enlisted at age forty-five, he was just over 5'11" and weighed 155 pounds. He was discharged October 8, 1864. He became a traveling salesman and moved around a lot, living in New York City, Chicago, Cleveland, and Geneva, New York, as well as East Varick,

Seneca County, New York and in Bloomington, Illinois. While in the military, he was a clerk in Office of the Commanding General of Prisoners, in Washington, D.C. from October 1864 through 1866. He would later suffer from chronic diarrhea, heart trouble, enlargement of liver, rheumatism and kidney disease. His pension records state his first severe attack of diarrhea was when "we were detached from Co. H with Capt. Wm. Arthur to Taneytown road north of Chain Bridge in Maryland. He was sick in quarters and was attended to by one of our own men. He got no better taken to Regimental Head Quarters at Fort Ethan Allen south of Chain Bridge, Va. where he was cared for by Surgeon Baylis in Headquarters tent by my (unreadable) Gen. Doubleday."

Ulysses D. Eddy (nephew, Civil War)

Ulysses D. Eddy was born October 21, 1843 at Jordan, New York and educated at the University of Illinois. He joined the Twelfth New York Infantry as a second lieutenant before re-enlisting as a first lieutenant, initially in Company F and later Company B of the Fourth New York Heavy Artillery March 4, 1862. He was eighteen years old when he traveled to Washington, DC and joined the artillery regiment for three years. Ulysses D. Eddy was placed on detached service when he was selected to be on General Whipple's staff from May through December of 1862 and continued to February 1863. During the battle of Fredericksburg, he was captured and later released at City Point February 20, 1863 and reported at Camp Parole, Maryland February 21-26, 1863. He transferred to Company B March 10, 1863 and was then detached again to Whipple's staff where he was the AAG for the Fourth Brigade located south of the Potomac River. The Fourth Brigade was ordered to defend the southern portion of the Washington, D.C. Following that duty, he served as Aide de Camp for Colonel J.C. Tidball, Commanding Artillery Brigade, of the Second Army Corps. This assignment lasted until April 1865 when he was discharged at the end of terms of service. In November 1864, he applied for a twenty day leave to visit his home in Bloomington, Illinois: "I wish to go home and arrange matters for my parents, who are old and infirm, in such manner that they can spare me; and to dispose of certain property by which I will suffer pecuniary loss, if not present in a few days to personally attend to it." His military life was over when he mustered out March 1865. Following the war he became a merchant, married, had three children and lived in New York City.

DOUBLEDAY'S STAFF MEMBERS

(This information can be found in pension and military records as well as newspapers.)

William Cullen Bryant Grey (Staff, Civil War)

William C.B. Grey enrolled in the Fourth New York Heavy Artillery January 4, 1862. He was twenty-three. Grey was commissioned as a first lieutenant. He served on Doubleday's staff, but his military career was short: He died of disease January 1, 1863 in Georgetown, D.C.

Eminel P. Halstead (Staff, AAG, Civil War)

Born August 13, 1833 Trenton, Oneida County, New York, attorney Eminel P. Halstead first joined as a captain in the Second New York Heavy Artillery. He later enlisted in the Fourth New York Heavy Artillery at Camp Arthur, Staten Island, as a first lieutenant October 1861 for three years. Halstead was twenty-eight years old, was 5' 11" with a florid complexion, had blue or gray eyes, and dark brown hair. He was appointed as an Assistant Adjutant General in April 1862. Halstead was wounded slightly at the battle of Antietam. He rose in the ranks to major by brevet March 13, 1865. He died February 13, 1912.

Henry T. Lee (Staff, ADC, Civil War)

Henry T. Lee joined Company A, Fourth New York Heavy Artillery as an Aide de Camp in August 1861 at Croton, New York. He was twenty-one years old and at some point in his life became an attorney. By August 1862 he became an Assistant Adjutant General on Colonel Thomas Doubleday's staff, but joined the staff of General Abner Doubleday later that autumn as an Aide de Camp. However, Lee suffered acute dysentery and chronic diarrhea and received ten days leave to go home in March with that leave being extended another twenty days. By 1871, he was an attorney in New York City.

Charles E. Livingston (Staff, Civil War)

Eventually becoming a colonel of the Seventy-Sixth New York Infantry, Charles E. Livingston first joined the Ninety-Second New York Infantry as a major December 20, 1861. He transferred to the Seventy-Sixth New York Infantry January 7, 1862. He was twenty-three years old. In May through June, he acted as military governor of Fredericksburg, Virginia. During the battle at Groveton, Virginia, (Second Battle of Bull Run) he was captured in action August 29, 1862. In September that year, Livingston took twenty-five days of sick leave to his home in Brooklyn, New York. In December 1862, he was attached to Doubleday's staff as an Inspector General (probably as acting assistant). He served in that capacity at least twice. Livingston had several heath issues that prevented him from certain forms of duty. In May 1863, Livingston was assigned to an examining board charged with reviewing qualification of commissioned officers to lead "Colored" troops. Major General Silas Casey was president of that board. He remained on that board until September 1864.

Benjamin F. Marten (Staff, ADC, Civil War)

Born in New York City, November 19, 1839, Marten enlisted in Company E, Forty-seventh New York Infantry, at age twenty-one, as a second lieutenant. He was later promoted to first lieutenant in April 1862. He soon became assigned as Adie de Camp for General Doubleday. Marten remained in that position until ordered to serve on the staff of General Augur April 1864, but resigned the next month. Long after his military service, Marten resided in Jersey City, New Jersey. His records describe him as 5' 4", 135 pounds, with brown eyes and a florid complexion. He never married, nor had children. Marten died June 18, 1908 in Jersey City, New Jersey.

George Freeman Noyes
(Staff, Commissary of Subsistence, Civil War)

Maine native, George F. Noyes enlisted April 21, 1862 as a captain with the U.S. Volunteer Commissary Department and served until March 22, 1864. He rose in rank until he reached that of lieutenant colonel March 13, 1865. He wrote a small book about his experiences with General Abner Doubleday *The Bivouac and the Battlefield*, New York, 1863. Like Doubleday, Noyes was the son of a congressman—Joseph C. Noyes who served in the Twenty-second and Twenty-fourth Congresses. Georg F. Noyes died January 9, 1868 and is buried in Portland, Maine.

Jacob Frederick Slagle (Staff, Judge Advocate, Civil War)

Jacob F. Slagle was an attorney in Pittsburgh, Pennsylvania when he joined Company D of the 149th Pennsylvania Infantry in August 1862 as a first lieutenant. He also served as a quartermaster in Washington, D.C. He served as judge advocate of the Third Division of the First Corps on General Abner Doubleday's staff until April 1864. Slagle was wounded with a ball in the face at the Battle of the Wilderness, and wounded again at Petersburg. He later accepted a presidential appointment as Major and Judge Advocate of the U.S. Army. After his military service, he served as Pittsburgh city solicitor until 1872 and as a judge for the Court of Common Please until 1897. He died September 6, 1900 and is buried in the Alleghany Cemetery in Pittsburgh.

ABNER'S ANCESTORS

Elisha Doubleday (French and Indian War)

Elisha Doubleday was born January 30, 1713 or 1714. He served in the Ninth Company of Captain Azel Fitch in 1759 and the Tenth Company under the same commander in 1762. He also served in the First Connecticut Regiment in September 1776. He married three times and fathered a total of twenty-five children. His first wife, Margaret Adams, was a distant relative of President John Adams and his son, President John Quincy Adams. Six of Elisha Doubleday's sons served in the American Revolution: Joseph (born December 27, 1737). Elisha (born April 15, 1740), Asahel (born March 31, 1752, Abner (born February 3, 1757), Ammi (born April 17, 1759), Seth (born August 15, 1761).

Abner Doubleday (Revolutionary War)

This Abner Doubleday is grandfather to the subject of this biography. "Captain" Abner Doubleday was born February 3, 1757. He was the father of Ulysses Freeman Doubleday. He served in Putnam's Third Regiment of Connecticut troops. He was also a corporal, then captain in the Eighth Connecticut Regiment. It is said that he was one of the many soldiers at Valley Forge. His first wife died, and he married Mercy Freeman, a daughter of Elisha Freeman, of Kinderhook, New York. He died December 28, 1812 and is buried in Lakeview Cemetery just outside Cooperstown, New York.

Ammi Doubleday (Revolutionary War)

Ammi Doubleday (April 17, 1759-January 31, 1839) enlisted at age eighteen, served as a private, corporal and sergeant in the Revolutionary War in the First Connecticut Regiment. "He applied for a pension in 1832 from Oneida County, New York and died in New Hartford, New York. (Source—*Lineage Book National Society of the Daughters of the American Revolution*, Vol. XCVIII, 1913, p 37 and 1908 revised edition) He also served on the Committee of the Chenango Canal. He married Susan Pierce February 5, 1814. One of their children was also named Ammi and was born the same year as the subject of this book.

Asahel Doubleday (Revolutionary War)

Asahel served in Sage's Regiment of Connecticut troops.

Elisha Doubleday Jr. (Revolutionary War)

Elisha Doubleday (April 15, 1740-1796) served as a Minute Man. "He was born in Boston; died in Connecticut." He was in the defense of New London. (Source—*Lineage Book National Society of the Daughters of the American Revolution*, Vol. CXXI, 1916 p.180, Vol. XL, p. 97)

Joseph Doubleday (Revolutionary War)

Served as a private in the Eighth Connecticut Regiment

Seth Doubleday (Revolutionary War)

"Captain" Seth Doubleday was born August 15, 1761 and served with the Connecticut Continentals. He married Barthena Clark and had eight children. He is buried in Pierstown, New York, not far from Cooperstown. Seth lived at 29 Pioneer Street (formerly known as West Street) in Cooperstown, the only Doubleday to live there, according to Marion H. Brophy, former librarian there. According to Judge William Cooper, Seth purchased two shillings of butter on May 25, 1792. Barthena died January 18, 1831 at age 69; Seth died October 8, 1836.

ABBREVIATIONS

The following abbreviations are used in the footnotes of individual chapters to save space.

AD   Abner Doubleday diaries, New York Historical Society, New York City. The page numbers often do not exist, or not in order and is one journal the book was turned upside down. Since the numbers are not in a logical order, I have opted to use no page numbers (n.p.). Other items written by Abner Doubleday will be source noted.

CCW   U.S. Congress, *Report of the Joint Committee on the Conduct of War*, Washington, D.C.: U.S. Government Printing Office, 1865

FNMP   Fredericksburg and Spotsylvania National Military Park

GNMP   Gettysburg National Military Park

GR   Army Generals Reports of Civil War Services M1098 Roll 8, Abner Doubleday

LOC   Library of Congress

MOLLUS   Military Order of the Loyal Legion of the United States

NARA   National Archives Records and Administration, Washington, D.C.

OR   U.S. War Department. *The War of the Rebellion: A Compilation of the Official Records of the Union and Confederate Armies.* 128 Volumes. Washington, DC, Government Printing Office, 1880-1901

          Written as OR, Volume, Part, Page. All are from Series 1 unless otherwise noted.

USAMHI   United States Army Military History Institute, Carlisle, PA

WP   United States Military Academy, West Point, NY

BIBLIOGRAPHY

MANUSCRIPTS

Adams County Historical Society, Gettysburg, PA
  Shriver family papers
The City College, CUNY, NY
  Gray, William C.B., papers
Columbia University, NYC
  Doubleday, Abner papers
Duke University
  Doubleday, Ulysses, papers
Franklin and Marshall College, Lancaster, PA.
  Reynolds, John F. papers
  Riddle, William, letter
Fredericksburg and Spotsylvania National Military Park
  Alsop, Lizzie Maxwell papers
  Blodgett, William O., papers
  Coye, James papers
  Hoover, Charles D. W., papers
Gettysburg National Military Park
  Batchelder papers
  Diary of Samuel Healy
  James Wadsworth papers
Harpers Ferry National Historic Park
  Doubleday, Abner papers
Library of Congress
  Anderson, Robert papers
National Archives, Washington, DC
  Record Groups 92, 94, 391, 407, 15, 49, 217, 24, 405
  Gales and Seaton's Register of Debates in Congress, US Government Printing
  Office
The National Baseball Hall of Fame, Cooperstown, New York
  Doubleday, Abner, papers
New York Historical Society, N.Y.
  Doubleday, Abner, papers

New York State Historical Society, Cooperstown, NY
Shaul, John D. papers
New York Public Library, New York City
Doubleday, Abner, papers
United States Military Academy West Point
Twenty-Fourth Annual Reunion of the Association of Graduates of the
United States Military Academy
Library, financial, record of demerits, Abner Doubleday
Newton, John papers
Cadet Application Papers, 1805-1866
Cullum's Register of Officers and Cadets of the U.S.
University of Rochester, Rochester, NY
Seward, William Henry papers
USAMHI, Carlisle, PA
Bowen, Isaac, papers
Bliss, Zenas, papers
Records of Courts Martial
Civil War Misc. Collection
Chamberlin scrapbook
General Court Martial Orders, War Department
Robert L. Brake Collection
Thomas R. Stone Collection
Warren, Horatio papers
Virginia Historical Society
Doubleday, Abner papers

NEWSPAPERS

Auburn Boston Evening Transcript, Boston, MA
Boston Evening Transcript, Boston, MA
Cayuga Patriot, Auburn, NY
Cayuga Republican, Auburn, NY
Charleston Mercury, Charleston, SC
Daily Record, Mendham, N.J.
Daily Pantagraph, Bloomington, Ill.
The Evening Star, Washington, DC
Freeman's Journal, Cooperstown, NY
Journal and Advertiser, Auburn, NY
The Kansas City Star, Kansas City, KS

New York Evening Post, New York City
New York Times, New York City
The Buffalo Daily Courier, Buffalo, NY
The Christian Banner
The Manchester Journal, Manchester, VT
The National Tribune, NYC
The New York Tribune, NYC
The Richmond Whig, Richmond, VA
Washington Chronicle, Washington, D.C.

BOOKS, ARTICLES, PAMPHLETS

Baker, Gertrude, *Marriages Taken from the Otsego Herald, Western Advertiser and Freeman's Journal, Otsego County, NY,* 1932

Bandy, Ken & Freeland, Florence, *the Gettysburg Papers,* Morningside Bookshop, Dayton, OH, 1978

Benedict, Col. G.G., *"A Short History of the 14th Vermont Regiment,"* September 16, 1887, USAMHI, Carlisle, PA

Beyer, Barry K., *The Chenango Canal,* (Norwich, N.Y., reprint by the Chenango County Historical Society; originally printed 1954 Carnegie-Mellon University, Pittsburgh, Pa.)

Cleaves, Freeman, *Rock of Chickamauga,* Greenwood Press Publishers, Westport, Connecticut, 1948

Crawford, Samuel Wylie, *The Genesis of the Civil War, The Story of Sumter,* New York, C. L. Webster & Co, 1887

Coker, Caleb, ed., *The News From Brownsville,* 1992, Texas State Historical Assoc., 1992

Crimmins, Col. M. L. *Fort McKavett, Texas,* Southwestern Quarterly, July 1934

Ferrell, Robert H. ed., Dana, Lt Napoleon Jackson Tecumseh., *Monterrey Is Our! The Mexican War Letters of Lieutenant Dana, 1845-1847,* University Press of Kentucky, 1990

Davis, William C., *Look Away! A History of the Confederate States of America,* The Free Press, New York, 2002

Doubleday, Abner; *Reports of the Battles of Gettysburg,* Walton's Steam Press, Montpelier, 1865

Doubleday, Abner, *Reminiscences of Forts Sumter and Moultrie in 1860-61,* Harper and Brothers, Publishers, NY, 1876

Eddy, Ruth, *The Eddy Family in America,* no publisher named, Boston, MA, 1930

Faibisoff, A Sylvia G., ed., *"Biography of Newspapers in Fourteen New York Counties"*; New York Historical Association, 1978

Faust, Patricia L. ed. *Historical Times Illustrated Encyclopedia of the Civil War*, Harper & Row, NY, 1986

Field, William T. Texas Military History, Fort Duncan and Old Eagle Pass, Vol. 6, Summer, 1967

National Guard Association of Texas, 1961-1970

Filler, Louis, *The Crusade Against Slavery 1830-1860*, Harper & Brothers, NY, 1960

Fish, Carl Russell, *The Rise of the Common Man 1830-1850*, The Macmillan Co., NY, 1950

Flayderman's Guide to Antique American Firearms, Norm Flayderman, Seventh edition, Krause Pub., 1998

Fleming, Thomas J., *West Point, The Men and Times of the United States Military Academy*, William Morrow & Co., New York, 1969

French, Benjamin Brown, *Witness to the Young Republic A Yankee's Journal 1828-1870*, Univ. Press of New England, Hanover, NH, 1989

Gibbon, John *Personal Recollections of the Civil War*, Morningside Press, Dayton, OH, 1988

Goldman, Perry M. and Young, James S., *The United States Congressional Directories, 1789-1840*, Columbia University Press, NY, 1973

Haskin, Wm. L., *The History of the First Regiment of Artillery Fort Preble, Portland, Maine*, B. Thurston and Co., 1879

Hertz, Emanuel, ed., *Lincoln Talks An Oral biography*, Brahall House, NY, 1986

Holmes, Clay W., A *Genealogy of the Lineal Descendants of William Wood*, Elmira, NY, 1901

Howard, Oliver Otis, Autobiography of Oliver Otis Howard,

Keller, S. Roger, *Events of the Civil War in Washington County, Maryland*, White Mane Pub. Co. Inc. Shippensburg PA, 1995

Kirk, Hyland, *Heavy Guns and Light, The History of the 4th New York Heavy Artillery.* C.T. Dillingham, NY, 1890

Kurtz, D. Morris, *Auburn, NY: It's Facilities and Resources*, The Kurtz Publishing Co., Auburn, NY, 1884

Ladd, David & Audrey, ed., *The Batchelder Papers*, Vol. II, Morningside, Ohio, 1994

Lader, Lawrence, *"Mad Old Man from Massachusetts,"* American Heritage, April 1961

Lane, Lydia Spencer, *I Married A Soldier*, Horn and Wallace, Publishers, Inc., Albuquerque, NM, 1964

Lapati, Americo D., *Orestes A. Brownson*, Twayne Publishers, NY, 1965

Lavender, David, *Climax at Buena Vista*, J.B. Lippincott Co., Philadelphia and New York, 1966

Leepson, Marc, *"Flag,"* Thomas Dunne Books, St. Martin's Press, N.Y., 2005

Lewis, Jon E., editor, *Mammoth Book of War Diaries & Letters*, Carroll & Graf Publishers, Inc, New York, 1999

Long, E.B., *The Civil War Day by Day*, by E.B. Long, Doubleday and Co., NY, 1971

McClellan, H. B., *I Rode with JEB Stuart*, Centennial Series, Indiana University Press, Bloomington, 1958

McClure LLD, Alexander Kelly, *Abraham Lincoln and Men of War-Times*, Philadelphia, The Times Publishing Company, 1892

McPherson, Edward, *The Political History of the United States of America during the Great Rebellion by Edward McPherson of the House of Representatives.* Second ed. 1865 Washington DC

Marshall, Jeffery D., ed., *A War of the People Vermont Civil War Letters*, University Press of New England, Hanover, NH, 1999

Martis, Kenneth C, *The Historical Atlas of United States Congressional Districts 1789-1983*, The Free Press, NY, 1982

Mayer, Henry, *All on Fire, William Lloyd Garrison and the Abolition of Slavery*, Martin's Press, NY, 1998

Meade, George, *The Life and Letters of George Gordon Meade*, Scribner's Sons, NY, 1913

Mearns, David C. *The Lincoln Papers*, Vol. 1, Doubleday and Company, Inc., Garden City, NY, 1948

Meirs, Earl Schenck ed, *Lincoln Day by Day A Chronology 1809-1865*, Washington, Lincoln Sesquicentennial Commission, 1960 (reprint Morningside, Dayton, OH, 1991)

Merrill, Walter M., ed., *The Letters of William Lloyd Garrison, Vol. 5, Let the Oppressed Go Free 1861-1867*, Belknap Press, Cambridge, Mass., 1979

Miller, William Lee, *Arguing About Slavery*, Random House, 1998

Monroe, Joel H., *Historical Records of Auburn for a Hundred and Twenty Years*, no printer listed, 1913

Moore, Frank, ed., *The Rebellion Record, A Diary of American Events*, G.P. Putnam, NY, 1862

Mulroy, Kevin, *Freedom on the Border*, Texas Tech University Press, 1993

Nolan, Alan T., *The Iron Brigade*, Michigan Heritage Library, Hardscrabble Books, 1983

Noyes, George F., *The Bivouac and the Battlefield*, New York, 1863

Oates, Stephen B., *The Fires of Jubilee Nat Turner's Fierce Rebellion,* Harper & Row Publishers, New York, 1975

Osborne, Seward R. ed., *"The Civil War Diaries of Col. Theodore B. Gates 20th New York State Militia,"* Longstreet House, Hightstown, NJ, 1991

Priest, John M., *One Surgeon's Private War Dr. William W. Potter of the 57th New York*, White Mane Publishing Co., Shippensburg, PA, 1996

Quaife, Milo M. ed, Williams, Gen. Alpheus S., *From the Cannon's Mouth*, Wayne State University Press and the Detroit Historical Society, Detroit, 1959

Randall, J. G. and Current, Richard Nelson, Lincoln *the President: Midstream to the Last Full Measure,* Da Capo Pr., 1997 reprint

Report of the Joint Committee on the Conduct of War, Washington, Government Printing Office, 1865

Robertson Jr., James I., *Stonewall Jackson*, Macmillan Publishing NY, 1997

Sandburg, Carl, *Abraham Lincoln The War Years*, Harcourt Brace Co., NY, 1939

Schlesinger Jr., Arthur M. *Orestes A. Brownson: A Pilgrim's Progress*, Octagon Books, Inc., NY, 1963

Schlesinger Jr., Arthur M., *The Age of Jackson*, Little, Brown & Co., Boston, 1953

Sears, Stephen W., *Chancellorsville*, Houghton Mifflin Co., Boston, 1996

Shaw, S.M., editor, *A Centennial Offering Being a Brief History of Cooperstown,* Cooperstown, New York, 1886

Sifakis, Stewart, Who Was Who in the Civil War, Facts on File, Inc., New York, 1988

Smith, A. P., *History of the Seventy-Sixth Regiment New York* Volunteers, Cortland, New York, 1867

Smith, George Winston and Judah, Charles, editors; *Chronicles of the Gringos*, The University of New Mexico Press, Albuquerque, NM, 1968

Snedeker, Lenora, *Memories at Willowbrook*, Oxford, N.Y., 1995

Sparks, David, ed., *Inside Lincoln's Army, The Diary of Marsena Rudolph Patrick,* Thomas Yoseloff Publisher, NY, 1964

Stanton, Henry B. *"Remarks of Henry B. Stanton in the Representatives Hall,"* Published by Isaac Knapp, Boston, 1837

Storke, Elliot G., *"History of Cayuga County, 1879,"* Syracuse, NY, 1879

Sylvester, Nathaniel Bartlett, *History of Saratoga County, New York*, Heart of the Lakes, Interlaken, NY, 1979 reprint

Thompson, Joseph Parrish, *Bryant Gray: The Student, The Christian, The Soldier,* A. D.F. Randolph, NY, 1864

Thoreau, Henry David, *On the Duty of Civil Disobedience,* 1849

Trefousse, Hans L., *The Radical Republicans,*

Unknown author, *"Diary of a Public Man,"* originally appeared as a series in *The North American Review* in 1879.

Warner, Ezra, *Generals in Blue*, Louisiana State University Press, 1988

Welsh, Jack D., MD; *Medical Histories of Union Generals*, Kent State University Press, Kent, Ohio, 1996

Wills, Barbara Pratt and Paula S. Felder, *Handbook of Historic Fredericksburg*, Historic Fredericksburg Foundation Inc., 1993

Williams, J.C., *"Life in Camp,"* Claremont Manufacturing Corp., Claremont, NH, 1864

Welcher, Frank J., *The Union Army 1861-1865 Organization and Operations*, Indiana University Press, Bloomington, 1989

Woodward, C. Vann editor, *Mary Chesnut's Civil War,* Yale University Press, 1993

Young, Jesse Bowman, *The Battle of Gettysburg*, Harper & Brothers Publishers, New York, 1913

Young, James Sterling, *The Washington Community 1800-1828*, Columbia University Press, New York, 1966

INDEX

ABNER AS THE FAMILY REMEMBERS HIM

Written by Charles Stewart Doubleday, grand-nephew of Abner

My research on the Doubleday family has shown that they have been in America for a long time from about 1670 in Boston. The immigrant ancestor was Roger Doubleday and he had two sons, named Elisha and Elijah. Even then the Doubleday's were in search of Freedom. In 1689 Roger was among those on military watch in Braintree. A couple of generations down, this family participated heavily in the Revolutionary War. Another Elisha had seven sons and two grandsons in this war for freedom. One of the soldiers was the grandfather of Abner who also was named Abner. He responded to the "Seven Day Alert" and marched from Lebanon, CT. to Boston. History records show that Abner participated in the Battle of Bunker (Breeds) Hill. As part of the 8th Connecticut Line Regiment, he fought at Germantown MD and then wintered at Valley Forge with Washington, 1777-1778. In mid 1779, Abner was part of General Anthony Wayne's victory at Stony Point. During the winter of 1779-1780, Abner's feet were frozen and he was unable to march and returned to Connecticut. But he wasn't done fighting and he signed on as a volunteer on the privateer sloop named Hibernia. Shortly after joining the Hibernia, they were captured by the British and placed in Sharon Prison. As Abner was a strong man, the British compelled him to serve on the ship HMS Hussar. While the ship was in Kingston, Jamaica, Abner escaped. He returned to Connecticut after the war, moved to upstate New York and became a tavern owner with his brother. That's where he met Abner's Grandmother Mercy Freeman and they moved to Cooperstown to take up farming. Abner's father, Ulysses Freeman Doubleday, was a newspaper publisher and had three sons, Thomas, Abner and Ulysses, plus a couple of daughters. Ulysses Freeman was a patriot who fought at Sackett's Harbor during the war of 1812. Ulysses was also a two-time congressman from his area and was involved with the railroad expansion in NY. This is where young Abner began to draw maps for this railroad expansion. The Doubleday's were always concerned with education and Abner was sent from Auburn, his home to Cooperstown to attend school and live with Amos, his uncle who was a judge in Cooperstown. Abner also played "ball" on James Fenimore Coopers front lawn as defined in Cooper's book, "Home As Found." From there he attended West Point from 1838 to 1842.

While Abner was growing up, he was very studious and liked the arts. There were some hints that his father was involved with the Congregational Church and was an abolitionist. After graduation, Lieutenant Abner wrote poems for his friends to help them in their romantic pursuits. He also wrote a poem to woo his bride Mary Hewitt. During the Mexican War Abner was the only officer that spoke Spanish. This helped him to obtain quarters in Mexico better than his commanders. Again he was very serious in everything he did in the military. During the war, he was always concerned with his family and visited them whenever possible. All three brothers were in the Union Army. Thomas was the Commander of the 4th NY Heavy Artillery. Brother Ulysses had several assignments and was Brevetted Brigadier general for gallantry in action and was Commander of several colored troops.

When Capt Abner was at Fort Sumter, he sent letters to his brother Ulysses, who hadn't entered the war yet. Abner's letters were coded so that the Rebs wouldn't know what was being said about the conditions at the Fort. The letters were decoded and Ulysses' forwarded them to Lincoln. So with this communication system, Lincoln knew exactly what was happening at the Fort. Copies of these letters are with the Lincoln records in the Library of Congress.

After the war, when Abner moved to New Jersey, he had many family visits. In fact, my grandfather James Stewart spent much of his school time staying at Abner's house. The family has copies of letters written by James to his father Ulysses, who then lived in North Carolina.

As stated in the United States Army Recruiting News, November 1938, an article by James Edward Kelly, described that "Abner was in height and weight considerably above the average; stood six feet, was a handsome brunette man, so striking in personal appearance that whether riding or walking, he would attract attention anywhere. Always dignified, his manners pleasing, ever courteous to all who came into contact with him. The general was so placid and free from any sudden impulse, that his staff call him "Forty-eight Hours." His habitual composure in a marked degree influenced the officers and men under him. Abner's heart and soul were in his profession as a soldier and it was as dear to him as life itself." He was always willing to help, especially his family and brothers. When his brother Ulysses was appointed Provost Marshall of the Capitol, Ulysses asked Abner to help him properly protect the capital, as Ulysses was a banker, not a military person. I have in my possession a detailed letter written by Abner to Ulysses describing the correct protection of the Capitol.

The Doubleday men in all of my research were tall and lanky, with ability to work with others to accomplish the necessary results. Most of the Doubleday men through the generations have served in the military to protect this freedom won from the Revolutionary War. It is also interesting to compare my children with these ancestors and recognize similar traits.

December 2007

Breinigsville, PA USA
18 September 2010
245667BV00002B/7/P